Mr. Broadway

Mr. Broadway

THE INSIDE STORY OF THE SHUBERTS, THE SHOWS, AND THE STARS

GERALD SCHOENFELD

APPLAUSE
THEATRE & CINEMA BOOKS

AN IMPRINT OF HAL LEONARD CORPORATION

Published in 2012 by Applause Theatre & Cinema Books
An Imprint of Hal Leonard Corporation
7777 West Bluemound Road
Milwaukee, WI 53213

Trade Book Division Editorial Offices
33 Plymouth St., Montclair, NJ 07042

Unless otherwise noted all photographs are from the author's personal collection.

Printed in the United States of America
Book design by F. Lynn Bergesen

Library of Congress Cataloging-in-Publication Data

Schoenfeld, Gerald, 1924-2008.
   Mr. Broadway : the inside story of the Shuberts, the shows, and the stars / Gerald Schoenfeld.
      p. cm.
   ISBN 978-1-55783-827-8 (hardcover)
   1. Shubert, Lee, 1873?-1953. 2. Shubert, Sam S., 1875-1905. 3. Shubert, Jacob J., 1878?-1963. 4. Theaters—New York (State)—New York—History—20th century. 5. Performing arts—New York (State)—New York—History—20th century. 6. Shubert Organization—History. I. Title.
   PN2285.S34 2012
   792'.0232'09227471—dc23
   [B]
                                                            2011053019

www.applausebooks.com

CONTENTS

HUGH JACKMAN

When people meet me, usually their lasting impression is of my wife... after all, she is in my opinion far funnier, more interesting, and definitely sexier! The type of person who turns heads in whichever room she is in.... Well, I have to say my first memory of meeting Mr. Schoenfeld was a little similar. It was at a fancy London hotel off Hyde Park, I was with my good friends Ben Gannon and Robert Fox, the producers of *The Boy from Oz*, and we were going to tell him of our plan to bring the show to Broadway. It was around six p.m., and Mr. Schoenfeld had plans to go to the theater, so we were going to shake hands before they went to the show.

I was surprised when we went into the hotel that we went straight up to the room. I thought we might have met in the lobby, but no... Jerry was always authentic and down-to-earth, and—as I would say to him later during our decade of friendship—he was to me an honorary Australian... a man of old-fashioned values, where a handshake was stronger than any contract.

Jerry welcomed us not as the titan of Broadway, as he had been described to me, but in a very warm, genial, and up-front way. "Nice to meet you, Mr. Schoenfeld." "Please call me Jerry.... Very nice to meet you, You"—Jerry always pronounced my name without the *H*... like a lot of genuine New Yorkers!—then straightaway said, "So... I know you are in movies, so are you really coming to Broadway with this show or what?"

Jerry always was to the point, and for the next ten years would say to me something similar: "Enough of all this movie shit, when are you coming home—when are you coming back to Broadway?"

I told him yes, we shook hands... apparently that was it, it was done, then barely two minutes into our meeting, Pat came into the room wearing her bathrobe: "Jerry, have you seen my…" And I can't remember the rest of the conversation. I immediately remembered I was in someone's hotel room, and Pat didn't blink an eyelid. We shook hands, I apologized for being there, and she told us to sit and relax, and I wondered how often things like this might have happened. For Pat it all seemed very normal. And like my wife, as big a personality as Jerry was, Pat somehow had that ability to turn heads effortlessly.

From that moment I knew we were going to be friends. I liked them both instantly, and very soon after, like would turn to love. Pat and Jerry invited me and my family to spend weekends with them upstate, we would go to the theater together, to restaurants, and all along I had that feeling that Jerry was not like a king but more like a father and brother all rolled into one.

The year I spent on Broadway doing *The Boy from Oz* was one of the greatest years of my life, with so many extraordinary memories. But one of my lasting impressions is the visits I would get from Jerry. Sometimes it would be just before I went onstage: "You," Jerry in a very loud stage whisper would say, "I need to talk to you about something." "Jerry, I am just about to go onstage." "I know—it won't take a second"…always made me laugh. But then, during the last song of the show, "Once Before I Go", two to three times a week I would look out to the wings and there Jerry would be, a lover of the theater and one of the greatest supporters I have ever had. He told me how much he loved the show…maybe it was the resonance of the show's themes of someone living their dreams, someone living life to the full, of having no regrets of the road traveled. And to me that was Jerry. Right up to his death Jerry was working…well, not that it was work to him. The theater was his domain, his church, his home. Talking to me about shows, sending me possible scripts for new shows, revivals… whatever.

The last night of Jerry's life, Pat and he came to the premiere of my movie *Australia*. He came and grabbed me after the movie was over, upset that Pat thought it not a good idea to go to the after party, and said, "Very good, You…now enough of this movie business, when are you coming back home…to Broadway?" It would be only nine months later, in a show called *A Steady Rain*, with Daniel Craig…a fourteen-week run, and in which theater? The Schoenfeld, of course!

I can't wait to read this book. I knew Jerry for only ten years. He changed my life in so many ways; now it is really time for me to learn about the other seventy years. Thank you, Pat, for making this book happen ... and secretly I will always picture you working on it ... in your bathrobe!

ALEC BALDWIN

It was twenty years ago, in the spring of 1992, that I was approached by a group of people about a Broadway revival of Tennessee Williams's *A Streetcar Named Desire*. The project had a good cast, with Jessica Lange, Amy Madigan, and Tim Carhart in the other lead roles. The smaller parts were rounded out by none other than the likes of James Gandolfini and Aida Turturro, who went on to star in *The Sopranos*. The director was Greg Mosher, who often wears the tag "The Smartest Guy in the Room" because he actually is. The costume designer was the remarkable Jane Greenwood. The executor of the Williams estate, the notorious Maria St. Just, lurked about during the rehearsals and beyond, trying to calm my nerves by reminding me how I could never hold a candle to Brando.

It was during this time that I met Jerry Schoenfeld. Schoenfeld, as everyone knows, was, along with Bernie Jacobs, the head of the Shubert Organization. Now many people give Jerry credit for "saving" the Broadway theater, the Great White Way itself, in the decade after J. J. Shubert's death. In the 1970s, the theater was in trouble, and Bernie and Jerry helped to resuscitate the business and return the Shubert group to profitability.

Jerry was a legend. He was tough. He was no-nonsense. But like other tough, no-nonsense guys I have worked with, like producers Marty Bregman and Lorne Michaels, once you sat across from him, you knew you were with a guy who succeeded at what he does because he has a gift for it and because he eats, sleeps, and drinks it. Jerry was a king in New York for those two reasons. He had a natural instinct for what defined Broadway, and a tenacity that was unequaled by his peers.

Jerry had what I call that "silk stockings" dialect. Which means he had that New York accent that sounded like FDR. (Film director John

Frankenheimer spoke the same way.) Keep in mind, all caps are for emphasis, not volume. Jerry was about well-timed emphasis. "My boy...," he'd say, "I want to have...a MEETING...with yooooooooou..., to DISCUSS...[lower the voice here for emphasis] a very important project that I truly believe you will find...[restore the volume here] MOST fascinating."

Jerry's head was bald and shiny. He never leaned back in a chair. He sat either erect or leaned in. And I could swear that on one or more occasions, he tried to reflect the sun or overhead lighting off of his dome and into my eyes, like something Richard Boone or Richard Widmark would do with a silver dollar in a Western movie. Jerry was a gentleman. He was formal and courteous, but also warm and sincere. But he was all business. "They're sending a car to pick you up and bring you to work at the Barrymore each night of the run," my agent informed me. "How nice!" I replied. "Forget nice," my agent said. "Jerry won't have you hunting for a cab to get to 47th Street."

I had the flu in July. I missed three shows. I could barely move.

I walked, no, crawled to the old Williams (how appropriate) Chicken on 86th and Broadway to get some matzah ball soup. The late-afternoon sun revived me a bit. At the corner across from Williams Chicken, an old lady stared at me, like a juror at a trial, then said, "Aren't you supposed to be on Broadway right now?" Was she a spy for Jerry?

My phone rang. "My boy...," said the Great and Powerful One. "Are you feeling that ill that you will...MISS...THE SHOW...this evening?"

"I'm half dead, Jerry," I said.

"Very well," he said. "There will be many cancellations tonight, as you know. MANY...refunds. If you like, I can send...a DOCTOR over to your apartment."

"No, I think I will be okay in a day or two. And thank you, Jerry."

"Not at t'aaaaaalll, my boy. I will ring you tomorrow."

Just the shift in barometric pressure created by Jerry's dissatisfaction was enough to get you out of bed.

That summer, I testified before the New York City Council in opposition to the carriage horse trade. The carriage drivers present at City Hall taunted me as I left the hearing. That night, they actually formed a protest outside the Barrymore. I got to the theater and the cops escorted me in. Jerry was waiting inside. "I will have some...SECURITY people in the house tonight," he said. "Who knows? These people are capable of anything. Maybe they'll buy a TICKET. I don't want someone flinging a bag of HORSE MANURE at you during the performance!"

That was Jerry. You often can tell a lot about a man by the woman he marries. Pat Schoenfeld has always been the kindest, most gracious, and elegant woman I have ever met in that orbit.

Meanwhile, all of New York, it seemed, knew we were reviving the show. Thanks to Mr. Schoenfeld. The fondest memories I have of my career come from *Streetcar*. Iced coffees to get revved up every night at the Edison Coffee Shop. Falling in love with Amy, literally, every performance. Spending those months learning from Mosher, a truly great director. Making fun of Maria over the PA system many nights, mocking her Blanche-like obsession with the past. Sitting in the wings to listen to Jessica's lovely readings of the greatest dialog written for an American actress. *Streetcar* was the best time for me creatively.

I owe that to Mosher. To Williams. And to Jerry, who gave me the wonderful gift of an enviable turn on Broadway, Shubert style.

ACKNOWLEDGMENTS

There are many people to thank for their help and encouragement with this book.

In the beginning, those people who encouraged Jerry to keep writing, writing, writing were Doris Kearns Goodwin, Jason Epstein, Frank McCourt, and all of our Connecticut friends who saw him working on the book every weekend and wouldn't let him give up.

My thanks, as well, to Heidi Mathis and Madeline Austin, both of whom were there for Jerry over the course of many years and too many late nights, recording his words and helping him put them into readable form. While this was going on, he asked a couple of trusted friends to read what he was writing and give him honest feedback. They did and I thank them both: Luciano Berti and Irwin Winkler.

My thanks as well for the support and encouragement I received after Jerry left us and I faced the daunting task of trying to bring Jerry's memoir to print. Among others, I am truly grateful to Marybeth Keating, Carol Flannery, and John Cerullo of Applause Books for bringing this to life.

Of course, none of this could have happened without the support of The Shubert Organization. My thanks, therefore, to Robert Wankel, Philip J. Smith, Wyche Fowler, Mike Sovern, Lee Seidler, and Stuart Subotnick. They stood by me and encouraged me.

Also at The Shubert Organization, and of indispensable help to me, were Maryann Chach, Reagan Fletcher, and Mark Schwartz from the Shubert Archives. Housed away on the top floor of the Lyceum Theater, Jerry and Bernie were instrumental in creating the Archives in 1976. Today it is the largest, most comprehensive theater archive of its kind, providing a repository for over six million documents related to the Shubert brothers and The Shubert Organization's theatrical activities.

The Archive's collection—which includes more than a century's worth of costume and set designs, scripts, music, publicity materials, photographs, correspondence, business records, and architectural plans—was an invaluable source of information, photos, and documents for this book.

Since Jerry's death and over the years I have spent on this project, so many friends have stood by me and willed me on. They include Robert L. Bernstein, Jason Epstein, Jeremy Gerard, Frank Rich, Helen Brann, and Peter Petre.

Alec Baldwin is also one of those friends, and right away he agreed to remember Jerry in his special way; and so is Hugh Jackman, who answered my calls and my emails no matter where he was in the world and has never forgotten Jerry.

Finally, there are no tributes that can adequately express my thanks to three special people, without whom this book would never have happened: Carrie Schoenfeld, my daughter and creative collaborator; Peter W. Bernstein, my agent and my guiding hand; and Jeffrey Robinson, who gave me invaluable editorial assistance while working with me on Jerry's manuscript and helping me to get it ready for publication.

Jerry would have been, and I am, eternally grateful.

—Pat Schoenfeld

PROLOGUE

Jerry and I were married for fifty-eight years, and in my mind one of the most amazing things about him was that he never saw himself the way others saw him. Too bad he couldn't have read his own obituaries.

They called him Mr. Broadway, and they called him the man who saved Broadway.

Frank Rich, the former drama critic of the *New York Times*, wrote, "Schoenfeld was so successful at turning a dilapidated sideshow of 20th-century show business into a modern corporation that impresarios of his old-school theatricality are now all but extinct."

In fact, the *New York Times* even published a full-page "in memoriam"—a single page, bordered in black, with just his name, his date of birth, and the date of his death, November 25, 2008.

They don't do that for kings or queens or presidents. In recent memory, they'd only done it for Luciano Pavarotti.

And they did it for Jerry.

He would have been astonished, because he never thought of himself in any of those terms.

It wasn't false modesty. He ran the largest, most important theater organization in the world for almost forty years. At the time of his death, the Shubert Organization owned or operated seventeen of Broadway's forty theaters, plus one Off-Broadway playhouse, in addition to operating theaters in Boston, Philadelphia, and Washington. He produced, or coproduced, or encouraged other producers to stage, some of the most memorable plays of the past five decades—from *A Chorus Line* to *Miss Saigon*, with *Cats*, *Phantom of the Opera*, *Equus*, *Amadeus*, *Pippin*, *Les Misérables*, *Evita*, *Godspell*, *Ain't Misbehavin'*, *Dreamgirls*, *Dancin'*, *Sunday in the Park with George*, *The Life and Adventures of Nicholas Nickleby*, *Glengarry Glen Ross*, *The Heidi Chronicles*,

The Gin Game, *Mamma Mia!*, and *Chess*—plays that changed the face of Broadway.

Nor was he a shrinking violet.

When he was fighting for something he wanted, like a new show, or when he felt something needed to be done, like the renovation of Times Square, or when he was battling City Hall because he thought it was doing something that would endanger his beloved Broadway, Jerry was focused and determined. He knew what he wanted to achieve, and he wouldn't give up until he achieved it.

Yet just about every time he achieved something, especially something major, when someone would slap him on the back and tell him how great he was, he'd look at me and whisper, "How did I get here?"

He was always saying that.

On our first trip to Paris, he decided to go out for a walk and found himself staring up at the Eiffel Tower. The next thing he knew, he tripped and twisted his ankle. He limped back to the hotel and told me, "I was looking up at the Eiffel Tower, and I kept thinking to myself, 'This is Paris, that's the Eiffel Tower, I'm Jerry Schoenfeld from West End Avenue—how did I get here?'"

He didn't realize the scope of his achievement, and didn't believe anyone would ever remember what he did.

But I never had any doubts. And as the years passed, I wanted him to get the recognition he deserved while he was still alive.

So, a few years before Jerry died, the idea came to me that the best way to honor his achievements toward the success and health of the American theater, and to recognize his contributions to the city of New York, was to have a Broadway theater named for him.

There had already been many tributes to his late partner, Bernie Jacobs, a man who'd also left an indelible mark on Broadway, but I felt Bernie should also have a theater named in his honor.

With that in mind, I went to see the media entrepreneur John Kluge, who was on the board of the Shubert Organization, and planted the idea with him. But I also warned John that Jerry must not hear a word of it. The plan had to be top secret, because I knew that if Jerry found out, he'd put an end to it.

John promised to talk quietly to the other board members and get back to me.

Obviously, it was difficult to discuss the idea without Jerry finding out. As chairman of the board of the Shubert Organization, Jerry played an integral part in all the board's actions, of course. It took some time for the board members to make such a big decision, but ultimately John came back to me to say that yes, the board had agreed. They proposed renaming the Plymouth and Royale Theatres, two historic Broadway houses that sat side by side on Forty-Fifth Street.

How perfect was that?

I was elated, and Bernie's family was equally thrilled. However, I had one more request. I wanted both theaters to have upright signs. The Booth, next door to the Plymouth, had an upright sign, as did the Golden, next door to the Royale. I felt that it was visually important that signs with the names Schoenfeld and Jacobs be consistent with those of the neighboring theaters. But because the Plymouth and Royale theaters were designated landmark sites by the city of New York, that took some doing. And because planning permission was necessary, inevitably the board had to tell Jerry.

He came home that night, astonished. "Do you know what they want to do?"

He had doubts, but I wasn't going to let him talk anyone out of it.

Once planning permission for the signs was approved, the New York State Assembly passed a resolution officially honoring Jerry for his vision and leadership in "rejuvenating the theater industry, Broadway, Off Broadway, and Off-Off-Broadway, and most importantly the economic and cultural health of New York."

Then came the big night: Monday, May 9, 2005.

It began with drinks and hors d'oeuvres at the Marriott Marquis hotel in Times Square.

Jerry stood at the ballroom door, greeting hundreds and hundreds of people who'd come to pay tribute to him.

Around the corner, the police had closed off Forty-Fifth Street. By the time we arrived, thousands of people were on the street singing along with recorded music blaring "Give My Regards to Broadway" and "There's No Business Like Show Business" and "42nd Street."

We decided that there wouldn't be any long speeches. We wanted to keep it short and sweet. So only a few people were on the podium. Jerry, our daughter, Carrie, and I stood with Bernie Jacobs's family, and with Hugh Jackman, who was the master of ceremonies. Mike Sovern was there representing the Shubert Organization, and so was the mayor of New York, Mike Bloomberg, who read a proclamation declaring the city's appreciation for all that Jerry and Bernie had accomplished. The mayor noted that Jerry was "the real deal."

That's when two puppets from the popular show *Avenue Q* suddenly popped up—except they were actually a Jerry puppet and a Bernie puppet—and from across the street, on top of the Music Box Theatre marquee, Dame Edna (the stage name for Barry Humphries) magically appeared to praise the work that Jerry and Bernie had done in restoring the Broadway theater and Times Square to their rightful place in American culture.

Mayor Bloomberg then directed everyone's attention to the large signs in front of the two theaters. The signs were covered with sleeves. The mayor pulled the cord, the sleeves fell away, and there were the names.

In red lights, "Schoenfeld," and in blue, "Jacobs."

Oh, my, you could see those lights all the way to the South Bronx!

I looked at my husband, who had once stared at the Eiffel Tower in awe and wondered how he got to Paris. Now he had the same look in his eyes as he stared at the huge lighted sign with his name on it.

He whispered to me, "How did I get here?"

Jerry finished writing this book just one month before he died.

How did he get here?

This is how.

—Pat Schoenfeld, New York City

PRELUDE

This is a story about the American theater and the dominant forces that shaped its growth and evolution throughout the last century. It's a story about the Shubert brothers—Sam, Lee, and J. J.—and their successors, and about how my life became entangled with the exceedingly strange Shubert family.

It is a story about family feuds, premature deaths, irrational behavior, regrettable choices, and odd coincidences, as well as invaluable assistance—all of which, for more than fifty years, made me an active participant in the survival of the Shubert legacy.

It is also a story about how the Shubert Organization brought huge box-office hits to the theater, shows like *A Chorus Line*, *Cats*, and *Les Misérables*, and how I learned to handle the massive artistic egos of Liza Minnelli, Bob Fosse, Jerome Robbins, and Stephen Sondheim, among so many others.

Finally, it is a story about my utter disgust with how dangerous and decadent the strip around Times Square had become in the 1970s, and how it drove me to help restore and revitalize midtown Manhattan, so that the Great White Way could once again provide safe, quality entertainment for millions.

How I landed a role in all this was a miracle. I was fired and rehired by the Shuberts more times than I can count. I was sued and investigated for long stretches. I was demeaned and discouraged by many. Yet from being a forty-dollar-a-week law clerk in 1949 at the firm representing the Shubert business, I rose to the unique position of chairman of the board of the Shubert Organization. From my office in what had formerly been Lee Shubert's bedroom above the Shubert Theatre on Shubert Alley in the heart of Broadway, I charted the course of this legendary American business.

I had no idea in my youth that I would have a career in law or theater, or that I would spend a lifetime working for Shubert. If someone had said the name Henry Ford to me as a young man, my immediate response, of course, would have been the automobile. For Thomas Alva Edison, I would have said the lightbulb or motion-picture camera. For the Wright brothers, airplanes. Yet during the entire twentieth century, the name Shubert was synonymous with Broadway and the theater, and I don't recall that in my youth I even knew the name existed.

Today, few remember the Shubert brothers, their many accomplishments, or their prominent role in the history of American theater. Even many currently in the theater business know little about their immediate predecessors.

The fact is that the theater is a business of transients: writers, performers, designers, actors, directors, theater owners, and producers. Some of the theater's greatest names—Tennessee Williams, Arthur Miller, Rodgers and Hammerstein—have endured, while a good many have faded into obscurity.

But the Shubert family and its legacy remains unique.

Their fights, vendettas, vindictiveness, and aberrant behavior set the Shuberts apart in the theater world. Whether they were liked or disliked, admired or shunned, trusted or not did not interest them. They were tenacious, remarkably devoid of loyalty, and extremely litigious. No one could intimidate Lee and J. J. (Older brother Sam met an untimely death.) Those who dared to try almost always regretted it.

They were bullies. They were demanding, and they almost always got what they were after.

To some degree, they were like the original Hollywood moguls, ruling as absolute monarchs and not giving a damn about their subjects. That attitude gave them a tremendous advantage over others who may have been more thoughtful and ethical. In business, the Shubert philosophy was "If we produce the show, we own it all." If they owned it all, they believed, there was no need to pay royalties, and they often refused to do so. Consequently, they were sued endlessly.

It's hardly surprising that Lee and J. J. were reviled. Lee, perhaps, got along with a few people, but I never knew anyone to be J. J.'s friend. The brothers so shunned publicity that any employee who spoke to the press was summarily fired. As a result, the few good deeds they may have done were never publicized. The brothers were so secretive that when they took a vacation, they didn't say when they were leaving or when they were returning for fear that the staff would slack off during their absence.

Yet despite their despicable behavior, there is no doubt that if it had not been for Lee and J. J. Shubert, American theater as we know it today would not exist.

They shared an all-consuming passion for Broadway, and that's what sustained them. From the 1930s and well into the 1950s, pretty much everyone working in American theater was on a Shubert payroll at one time or other. Maybe not ushers in Boise, Idaho, but in the relative mainstream theaters, yes.

The Shuberts produced plays with, and made stars of, Sarah Bernhardt, Lillian Russell, Paul Robeson, Cary Grant, Fanny Brice, Mistinguett, Al Jolson, Uta Hagen…the list goes on and on. They produced plays, bought plays, stole plays, created stars, drove people to drink, and ruined careers. They ruled tyrannically and crushed their rivals, rising from extreme poverty to great riches. They pandered to no one.

Despite my many misgivings about the Shuberts themselves, I am proud to have shared in their legacy. Yet in recounting my part of the Shubert story, I know full well that if Lee or J. J. were alive today, their reaction to my accomplishments in the Shubert business would not evoke even a sigh of appreciation or satisfaction.

Instead, the Shubert brothers would demand to know: "What damn right did you have to do what you did to our business without getting our permission?"

———— •◦• ————

As I became immersed in the Shubert business, I became more infatuated with the theater. My life with the Shuberts was a wild ride, full of platonic flings with thousands of people and all the highs and lows of dealing with huge theatrical successes and massive failures. There were ceaseless negotiations with money men, and all the many joys and frustrations of combining the creative side with the practical. There was no shortage of putting on the kid gloves to deal with prima donnas—actors, writers, directors, choreographers, producers.

There were also times of rejection and disappointment, times of birth and renewal, times of cruelty and of serious personal depression.

And mostly there were never-ending battles, a procession of confrontations and conflicts that could not be ignored. Some were brush fires; others were frontal attacks. Some irrational and absurd. Others inevitable. All were costly, time-consuming, and terribly debilitating. In some cases, defeat would have meant the end of the Shubert Organization, my professional career, and the Broadway that I'd come to love and cherish.

I can't actually remember when I started to go to the theater. My first memory of seeing a significant theatrical attraction was *A Streetcar Named Desire*, probably sometime in 1949, when I was twenty-five. Written by Tennessee Williams and directed by Elia Kazan, it starred Marlon Brando, Jessica Tandy, Kim Hunter, and Karl Malden.

I also recall seeing another Tennessee Williams–Elia Kazan classic, *Cat on a Hot Tin Roof*. But that was some years later, in 1955, around the time I saw *Inherit the Wind*. The following year, I saw *My Fair Lady* with Rex Harrison and Julie Andrews. Up to that point, I was only an occasional theatergoer. It wasn't until I became more entrenched in the Shubert business that I started attending the theater regularly, sometimes four or five nights a week.

As my role in the business grew and my love for the theater became a passion, I recall countless occasions of pure exhilaration.

Gypsy with Ethel Merman absolutely electrified me. One of the greatest American musicals ever, it opened in May 1959 in the Shuberts' Broadway Theatre. It was brilliantly directed and choreographed by Jerome Robbins, with music by Jule Styne and lyrics by Stephen Sondheim. I was so captivated that I would stand in the back of the theater night after night just to hear Ethel close the first act as she belted out "Everything's Coming Up Roses."

Hundreds of other dramas, comedies, and musicals have made my heart beat faster.

Sitting with my wife, Pat, in our aisle seats, in a beautiful rococo room buzzing with excitement as the lights dim and the curtain comes up . . . there is nothing like it.

We have sat through, literally, thousands of overtures and curtain calls. Some have been very good, some very bad, some just all right, but many have been so exceptional that they have enriched our lives.

And then there are a few that stand out as extra special.

I'm thinking of *A Chorus Line, Cats, Les Misérables, Sunday in the Park with George, Phantom of the Opera, Passion*, and *Miss Saigon*.

These are some of the shows that created a fabulous new chapter in Broadway theater, shows that have withstood the test of time and are still performed so many years later.

These are also shows that, in their popularity and profitability, literally saved the Shubert Organization from extinction.

The business we took over took from the Shuberts in 1972 was out of touch and teetering on the edge of bankruptcy. It was mired in lawsuits, the vestiges of the Shubert brothers' tyranny and constant family feuds. The very name Shubert was despised by many in the theater business and considered a dinosaur by many outside the business.

By 1975 we were a sinking ship, in desperate need of a show that would produce sufficient revenue to keep us afloat. But box-office hits are notoriously few and far between, and finding one that would propel us into the future was easier said than done.

A hit show can't be grown or manufactured, like many products. We can't do market research to learn how it tastes, smells, looks, moves, or will compare with the competition. We don't know if customers will like it. We don't even know if there is a market for our product. And after our investment is made, aside from our customers we also have to satisfy a small powerful cadre of people called critics, most especially those who write for the *New York Times*. We can't predict what they will say, because we don't know what they will like, or even if they'll agree with each other. Yet we raise millions of dollars to bring our product to market with the full understanding that the investment could evaporate overnight. In reality, it's easier to strike oil.

But sometimes the process works beautifully, and in the mid-1970s, just as the Shubert Organization was teetering on the brink, *A Chorus Line* came along.

The musical was directed and choreographed by Michael Bennett, who had joined forces with Joe Papp, founder of the New York Shakespeare Festival, then the most important not-for-profit Off-Broadway theater group in New York. Their mission was to put on a new type of musical.

Set on a bare stage, it's the story of nineteen dancers auditioning for spots in a show. As the dancers perform, they show traces of their personalities, their lives, and events that led them to become dancers.

Word spread quickly throughout the theater community that Michael and Joe had a potential hit on their hands. But at first it was purely an experimental project. And by the time *A Chorus Line* was in rehearsals at the Public Theater, Joe let Michael know that he would have to close it for financial reasons.

In desperation, Michael came to our offices so that we could hear several songs. His hope was that we would fall in love with them and step in and save the show.

It worked. My longtime partner, Bernie Jacobs, met with Joe and worked out an arrangement in which Joe agreed to fund the balance of rehearsals and open the show downtown.

By the time the show opened on Joe's stage in lower Manhattan on May 21, 1975, it was an eagerly anticipated event. The short run sold out immediately.

Michael invited Bernie and his wife, Betty, to an early performance, and they were enamored. Pat and I saw *A Chorus Line* immediately afterward and were overwhelmed by it. But Bernie was so smitten that he saw it innumerable times, often taking guests with him. By then the show was completely sold out, and Bernie and friends frequently sat on aisle steps because no seats were available.

Not surprisingly, Bernie and Michael had already started conversations about moving the show to Broadway.

Michael decided that the Shubert Theatre was his theater of choice, and whatever Michael wanted we were determined to give him. However, as often happens in the theater business, the Shubert was already booked—with Tennessee Williams's *The Red Devil Battery Sign*.

Although our Broadhurst Theatre—which seats 250 fewer than the Shubert and, some might say, is a little less grand—was available, we weren't sure Michael would agree, and we hated the possibility of losing *A Chorus Line*. But our fears were alleviated when Michael, purely out of friendship, accepted the Broadhurst.

In the end, as luck would have it, the Tennessee Williams play closed in Boston, never making it to New York. Michael got the Shubert after all.

Moving *A Chorus Line* uptown to Broadway was going to cost $700,000, and Joe Papp's Shakespeare Festival didn't have the funds. We wanted the show so badly that we offered to pay for the move, not knowing how we would raise the money. Fortunately, while our offer was appreciated, it was not accepted. LuEsther Mertz, a major supporter of the Shakespeare Festival, stepped in to foot the bill.

A Chorus Line was heralded in the press and anxiously awaited on Broadway.

The show started its preview performances on July 25, 1975, and was scheduled to have its official opening on October 7. But a strike intervened, and every show opening on Broadway got pushed back. Instead, *A Chorus Line* opened on Sunday night, October 19.

That night, after the songs were sung, the dances danced, and the lights back up, Bernie and I were ecstatic. So was the audience. And when the reviews appeared, they were raves.

Clive Barnes wrote in the *New York Times*, "It was not exactly an opening. It was more of a celebration. . . . 'A Chorus Line' is still one of those musicals you will sing about to your grandchildren. It is an occasion of joy, an affirmation of Broadway and a smoke-signal to the world that the musical can touch unexpected depths in the human heart."

A Chorus Line was a hit of mammoth proportions. It was nominated for a dozen Tony Awards and won nine. The show won the New York Drama Critics' Circle Award for Best Musical of the season as well as the 1976 Pulitzer Prize for Drama, one of only a few musicals ever to receive that honor. When it finally closed, after fifteen years and 6,137 performances, it was the longest-running show in Broadway history.

For everyone connected with *A Chorus Line*, it was New Year's Eve every night. The cast was the toast of the town. Michael Bennett was the toast of Broadway. And Bernie was so proud of Michael that he mentioned him in every conversation as the musical theater's greatest-ever director.

A Chorus Line was also Shubert's salvation. The show's record-breaking run on Broadway, and across the country, was the beginning of a new era for the company.

In the wake of *A Chorus Line* came the British invasion. It had begun, timidly, with Andrew Lloyd Webber and Tim Rice's *Jesus Christ Superstar*. But then came their *Evita*, followed in full force by Andrew's *Cats*, Cameron Mackintosh's *Les Misérables*, Andrew's *Phantom of the Opera* and *Starlight Express*, and Cameron's *Miss Saigon*.

These musicals have been described as "pop opera," "the sung-through musical," and "the musical spectacular." But whatever they're called, the genre created a new era of musical theater—a new golden age—which continues today with *Beauty and the Beast, The Lion King, Mamma Mia!, Wicked, Spamalot*, and *Jersey Boys*, to name a few.

This new golden age is a far cry from the Broadway and the Shubert family business that I first stepped into all those years ago.

ONE

THE SHUBERTS AND THE FIRST "GOLDEN AGE" OF BROADWAY

The Shubert family story begins in the late 1870s, in Syracuse, New York, where the impoverished immigrant family was trying to scratch out a living.

David Shubert, a brandy drinker and absentee father and the black sheep of the family, had immigrated to America. In his native town of Neustadt, Germany, he'd been an itinerant peddler who smuggled tea across the Polish border. In America, he settled first in New York City and soon after with relatives in central New York State. His wife, Catherine, their two daughters Fannie and Sara, and three sons—Lee, Sam, and Jacob John—soon followed him to their new country, paying for their passage with gifts and loans from friends and a family rabbi. A third daughter, Dora, might have been born in Syracuse. A fourth girl, said to have been called Lisa, supposedly died of malnutrition at an early age.

The brothers' infatuation with the theater began early. Their strong-willed mother sent Sam onto the streets to hawk newspapers on a corner directly across from Syracuse's Grand Opera House. By the time Sam was nine, the manager of the opera house had hired him as an usher and allowed him to sell refreshments and souvenirs in the balcony during evening performances.

Two years later, Sam was promoted to chief usher and started earning a weekly salary. The following year, with the help of a local clothier who had theatrical financial interests, Sam became the box-office treasurer of Syracuse's first-class Wieting Opera House.

Lee also started out selling newspapers but then got a job sitting in the window of a cigar store wrapping cigars.

At age seven, Jacob John, known as J. J., was also dispatched by Catherine to sell the morning paper, which meant he had to be on the streets by four a.m. Following in Lee's footsteps, he also later worked in the cigar store, but before long, with Sam's help, both brothers landed jobs in local theaters. While still a teenager, J. J. was working in five different theaters, in addition to selling tickets for a local baseball team during the summer.

Sam soon developed an interest in producing plays and while in his late teens and early twenties produced two successful road tours before departing Syracuse for New York in 1900. With the help of financial backers in Syracuse and New York, he gained a foothold in the theater community by leasing the Herald Square Theatre on Thirty-Fifth Street and Broadway, then the heart of the theater district.

Lee joined him in New York City, and the firm of Sam S. and Lee Shubert was born. A year later J. J. arrived to work with Sam and Lee.

Believing that real estate was the key to wealth, the brothers acquired additional New York theaters, launching what would become the largest theatrical empire of the twentieth century.

Then, in May 1905, a catastrophic accident tore the family apart. A train bound from New York to Pittsburgh carrying Sam, his booking agent Abe Thalheimer, and his attorney William Klein, collided with a freight train filled with dynamite. Sam was killed, despite Thalheimer's and Klein's best efforts to help save him. Sam was buried in the Salem Fields Cemetery in Brooklyn.

Sam had been the adored brother and the family's guiding light, and there was no love lost between Lee and J. J. Fortunately, they did agree that in order for the business to continue after Sam's death, it would need an infusion of capital. Their mother Catherine, worshipped by both Lee and J. J., was the beneficiary of Sam's $200,000 life insurance policy. Catherine knew that there were hard feelings between Lee and J. J. and told the brothers that she would lend them the insurance proceeds only if they pledged to stay in business together. They agreed. For his efforts to save Sam's life in the train wreck, attorney William Klein was rewarded with the position of legal representative for the Shuberts, a job he held for more than fifty years.

The new firm's first priority was to acquire theaters, and the brothers embarked on a nationwide expansion in key markets. But the Shuberts' emergence as important players in American theater pitted them against barriers erected by the formidable Theatrical Syndicate, a monopoly that virtually controlled the industry at the turn of the twentieth century.

In 1896, the six largest theater owners and operators in the country had met secretly in New York to pool their resources. Led by an ambitious theater owner and producer named Charles Frohman—along with Abraham Lincoln Erlanger, Al Hayman, Marc Klaw, Samuel Nixon, and Fred Zimmerman—the group brought most of America's theaters into a franchise agreement. The arrangement combined all their booking offices and standardized their contractual terms. Franchisees were required to present attractions booked by the syndicate. They had to use the syndicate's booking office to book attractions, even those originating in their own theaters, and they had to present shows in the syndicate's theaters. The syndicate forced independent owners, producers, business managers, and even actors to work under their conditions. The only alternative was to not work at all.

Frohman and his friends claimed that their goal was to make the theater more profitable for everyone, but in reality they were simply eliminating competition and increasing their own profitability.

The Shuberts wouldn't play by the syndicate's rules, and a war between the brothers and the syndicate raged for nearly twenty years, encompassing many battles, several peace treaties, and then more battles. It was terribly damaging for everyone. One upside for American theater, however, was that because the Shuberts were locked out of the syndicate's theaters, the brothers had no choice but to build new theaters across the country.

The beginning of the end of the syndicate war came unexpectedly on May 7, 1915. Frohman was on his way to London to meet with the playwright J. M. Barrie—of *Peter Pan* fame—when the ship he was sailing on, the *Lusitania*, was torpedoed and sank. With Frohman's death, the syndicate gradually lost its stranglehold. By June 1924, when Lee and J. J. formed the Shubert Theatre Corporation, the brothers had become the dominant force in the American theater. They owned and operated 104 theaters in twenty-nine American cities, plus seven theaters in London. To fill their theaters, they produced numerous new shows, and booked attractions in more than a thousand theaters from New York City to Portland, Oregon.

The so-called "legitimate theater" and vaudeville, a group of separate variety acts, were the principal forms of entertainment at the time, and their popularity rapidly expanded throughout America. Within a quarter century, Shubert grew to be America's largest producing and theater-owning firm, presiding as it did over the nation's most important sources of entertainment.

Lee and J. J. were emperors during this first golden age of Broadway.

Then came 1929 and the Great Depression. Hundreds of theaters across the country quickly closed their doors. By 1932, the Shuberts were forced into receivership. Lee was named as one of the two receivers. The Irving Trust Company was the other.

Undeterred, the two brothers formed the Select Theatres Corporation.

Thanks to the receivership, in fact, the Shuberts were ultimately allowed to cancel undesirable theater leases and contracts. The receivership also allowed the Select Theatres Corporation, as the sole bidder for the Shubert Theatre Corporation, to buy the remaining desirable theaters for the reasonable sum of $400,000. When the receivership ended in 1935, Select Theatres Corporation emerged with fewer playhouses, but the Shubert business, which included many valuable theaters and nontheatrical properties privately owned by Lee and J. J., was still the country's largest, most powerful theatrical force.

The Shuberts' business soon began to rally.

Drama was primarily Lee Shubert's domain, while the musical was J. J.'s. He especially liked foreign musicals and traveled to Europe to catch operettas, such as *Das Dreimaiderlhaus*, which he brought to the United States as *Blossom Time*, and *Alt Heidelberg*, which ultimately became *The Student Prince*.

Unfortunately for writers, J. J. believed that if he produced a work, he owned it. Copyright laws did not apply to J. J. For instance, while there was some litigation involving *The Student Prince*, the Shubert business still gets royalties on it. At one point, the Shuberts had thirteen companies touring the United States performing *The Student Prince*.

In the 1937 to 1939 theatrical seasons, three shows arrived in Shubert theaters: *Hooray for What!*, a Harold Arlen musical starring Ed Wynn; the musical revue *Hellzapoppin'*; and the Bud Abbott and Lou Costello musical *The Streets Of Paris*, which debuted a young dancer and future award-winning director-choreographer, Gower Champion. All three were major hits, enabling Lee and J. J., with the help of loans as well as savings from unpaid federal income taxes, to survive the tough times.

The 1940s, which included the war years, brought a series of exciting plays and actors to Shubert houses: Thornton Wilder's *The Skin of Our Teeth*, with Tallulah Bankhead; Noel Coward's three plays *Blithe Spirit*,

five. Since I'd graduated number two in my class, I took a deep breath and came up with "Forty dollars."

Working in my favor was the fact that, typical of many theatrical fee arrangements, Weir's salary was based on a percentage of gross revenues. As a result, neither my salary nor that of others in the firm was of any concern to Weir. Whether I was paid ten dollars a week or two hundred dollars a week didn't affect him. So, he just nodded and said, "Done."

On July 11, 1949, my employment as a law clerk at Klein & Weir began.

Weir was a wiry man in his mid-fifties with intense eyes. His senior partner, William Klein, the fellow who'd tried to save Sam Shubert's life in the train wreck, was recovering from a serious illness. He didn't know about my arrival until he returned to the office three months later. Since Klein's compensation from the firm's practice was based on net profits—unlike Weir's gross-profit deal—he wasn't too happy about Weir having hired me at the forty-dollar weekly salary.

A tall, thin, patrician-looking man with a dictatorial presence, Klein only began to tolerate me when he heard that my father was a furrier: he assumed we were wealthy, which we weren't.

Klein had been the Shuberts' lawyer for so many years that he reported to work but did no work at all. The work was done by Weir and the firm's junior partner, Adolph Lund, a very small man with a round bald head who resembled my grandfather.

My "office" on the twelfth floor at 1440 Broadway consisted of a glass-topped table in a corridor. I had no telephone, no secretary, no file cabinet. I didn't even have a wastepaper basket.

With nothing much to do, I spent most of my time sitting in Adolph's office. I watched him dictate contracts, affidavits, and briefs for litigation, opine on literary rights and labor problems, and prepare for meetings with clients. He was my mentor.

While Lund dealt with the nitty-gritty of the firm's business, Weir spent mornings in the office, then disappeared, not returning until late afternoon or early evening. Weir's daily routine was to see Lee and J. J. separately in their respective offices. J. J.'s office was on the sixth floor of the Sardi Building on the south side of Forty-Fourth Street. Lee's was directly across the street on the second floor of the Shubert Theatre building.

Weir had to see them separately because they did not speak to each other.

My job consisted mostly of taking the subway or bus to the courthouse at Foley Square in lower Manhattan to file legal papers, making copies of documents, researching cases in which the firm had some interest, and worrying about the transoms over our law-office doors. There was no air-conditioning in the office, and in the summer the only way to get air circulating was to open the transoms above every door. But someone had once climbed over the transom and robbed the office, so after everyone left in the evening, it was my job to close the transoms.

Three or four times a week, I'd come home at night and worry that I'd forgotten to shut them. I would then hop on the crosstown bus back to Broadway, and on another bus up to Fortieth Street, a twenty-minute trek each way, to check that the transoms were closed. That soon became a real chore.

My first responsibility as a lawyer, at least the first one that I remember, was to defend a lady friend of J. J.'s son, John. She was accused of yelling, screaming, and interrupting a performance in a movie theater on Fifty-Ninth Street. Police had arrested her for disorderly conduct.

I cross-examined the prosecution's witness about whether or not anyone watching the movie had actually heard her screaming and yelling, but no one had. At the end of the trial, which wasn't long, the judge said to me, "You can now make your motion." I hadn't the faintest idea what he meant. He said, "Do you move to dismiss for failure to prove prima facie case?"

I said, "I do."

He said, "Motion granted," and that was the end of that case.

With that success behind me, by the end of the year I got a raise to fifty dollars a week.

Life changed radically for me on February 20, 1950, when a complaint came in from the U.S. Department of Justice. It was an antitrust action against Lee and J. J. Shubert, the Select Theatres Corporation, and a man named Marcus Heiman, who was their partner in the United Booking Office, which was the sole theatrical booking office in America. Weir handed me the complaint and told me to prepare an answer.

I was stunned. I knew next to nothing about antitrust law. Nor did I have any experience drafting answers to complaints. I faced a dilemma.

I could move forward in total ignorance, or I could admit that I did not know what I was doing. I chose the former.

Looking back, I shouldn't have. I didn't appreciate the significance of the case or what was ultimately at stake. I didn't understand that if we lost this case, Klein & Weir would not only lose the Shuberts, their most important client, but that the course of American theater would be altered significantly.

The suit alleged that the Shuberts' business methods violated the Sherman Antitrust Act, the 1890 law designed to prohibit nefarious dealings that could create a monopoly or somehow keep prices artificially high. The government believed the Shuberts had too much control over the production of shows, where the shows played, and how they toured. In the government's view, there was no real competition in the theater business.

As a remedy, the Justice Department demanded that Lee and J. J. divest a number of theaters in various cities. At this point, the Shuberts owned twenty-six in New York and seventeen in other parts of the country. The government also made other specific demands of the Shuberts: close down the United Booking Office, which put shows into more than a thousand theaters nationwide; stop booking attractions in theaters other than their own; disengage from all theatrical partnership interests; and stop acquiring any more theaters without the prior approval of the Justice Department.

The ramifications of losing the case were grave enough. But under the surface of those troubled waters was even greater turmoil. The Shuberts could be exposed to countless antitrust actions from private litigants seeking treble damages, attorneys' fees, and further penalties.

Losing the case would seriously dismantle the empire the Shuberts had built, in effect putting them out of business.

The government's charges were reportedly based on complaints by several producers who had refused to enter into agreements to use the United Booking Office.

At one point the FBI showed up at the Shubert offices and made photostats of every contract, letter, and document that might possibly support the government's case.

The Shuberts never threw out a single piece of paper, so the FBI had a feast.

To prepare our answer to the government's case, I also had to look at those papers—thousands of booking contracts, franchise agreements, correspondence, production contracts, leases, and financial records, going back more than twenty years.

A de facto history of the Shuberts, those papers revealed their business methods.

A producer who arranged to present a play outside of New York was required to sign a contract with the United Booking Office, which franchised the most desirable theaters. The setup meant that the Shuberts had control over what shows were produced in which theater, even if they didn't own the theater. Once the show came to Broadway, the producer had to book a Shubert theater. And if the producer opened on Broadway and later took his show on the road, he was required to book the tour through the United Booking Office. What's more, for the privilege of doing business with the United Booking Office, the producer paid a booking fee equal to 5 percent of the gross weekly box-office receipts. The Shuberts got their cut right off the top.

The Shuberts got away with it because they controlled the best theaters in America. They were essentially the only game in town—you dealt with the Shuberts or you dealt with no one. It was quickly clear to me that this practice would be almost impossible to defend at trial.

We had only sixty days to answer the complaint, and the more I studied the case, the more I realized I needed more time. But I was intimidated and frightened to death to ask the other side for an extension. I didn't even know how to go about it. I mentioned my dilemma to Adolph Lund, and he got me an additional sixty days.

Our office law library had almost no information regarding federal cases, so Adolph arranged for me to work at the bar association's library. I spent four months holed up there. During that time, neither William Klein nor Milton Weir ever asked me for any progress reports. Nor did Milton ever ask to see any of the work I had done.

Adolph, however, sent me to confer with a prominent lawyer named Alfred McCormack and several of his associates at one of the country's leading law firms, Cravath, Swaine & Moore.

McCormack, who had served during World War II as assistant to the secretary of war, was around fifty when I met him. He may have been a senior partner at a very formal, stuffy firm, but there was nothing formal or stuffy about him. McCormack represented everything that Cravath, Swaine & Moore did not. He was a maverick. He loved eating lunch at the printer's, where he went to dictate briefs, accompanied by two stenographers and young assistants who carried his law books. He would do some work, then order in a Nova Scotia salmon and sturgeon from a local Jewish delicatessen. One day when I was with him, a young assistant pointed to the salmon and asked, "What's that?"

McCormack told him, "That's lox, you dumb goy," using the Yiddish word for a gentile, which he was himself, of course.

McCormack and I got along extremely well. He had faith in me, which helped build up my own self-confidence. He even invited me to join his firm, a genuinely brave act since he knew I was Jewish and Cravath was not a firm that hired Jews.

At this point, I still had not actually met the Shuberts. I did not know their executive staff, or lower-level staff, nor did I know their competitors, producers, managers, box-office personnel, out-of-town Shubert theater managers, labor-union executives, agents, performers, writers, directors, or choreographers. I was a hired hand, just one spoke in the wheel that drove the response to the government's allegations.

Most of my time at the bar-association law library was spent boning up on antitrust law. But then I found a book called *The Business of the Theater*, by Alfred L. Bernheim, who had apparently been commissioned to write it by Actors' Equity in 1932. It laid out the evolution of the American theater from the nineteenth century, with many chapters devoted to the Shuberts and their ascendancy. That became my primary reference.

From the book I deduced that if, indeed, the Shuberts had a monopoly, that position had been thrust upon them after their publicly listed Shubert Theatre Corporation went bankrupt in 1931 and a large number of their theaters, mostly outside New York, had to be put up for auction.

Lee Shubert had then used funds that he had loaned to the bankrupt corporation to bid on the Shuberts' more valuable assets. And because Lee was the only bidder, the brothers' newly formed Select Theatres Corporation had ended up with a large number of desirable theaters.

My response to the government, then, claimed that the Shuberts had not purchased the theaters to drive competitors out of business. Instead, a monopoly had been thrust upon them as a result of their original company's bankruptcy.

This "thrust-upon monopoly" defense, to my knowledge, had never been used before. It was totally my invention. I also conceived six or seven other defenses, including the "clean hands doctrine." In that defense, I alleged that the government had not come into the case with clean hands, since before the current case it had already tried to break up the Shubert business. Unfortunately, I would later learn that "clean hands" is no defense against the government.

I must say I was quite self-satisfied at having devised these various responses. We met our 120-day deadline, which bought us more time, as the government prepared its response to us.

By 1952, however, it became apparent to Milton Weir and Adolph Lund that they needed more seasoned counsel than I to work on the case. Lee Shubert, now an active participant in the litigation, took Weir's advice and retained a cocounsel, Ernest S. Meyers, once head of the judgment section of the Antitrust Division at Justice. His fee was a hefty $5,000 a month, and whenever his monthly bill arrived, Lee or J. J. would launch into a diatribe against lawyers in general and Klein & Weir in particular.

Shortly thereafter, I was invited to participate in a meeting about the case with Lee. It would turn out to be my first and only encounter with Lee Shubert. I joined William Klein, Milton Weir, Ernest Meyers, and two other executives of the company in Lee's second-floor office above the Shubert Theatre. In the course of the discussion, during which I never uttered a word, Klein said to Lee, "I don't know whether we should do that."

Lee, a small man with a receding hairline and dark, piercing eyes, snapped at Klein, "We? We? Since when did I make you my partner?"

This public humiliation effectively silenced Klein, and left me in a state of bewilderment over the nature of the Shubert brothers.

Two

A FOREIGN WORLD

The Shubert world was foreign to me. Nothing I'd ever done and no one I'd ever met had prepared me for the Shuberts.

I was a good boy from a comfortable middle-class Jewish family on New York's Upper West Side. My father, Sam, was a furrier. My mother, Fanny, was a small, elegant, very good-looking woman with white hair. Sam was a happy-go-lucky fellow who enjoyed betting on baseball, football, the horses—in fact, on anything. Fanny was a rather negative, cautious person.

My own sense of insecurity comes from Fanny. Sam was loose with money and loved having a good time. Fanny was always nervous about money and worried about Sam's gambling. She looked at things in an odd way and always punctuated comments with "if all is well." Every plan we ever made was followed by "if all is well."

It took me years to understand that she wasn't worried about some future autumnal season: "If fall is well."

Unlike most of my friends' parents, mine were so open that everybody always called them by their first names. Even my brother, Irving, and I called them Sam and Fanny.

The building where I grew up, 400 West End Avenue, is still there on the northeast corner of Seventy-Ninth Street. Everyone in the neighborhood knew the building because Joe DiMaggio lived in the penthouse with his first wife, Dorothy Arnold. One Sunday, my father took me to Yankee Stadium, and I saw Joe hit the winning home run. When we got home, I waited outside for him. As he arrived, I stuck out my hand to congratulate him. He said, "Hello, kid," and walked right by. It was a rejection by an idol that I never forgot.

My brother, Irving, eight years my senior, was a rebellious teenager—he once took off for Florida to pick oranges, returned, and eventually moved to California. Fanny saw me as the serious one and doted on me. I saw Irving as the person who terrorized me. I was already an easily frightened child. Frightened to be alone in the house, frightened to sleep in the dark, frightened to make decisions. Irving delighted in teasing me unmercifully, thereby heightening my anxieties. I don't think I ever overcame my anxieties; they plagued me for a good part of my life.

As a young boy, I attended P.S. 87 on West Seventy-Eighth Street. We had a student government: there was a mayor, a district attorney, a judge, a patrolman inside the school, one at the outside crosswalks, and one in the playground. A student caught talking on the stairways, for example, was given a summons and a trial. Students who were found guilty were sent to the detention room for a half hour after class. I was the judge.

I was also the school orator. Irving had often recited poetry to me, sometimes for entertainment, but mostly with the goal of frightening me. From seventh grade on, there were regular poetry-reading contests. Thanks to Irving and all the poetry he had read to me, I always won. I would often recite the Gettysburg Address or "The Ballad of East and West," which was so long it put listeners to sleep. One happy consequence of my oratorical skills was that I won an important contest and the Child Welfare League of America asked me to speak at their annual luncheon.

There I was, twelve years old, in the grand ballroom of the Waldorf-Astoria, sitting between Mrs. Sara Delano Roosevelt, the president's mother, and Joe E. Brown, a famous comedian of the day. Mayor Fiorello La Guardia was there, as was Robert Ripley, the cartoonist who created *Ripley's Believe It or Not!* During the after-lunch speeches, I was introduced as the "representative of America's children." From memory I delivered a long address, pledging the cooperation of the nation's children in making America a better place. I stated that what we children needed most was a world full of cautious automobile drivers. Honestly, that's what I said.

The next morning's *New York Times* wrote that a twelve-year-old schoolboy had stolen the show. Another paper's headline put it, "Lad Wins Applause of 1,000 at Luncheon Here."

After grade school, I had a rather undistinguished four years at DeWitt Clinton High School in the Bronx. I wasn't a particularly good student. I was small in size, not especially good-looking or sought-after.

Although I had a girlfriend for a time, she left me for another boy. A question in the yearbook asked, "What do you wish to be when you grow up?" All I could think of was "president of General Motors."

Paradoxically, despite my insecurities I have often made decisions that run contrary to my basic nature. The earliest and most important decision I was faced with was where to attend college. Irving urged me to go out of town, insisting that I would ruin my life if I remained at home. He'd been to Chicago and talked me into going to school there. So in August 1941, I enrolled at the University of Illinois in Champaign-Urbana. I was not yet seventeen, and totally alone. I wasn't shy, but the idea of being so far from home frightened me. I didn't know anyone and didn't know where I would live. Still, I went. It was so unlike me.

Shortly after I arrived, I joined a fraternity. But that December, World War II started, and by the following June many of my fraternity brothers had been called to serve. I decided to take classes at Columbia University in New York that summer, and when I returned to Illinois in the fall, I switched from the College of Commerce to the College of Engineering.

I didn't know my way around engineering and wasn't good at math, but I figured that engineering courses would land me some sort of specialty assignment in the army. I was getting by, but I was struggling. Then one day I saw a bulletin board: "Wanted: Applications for meteorology program, U.S. Army Air Corps." I applied and to my amazement was accepted. By February 1943, I was in the Army Air Corps.

First, I was sent to Camp Upton in Patchogue, Long Island. It could have been in the middle of Timbuktu, as far as I was concerned. Whoever heard of Patchogue? Who knew the Long Island Railroad went out that far? Six days later I was sent to Atlantic City and assigned to the Ritz-Carlton Hotel for basic training. My room had double-decker bunks and salt water in the bathtub. At two and three o'clock in the morning we had drills that involved jumping out of bed, running down twelve flights of stairs, and standing on the boardwalk in the cold.

One month later, I was sent to the Massachusetts Institute of Technology, where, for the next ten and a half months, I studied advanced algebra, differential calculus, integral calculus, advanced calculus, and differential equations. I had to take physics, oceanography, climatology, geography, descriptive meteorology, dynamic meteorology, and synoptic meteorology. I didn't know whether I was coming or going. I flunked out. Not because of the math, but because I couldn't draw my maps well enough. They expected good hand-eye coordination from someone who couldn't even tie shoelaces until he was eight. Obviously, though, placing the weather front in the wrong spot on the map would mean big trouble for anyone relying on your forecast.

It was around that time, while I was asleep in my room, that I suffered my first panic attack. I felt as if I were about to explode. I jumped out of bed, ran across the hall to another fellow's room, and woke him up. I just had to talk to someone. After awhile the fear subsided, and I went back to my room and fell asleep.

From MIT, I was put on a train to Tyndall Army Air Field, an aerial gunnery training base in Panama City, Florida. There I started a six-week course to become a Sperry lower-ball-turret gunner on a B-17 Flying Fortress. The fact that B-17s were flying daylight, deep-penetration, precision-bombing missions over Germany was a sobering thought. The potentially fatal prospects did not escape me. I was just nineteen, and I would read headlines in the papers that said "Raid on Schweinfurt: 55 Bombers Shot Down" and "Raid on Regensburg: 52 Bombers Lost." Because we didn't wear parachutes, I had visions of a plane door falling off and me tumbling out into space with nothing to save me.

I said to myself, "I am really in serious trouble here."

In the fifth week, I had to take a phase check, which meant removing both .50-caliber machine guns from the turret, disassembling them, and then reassembling and replacing them in the turret. I failed and had to take the test again. Rumor had it that if you failed the second test, you would be transferred to the infantry and three weeks later would find yourself in the jungles of New Guinea.

Once again I was in a high state of anxiety, and once again I failed. But fate intervened. It rained the sixth week, preventing the gunnery class ahead of mine from engaging in air-to-air firing, an essential part of the training. As a result, every class was washed back one week. My second failure was erased, and I took the test a third time. Miraculously, I passed.

Instead of being shipped overseas, I was sent to gunnery-instructors' school at Laredo Army Air Field in Texas before coming back to Tyndall as an instructor. I then spent some time at the Eastern Flying Training Command headquarters in Montgomery, Alabama, and the Central Flying Training Command headquarters in Fort Worth, Texas, before being discharged on February 6, 1946, never having fired a shot in anger.

Thanks to the courses at MIT, I'd earned fifty-nine credits. So, having left Illinois as a lower sophomore, I returned that fall as an upper senior. I had also matured and was in a more serious frame of mind. I got nothing but As.

Back in New York after graduation, my father asked me about my future plans. I told him, "I don't know. I'll go into your business. I'll be a furrier."

He said, "You're not going into the fur business. You should go to law school. Law school will never hurt you."

As I've said, the only lawyer I knew was Bernie Jacobs. He'd gone to Columbia Law and was happy to recommend me. His recommendation counted. But Columbia started in September. At NYU Law School I could start in February, so I enrolled at NYU.

I was living at home, when one night during my second year in law school I had a date with a girl named Cynthia Miller, who lived around the corner. I remember the evening well because it was the night of the blizzard of 1947. The city was completely crippled. I also remember it well because Cynthia had a younger sister named Pat, who also had a date that night, with a boy who lived in their building. So the four of us went out to walk in the snow.

Cynthia and I never went out again. But months later I ran into Pat at the Seventy-Ninth Street and Broadway subway station on her way to NYU, where she was an undergraduate. She was relaxed, fun, and easy to get along with. In fact, we started running into each other there fairly regularly. In the subway entrance, there was a gum machine with a little mirror on the front. I'd stop there to check my face, and Pat was always catching me in the act and laughing. The idea of having a steady girlfriend never entered my mind. We were friends. Nor did Pat seem to have any particular interest in me as a boyfriend. We would sometimes meet at a luncheonette near NYU, or make casual plans to ride home together on the subway. We didn't really date; we just sort of hung out together. It went on like that for quite a while.

Everything started to change one day as we were walking across Washington Square on our way to the subway. I mentioned that my parents were in Florida, and she invited me to dinner at her house.

I said, "I don't go to girls' houses for dinner."

She told me, "My parents always have our friends over for dinner."
So I went for dinner.

After dinner, we went dancing with some friends at the Hotel Pierre, where there was a small downstairs room with a combo. We danced and had a few drinks, and when I brought her home, we kissed good night.

That first dinner at Pat's house led to a heightened sense of awareness on my part that something might be brewing between us. What she didn't know at the time was that I suffered from those panic attacks.

One night, I was home alone when our doorman sneaked into the apartment thinking it was empty. I heard him, grabbed a baseball bat, and ran after him. He was looking for whiskey. I was so terrified that after that I couldn't stay home. Before long, I confided to Pat about my panic attacks and my fear of being alone. The next time Sam and Fanny went to Florida, to my amazement Pat insisted that I stay at her house. I slept on the couch in her living room. Being invited into her family like that was pretty unusual for those days. We weren't engaged yet; we were just going out. Still, she was always very caring, and she was very patient.

At exam time, especially when I was studying for the bar exam, I told Pat that I couldn't see her. I didn't feel right saying, "Don't see anyone else," but for three months I knew I wouldn't be taking her out, except for her birthday. My system for studying was to put my books above my desk and go through them three times. As I finished one, I put it on top and reached for the one on the bottom. Every so often, I would call Pat and say, "I'm taking a three-and-a-half-minute break; come on over."

She only lived around the corner, so she would run over for the three and a half minutes, we would have a chat, and then I'd say good-bye. She would leave, and I would go back to studying.

But we were not going steady, and Pat was occasionally seeing a young man from Connecticut named Mort, who drove a Chrysler convertible with station-wagon sides. Not only did I not have a car, but I couldn't even drive. He came to pick her up one Saturday night, which happened to be her parents' twenty-fifth wedding anniversary, bearing a silver dish as a gift for her parents. As soon as Pat saw it, she ran inside to phone me. "Mort just bought my parents an anniversary present," she said, "and there's no doubt he's serious about me. What do I tell him?"

I said, "Don't rush into anything. Let's talk about it."

She said, "All right, then tomorrow I'm coming over, and you're going to tell your parents that we're going steady."

I agreed.

This was a big step, because in 1949, "going steady" meant you were sort of engaged to be engaged.

As our relationship deepened, I still had no thought of marriage. I was totally satisfied with the going-steady status quo. But she wasn't. By now I'd passed the bar and was working. However, since my job was paying only forty dollars a week and she was still in school, imminent marriage was out of the question. There was no way I could support a wife.

As Pat approached her twenty-first birthday on April 4, 1950, tensions developed. In those days, twenty-one was a year of demarcation. There was marriage and there was impending spinsterhood, with not much in between. I asked her what she wanted for her birthday, and she brazenly said she wanted to get engaged.

"Oh," I teased her, "I was thinking of getting you a pair of gloves."

I didn't find out until later that she asked her mother, "What do I do if he buys me gloves?"

Her mother said, "Patsy, darling, if Gerald is buying you a pair of gloves for your twenty-first birthday, I don't know how serious he really is."

I was a nervous wreck about getting engaged, although I took solace in the fact that no wedding date was set.

On the Friday night before her birthday, we had dinner at her folks' house. Afterward, we went to my house, where my parents were sitting around the table with some friends. I had alerted them about the engagement. In fact, Fanny had given me her own diamond engagement ring, which she wanted me to put into a corsage box and present to Pat with great ceremony.

I kept telling Pat about the pair of gloves in store for her. But when we got to my parents' house, I said to her, "Tell my folks what you want for your birthday."

She said, "To get engaged."

On cue, I unceremoniously brought out the ring and slapped it down on the table. Pat was thrilled. But Fanny was annoyed that I had not followed the prepared script and gone through with the ceremony.

Ten weeks later, on June 25, the Korean War started. Every man in the country between the ages of eighteen and a half and thirty-five was eligible for the draft. I had already served, but the government was also considering calling up World War II veterans. Married men, however, would be less likely to get called. So we set a date: October 29, 1950.

I was frightened about getting married. I had financial concerns. We had nowhere to live, and because Pat was still in school, we couldn't afford to rent a place. My worries raised my anxiety level to the boiling point, and I suffered another panic attack.

October 29 finally arrived. We had a wonderful small wedding at the Hampshire House, followed by a week's honeymoon at Grossinger's Hotel, a popular resort in the Catskills. We had no money, so Pat's parents gave us five hundred dollars for the honeymoon.

I confided in Pat completely about my fears and anxieties. I wondered how she could still love me, convinced that only massive psychotherapy in some institution could make me a worthy person. She obviously saw something in me that I couldn't see. She was so young and confident. I was on life support, and she was my life preserver.

For the next six months we lived in her parents' home, which I didn't mind at all. Her mother was good to me, my meals were prepared, the beds were made, and we had no rent to pay. It suited me fine. But Pat hated it. So as soon as we could, in spring 1951, we rented a one-bedroom apartment in Peter Cooper Village on East Twentieth Street.

It was a great place on the tenth floor overlooking the East River. But it cost the then-unimaginable rent of $110 a month. Pat received her bachelor's degree in education from NYU in June 1951 and started teaching in a city public school on the Lower East Side. She was earning fifty dollars a week. By then I was earning just a little more. But in those days landlords didn't consider a woman's salary in calculating whether you could afford the rent. The norm was that one week's salary equaled one month's rent. Since my salary alone didn't qualify us, our fathers subsidized us, pitching in twenty-five dollars each per month.

Pat's father, Peter, drove a Cadillac, which in my naïve experience stamped him as a rich man. He wasn't. Every morning, he would come in the Cadillac to pick up Pat and drive her to P.S. 97 on Mangin Street, off Houston Street. One day Pat's principal saw her getting out of the car and asked if the driver was her sugar daddy. From then on, Pat insisted that her father drop her off two blocks away so no one from the school would see her.

Pat had to be downstairs every morning at exactly three minutes to eight to satisfy her father, who was a stickler for time. I didn't get into my office until nine thirty, so Pat decided that if I wanted her to fix breakfast, make the beds, and clean the bathroom, I had to be up as early as she was. "If you'd rather sleep the extra half hour, then you have to make the bed, clean the bathroom, and make your own breakfast," she said.

Given the choice, I decided to sleep the extra half hour. The arrangement amazed our friends. In the early 1950s, after all, a nice married lady did not tell her husband to make the bed. But I preferred and still prefer my way of making the bed, the way I was taught in the army.

One day, early in our marriage, William Klein asked me about meeting Pat. When I told her, she suggested we invite Klein to our apartment for dinner. We also invited his brother, Jacob; the Weirs; and Adolph Lund and his wife, Esther. Obviously, bringing the bosses home for dinner was an important event, especially since William Klein fancied himself a gourmet. So much so that whenever the *Ile de France* ocean liner docked, he sent his sister to the piers to get real French bread. He also dispatched her to a spot in the South Bronx that he'd decided was the only place to buy chopped liver.

Pat was teaching every day, so she set the dinner table the night before our guests were due to arrive. Then she got up at five the next morning to bake and make other preparations. She cooked pot roast, potato pancakes, and a flaming pineapple dessert for the dinner. It was a lot of work, but it turned out to be a wonderful meal. We both agreed that the evening was a success.

The next day, Klein called me into his office. I was hoping he would tell me he had enjoyed the evening and how glad he had been to meet Pat. Instead he said, "Pat is very nice, and dinner was very nice, but couldn't she have served a little soup?"

While my home life was peaceful, work on the antitrust case intensified. The more time I spent working on it, the more I realized just how much was at stake. I came home every night and told Pat everything that had happened that day, the good and the bad. But I'm afraid I became somewhat of a specialist in delivering bad news.

Pat used to say she could tell what kind of day it had been simply by the way I put the key in the door.

THREE

LEE, J. J., AND JOHN

We were anxiously awaiting Judge Knox's decision on the antitrust case when, on Christmas Day 1953, I heard a shocking announcement on the radio: Lee Shubert had died from a stroke.

His funeral took place in Temple Emanu-El, a Reform synagogue at Sixty-Fifth Street and Fifth Avenue, even though neither Lee nor J. J. had ever made known their Jewish heritage. They didn't attend synagogue. In fact, J. J. often expressed hostility toward members of his own faith. If a Jew could be called an anti-Semite, J. J. deserved the title. He never attended funerals and was notably absent from his own brother's. Still, in his own way, J. J. mourned Lee, despite the bitter rivalry and lack of communication between them.

Lee's death revealed serious fault lines in the Shubert family structure.

The day after the funeral, the son of J. J.'s sister Fannie, a man who called himself Milton Shubert but whose real name was Milton Isaacs, took over Lee's office, Lee's desk, and Lee's chair. J. J. despised this man. Making matters worse in J. J.'s eyes, Milton Weir was in there too, claiming that Lee's will had made Milton Shubert his rightful successor. It was true that Lee's will expressed his wish that Milton Shubert succeed him, but that was in no way binding on J. J. What's more, J. J. had already brought his son, John, into the business, and in his view, it was John who would be the heir. Upset, J. J. ordered Adolph Lund to investigate the situation.

Worried that Milton Shubert might have a rightful claim, Adolph asked J. J. if he had any written agreement with his brother, to which J. J. replied, "I do but I won't show it to you."

Adolph responded, "If you don't show it to me, I can't advise you."

The next day, J. J. handed Adolph a copy of an agreement with Lee that basically set out terms of a fifty-fifty partnership. Based on the letter,

Adolph told J. J. that as the surviving partner, he owned the Shubert business. All he had to do was pay Lee's estate half of the company's total value as of the day of Lee's death.

J. J. then asked, "Can I throw my nephew and Weir out?"

As owner of the business, Adolph said, J. J. could do as he wished.

Putting on his hat and coat, J. J. walked across the street to Lee's office. Adolph brought along copies of the partnership agreement and the New York statutes governing partnerships. They found Milton Shubert sitting in Lee's chair, with Milton Weir standing beside him.

A man whose furious temper could melt the paint off walls, J. J. demanded of his nephew, "Get out of the office and take Weir with you."

Milton Shubert told J. J., "We won't leave."

J. J. turned to Adolph. "Tell them what my rights are."

Adolph explained that the letter of agreement clearly made J. J., as the sole surviving partner, the owner of the business, and that as such he had the right to fire them. Weir was dumbstruck. In all the decades of representing the Messrs. Shubert, he had never known about the agreement's existence.

Milton Shubert protested, but J. J. shouted at him, "You're a thief! When my son John was a child, you stole his piggy bank and ran down the street with it!" Again he ordered Shubert and Weir to leave.

The two Miltons stood their ground.

Turning to Adolph, J. J. asked, "Can I call the police and have them arrested for trespassing?"

Adolph said, "You can do whatever you want."

With that, J. J. ordered, "Adolph, call the police."

Enraged, Milton Shubert and Milton Weir stormed out. Shortly thereafter, Milton Shubert dismissed Weir as his lawyer.

The following day, J. J. summoned Adolph into his office and told him in no uncertain terms that Weir was no longer working on Shubert affairs. "You have a choice to make," J. J. told Adolph. "Remove Weir, or you, too, will have no future in the Shubert business."

Adolph Lund and Milton Weir were honorable men, who had worked together for twenty years. The decision was agonizing for Adolph. He could remain with Weir and lose Shubert as a client, or he could retain Shubert and dissolve his partnership with Weir. Without the Shubert revenues, the partnership could not be sustained. Adolph proposed that he retain Shubert and a client who paid an annual $1,200 fee, and that Weir retain all the firm's other clients. Weir agreed to the arrangement. The new firm called itself Klein & Lund.

I was in the uncomfortable position of being caught in the middle.

Milton Weir had hired me, and I felt a sense of loyalty to him. But Adolph was my friend and mentor, and I felt a sense of loyalty to him, too. We weren't contemporaries—he was fifteen years older—and we certainly weren't equals in the senior partners' eyes. But I worked more closely with him, and he always encouraged me. Pat and I spent time with him, his wife Esther, and their children. It was a worrisome time for me.

Suddenly, on December 30, 1953, just five days after Lee's death, the clouds parted, albeit briefly. Judge Knox rendered his decision in the antitrust suit, writing that he could see no valid distinction between the facts in our case and *Toolson v. New York Yankees*, a ruling that effectively let the baseball business continue to operate outside antitrust laws. He announced, "Upon the authority of these adjudications, the complaint in the above-entitled action will be dismissed."

We won.

Our elation was short-lived, however. The government immediately appealed to the United States Supreme Court.

———•◦•———

J. J.'s son, John, was forty-five when his uncle Lee died. Raised by his mother, Catherine, whom J. J. had divorced in 1915, John grew up watching his parents fight bitterly over money. Catherine, who bore the same name as J. J.'s mother, had been a chorus girl and exquisitely beautiful as a young woman. J. J. loved John but was not paternal or outwardly affectionate toward him. At whim, J. J. would cruelly deprive his ex-wife and son of money, or he would turn around and lavish it on them. John was well educated at private schools, graduated from the University of Pennsylvania, and attended Harvard Law School. He was respected by his uncle Lee.

John entered the Shubert family business before the war, and after serving in the army went back to work in the United Booking Office. Gradually, J. J. allowed John to assume greater responsibility, but he never ceded total authority. J. J. would send memos to his son incessantly. The memos were reminders to John to consult his father before making any decisions, and not to dare act without his permission.

John's office was on the sixth floor of the Sardi Building, at the opposite end of the floor from his father's—that is, until J. J. decided to move his son into the office adjoining his. The new office contained the "Holmes Room," a protected area that housed a number of safe-deposit boxes. The room was named for the security company that controlled it. I never entered that room until after John's death, although I often saw John go in there. I imagine that the boxes contained wads of cash.

J. J. was always wandering into John's office. If you happened to be with John when J. J. appeared, J. J. would suspect that you and John were hatching some plan or other. You had to be prepared to tell J. J. just why you were there. John often fended off his father's questions. But if the response was something J. J. didn't already know, or had forgotten, he would demand to know why he hadn't been told. Inevitably, the confrontation would lead to acrimony.

Back in 1937, John had married Kerttu Helena Eklund, known to everyone as Eckie. He had kept the marriage a secret from his parents. When Catherine found out, she decided she despised Eckie with a vitriolic hatred. Eckie reciprocated the sentiment but without the same viciousness. John bought a mansion in Byram, Connecticut, a beautiful place near the water on a peninsula. Before long, he built a ranch house on the grounds for Catherine. Maybe he was hoping for a truce between his wife and mother, but that never happened.

Everyone always addressed John by his first name. I didn't. He called me Mr. Schoenfeld, and I always called him Mr. Shubert. If he had one fault, it might have been about spending money. I can't say he was cheap, but I think he had a serious problem when it came to money, possibly as a result of the financial hardships his father had imposed on him and his mother.

Pat and I got to know John when he invited us to see a show he was producing, one of the old Shubert properties, Sigmund Romberg's *Blossom Time*. It was during a summer-stock run in New England. Pat never forgot that when she first met John, a tall, nice-looking man with salt-and-pepper hair, he was wearing chinos tied with a rope. "Couldn't he afford a belt?" she asked me.

Unlike his father, John was always very polite. One night, he phoned our home at eleven p.m., and the first thing he asked Pat when she answered was, "Am I disturbing dinner?" She never got over the fact that someone thought we were having dinner at eleven o'clock at night.

I always thought John was a very nice man, dedicated to rehabilitating the image of his father and uncle. However, Lee's death highlighted the deep divide in the company. With Lee gone, many executives who had worked with him over the years departed. Some were fired, but many quit, unwilling to tolerate J. J.'s wrath. The executives on J. J.'s side of the street were, by this time, immune to J. J. Just about everyone's fate at Shubert had been determined by the north-south geography of Forty-Fourth Street.

Surviving a J. J. purge did not at all mean that he embraced you. If you stayed, you lived in fear of coming within his sight or into his mind. At this time, had it not been for John, the business might have disintegrated.

One bizarre instance that I personally witnessed occurred during a Saturday morning meeting—I always worked on Saturdays. The name Jack Small was mentioned. Small was the "booker," the executive who brought shows into the Shuberts' theaters. His name didn't have any particular relevance to the conversation, other than being mentioned.

J. J.'s reaction was, "Get him in here."

One of the secretaries found Small at his country club playing golf. The message went out: "Mr. Shubert wants to see you."

If he dared say, "But I'm on the golf course," he'd be dead. If he dared not come in, he'd be dead. So Small showed up, still wearing his cleated golf shoes. By that time, J. J. didn't remember why he wanted him.

Unfortunately for the Shuberts, animosity toward them had been seething in the industry for years before Lee's death. J. J. had few relationships with the new faces that would become forces in the changing theater world. He refused to relinquish full power to his son, or to anyone. But day-to-day business had to be conducted, and it was John, Jack Small, and Adolph Lund who interacted with the new generation of theater people. They opened Shubert doors to those who had never crossed the threshold. At the same time, the trio remained subject to J. J.'s whims, paranoia, and temper tantrums.

In the ensuing months, J. J. began to pressure Adolph Lund unmercifully to relocate from our law offices at 1440 Broadway to Lee's former apartment in the Shubert Theatre building. During this period, I was mostly at the Cravath offices, working with Alfred McCormack and his associates on the antitrust case. It was Adolph who spent his days largely on Shubert business.

By now, Adolph was paying my salary, which under normal circumstances would make it obvious where my future lay. But in reality I was in limbo, with no identity of my own within a firm that had just imploded.

In May 1954, J. J.'s pressure on Adolph to display his loyalty finally reached the boiling point. He demanded that Adolph either work out of Lee's former apartment or sever their relationship. The move carried with it William Klein and his brother, Jacob, the office secretaries, the receptionist, the library, the telephone number, and me. It was just assumed that I would go along, so I did.

To the outside world, it appeared that the renamed firm of Klein & Lund was basically Shubert's in-house counsel.

Adolph generously gave Lee's bedroom to William Klein to use as his office, together with its private bath and shower, cedar closets, upholstered furniture, vanity, and chest of drawers. William Klein sat there day after day with nothing to do except review his family's financial matters with his accountant. Adolph occupied the dining room. A small office was given to Jacob Klein.

The living room housed an old dining table, a few chairs, and some upholstered pieces. That became the law library and my office. The dining table was my desk. A telephone extension was placed near the window. Situated as it was between Adolph's office and William Klein's office, my space was the thoroughfare that people traversed, occasionally lingering to chat with me.

J. J. demanded that Adolph itemize all our office expenses, from telephone bills to the cost of stationery, and only after that accounting did he decide what he would pay for our legal services. The fee included salaries for two secretaries, and my salary, which had now risen to $10,000 a year. J. J. made several reductions to the items on Adolph's list and would not allow Adolph the luxury of a receptionist.

No sooner were we settled in when J. J. renewed his war with Milton Weir. It wasn't enough that Weir was no longer a member of our law firm; J. J. wanted the Broadway League to fire Weir as its lawyer. Klein & Weir had long been counsel for the League of New York Theatres, the precursor to the League of American Theatres and Producers, now known as the Broadway League. Its offices were on the seventh floor of the Sardi Building. To get at Weir, J. J. told Adolph he wanted the League out of the building.

The idea of capitulating to J. J.'s demands was anathema to most people in the business. The League decided to tell J. J. to go to hell. They moved out, taking Milton Weir with them as their lawyer.

The furor had no effect on J. J. whatsoever.

From my earliest days, and then as I gradually learned more and more about the Shubert brothers' monstrous behavior, I always rationalized that despite their personal shortcomings, they had possibly single-handedly saved the American theater from destruction during the Great Depression. While others had abandoned theaters, demolished them, or converted them to other uses, Lee and J. J. had steadfastly committed energy and resources to save their theaters.

That said, dignity did not accompany our move into the Shubert offices. We were captives, working for an unrelenting master. It didn't seem to matter much to Adolph if I was in the office or at Cravath, because he was too busy shuttling back and forth from the north side of Forty-Fourth Street to the south side, ten or more times a day. His footprints were figuratively in the street between the offices. Nor did it matter to J. J. how many times Adolph came to see him or how recently he had last seen him. Whenever Adolph's name was mentioned, a call came from J. J.'s secretary, Belle Jeffers, summoning him to J. J.'s office. And each visit was filled with anxiety.

I couldn't relieve Adolph by making any visits for him. At that point, J. J. didn't know me. I wondered if he even knew I was just across the street.

FOUR

THE SUPREME COURT DECIDES

The U.S. Supreme Court heard arguments on our antitrust case in November 1954. Adolph invited me to go to Washington with him and at the same time told me to prepare an application for my admission to practice before the Supreme Court. I had difficulty comprehending that in five short years, I'd gone from a forty-dollar-a-week law clerk to someone deeply absorbed in the fortunes of the Shuberts, and eventually to being admitted to the bar of the highest court in the land.

Pat accompanied me for our appearance there. I sat down at the defense table and looked at the nine robed men sitting on high at the bench, legendary justices like Earl Warren, Felix Frankfurter, and William O. Douglas. Frankly, it took my breath away. I had one of those "how did I get here?" moments.

We thoroughly laid out our case as to why *Toolson v. New York Yankees* applied, and left Washington thinking that we had argued convincingly. Unfortunately, on January 31, 1955, our hopes were dashed by a unanimous opinion in favor of the government. The justices held that the legitimate theater could not rely on *Toolson v. New York Yankees*, and that the antitrust laws did in fact apply to us.

Now either we had to settle, or we had to take our chances at trial.

The government's attorney, Philip Marcus, was a Javert type—that is, like the prison guard in *Les Misérables*, he wanted to win at all costs. His zeal was marked by an obvious antipathy toward the defendants and their attorneys. The heat of his breath served as a catalyst for negotiating a settlement. We knew, as did Marcus, that if we took the case to trial, we would be opening ourselves up to private litigants who might be lurking in the wings. These potential litigants could use a government victory as prima facie evidence in a treble-damages antitrust case against us. We were left with little room to negotiate.

But J. J. didn't give up easily, and he wanted to fight the decision, even though the government had left him with very few options. Above all, J. J. was determined that he would not sell any theaters.

Fortunately, John was on our side, and with his help Adolph was somehow able to talk J. J. out of proceeding with a trial. I don't know if J. J. ever fully understood the risks of a trial. I suspect that he backed down mostly because of the expense involved in a protracted fight. After all, this was a man who went crazy whenever a legal bill arrived.

J. J. finally ordered us to "get rid of it."

Our negotiations with the government lasted more than a year, ending in February 1956 with a "consent decree," a settlement in which we agreed to take specific actions without admitting to any wrongdoing.

The demands were brutal. Shubert was required to divest twelve theaters: four in New York (the St. James, the National, the Ritz, and the Maxine Elliott); two each in Boston (the Colonial and the Wilbur), Chicago (the Great Northern and the Erlanger), and Philadelphia (the Locust and the Shubert); and one each in Detroit (the Cass) and Cincinnati (the Cox). Partnerships in two Detroit theaters and one in Philadelphia had to be dissolved. And, in addition to various other restrictions on how the Shubert business could operate, we were forbidden to acquire more theaters.

Finally, the decree ordered the termination of the United Booking Office. That was the easy part. J. J. and Marcus Heiman, his partner in the enterprise, shut it down and replaced it immediately with the Independent Booking Office, which they operated out of the League offices. Divesting the theaters and separating the various partnerships was not so easy.

By then, I often accompanied Adolph across Forty-Fourth Street to meet with J. J. and frequently to meet with John. As far as selling off theaters, neither Adolph nor I knew how to attract prospective buyers. The best we could come up with was to place an ad in *Variety* announcing that some Shubert theaters were for sale.

It was not a boom time, and replies were sparse.

Some of the theaters were obsolete and badly in need of repairs. Neither J. J. nor Lee practiced preventive maintenance. The sole ray of sunshine was that, because Broadway was undergoing one of its periodic declines—dramas were particularly affected—liquidating some of those run-down theaters would save the Shubert business plenty in carrying costs.

The consent decree stipulated that, when it came to owning a theater, the Shuberts could not have any partners. The one exception was the Music Box on West Forty-Fifth Street. Its control and management were left to the Shuberts and their partner, the great composer Irving Berlin.

Berlin hated the Shuberts, and I think in turn they hated him. We felt that the Music Box was in a terrible state of disrepair, and that our management policies were more efficient and less wasteful than his. Furthermore, as long as the government wasn't forcing us to sell our share, we wanted to buy it. But Berlin and his family weren't interested in selling.

Our attempts to get the Music Box dragged on for years, until well into the 1980s, as Berlin approached his hundredth birthday. By then we had decided that picking a fight with the American icon who had written "God Bless America" was not a good idea. It wasn't until after Berlin's death in 1989 that Shubert, with the consent of the executors of Berlin's estate, assumed control and management of the Music Box. Later, around 2007, the Shubert Organization bought out the Berlin estate's 50-percent interest.

As the consent decree required, the theater divestitures were all accomplished within a two-year period.

Most noteworthy was the sale of the National on West Forty-First Street off Seventh Avenue. A Broadway producer named Harry Fromkes bought the National in September 1956. The purchase was partly funded by a $700,000 mortgage, which was held by the Shuberts. Fromkes later placed two additional mortgages, one for $200,000 and one for $100,000, on the property. Soon afterward, Fromkes contracted to buy a non-Shubert theater, the Playhouse on West Forty-Eighth Street. Unfortunately, he ran out of cash and, to close the deal, improperly used $17,000 from advance ticket sales. But it wasn't enough. As the pressures on Fromkes continued to mount, he could neither service the mortgages nor repay the $17,000. A few years after he bought the National, he fell to his death from a twelfth-floor window in his West Ninety-Second Street apartment. He was fifty-three. John Shubert and other theater owners contributed the missing $17,000.

As a result of these sorry events, the Shuberts instituted a mortgage foreclosure proceeding. I appeared on Wall Street at the foreclosure auction of the National Theatre, prepared to bid $700,000. To my surprise, Billy Rose was also there. Billy was the creator of the *Aquacade* at the

1939 New York World's Fair, the owner of New York's Ziegfeld Theatre, a songwriter, an art collector, a friend of presidential confidant Bernard Baruch, and a major AT&T stockholder.

I asked Rose, "Are you going to bid?"

He said no. However, after I bid $700,000, Rose bid $700,001.

A third bidder appeared with an additional $200,000, and Rose upped his bid to $900,001. The third bidder went to one million, and Rose won with a bid of $1,000,001. Almost immediately, he changed the name of the National to the Billy Rose.

After the sale, but before Rose received the deed to the theater, J. J. was advised that he was due an interest payment on the mortgage. J. J. ordered me to collect his money. So I phoned Rose to say that Mr. Shubert wanted payment. Rose replied, "Tell that no-good bastard son of a bitch I have a grace period."

I explained, "The grace period doesn't apply to the interest, only to the principal."

That didn't stop Rose from responding, "Tell the SOB to drop dead."

I reported the conversation to J. J., omitting Rose's tender sentiments. J. J. responded, "Tell Rose I don't know anybody named Grace and I want my money now."

I did. That afternoon Rose sent over a check.

Shortly thereafter, on a Sunday morning, I was summoned to J. J.'s office, where I found Mike Todd, the noted theatrical and film producer—and Elizabeth Taylor's third husband—with his attorney, Herman Odell.

J. J. turned to Todd and said, "Tell my lawyer what you just told me."

Todd wanted to buy out the Shuberts and explained his terms. I translated the proposal into language that J. J. could understand—it was strictly a Mike Todd proposal, all for him and nothing for J. J. At that point, J. J. put his finger under his nose and admonished Todd: "You are a bad boy."

That ended the discussion.

Annoyed that I'd told J. J. the truth, Todd turned to me on his way out and said, "When I take over here, the first thing I'm gonna do is fire you."

He never got the chance.

Then came the most painful divestiture: the St. James, a large musical theater on Forty-Fourth Street between Broadway and Eighth Avenue.

We started discussions for the sale in mid-1956 with a man named Sam Schwartz, a former general manager at several theaters. He came to see John Shubert, representing William Lester McKnight, who was interested in buying not just the St. James, but also our Colonial Theatre in Boston, and our Shubert Theatre in Philadelphia. We found McKnight's financial credentials impeccable. He was the founder and major shareholder of Minnesota Mining and Manufacturing (3M). *Fortune* magazine had estimated his worth at more than $400 million.

Suddenly another buyer emerged for the St. James. John consulted with his father about this purchaser and his offer of $2.1 million, of which $300,000 would be cash and the balance secured by a mortgage. J. J. didn't want to finance the transaction, and there were no further negotiations with him. John told Schwartz that J. J. would be receptive to an all-cash offer, and Schwartz replied that McKnight would pay $1.6 million, all cash, for the St. James.

J. J. called me in, saying he had never heard of McKnight and wondering if I believed he could pay all cash. I told him about McKnight's ranking in *Fortune* magazine, and he told me to proceed with the transaction. The contract was signed, but before the closing, McKnight's lawyer announced that he preferred to pay the entire purchase price in 3M shares, instead of cash. When I reported this to J. J., he said, "I thought you told me McKnight was so rich. If he's so rich, he can pay cash."

McKnight paid cash. The sale of the St. James closed on July 29, 1957. Three years later, the stock of Minnesota Mining had tripled.

I never mentioned it to J. J.

FIVE

THE MADNESS OF J. J.

In spring 1956, Broadway was abuzz with the long awaited arrival of *My Fair Lady*.

The musical, starring Rex Harrison and Julie Andrews, was scheduled to open at our Broadway Theatre on March 15, 1956, after it concluded its engagement at Shubert's Forrest Theatre in Philadelphia. But its producer, Herman Levin, was concerned about the size of the Broadway. He believed it was too large and lacked intimacy. He sent a telegram to John Shubert suggesting that the theater be made smaller by removing the last three rows of orchestra seats.

John showed Levin's telegram to his father, after which a reply was sent to Levin: "You have no business telling us how to run our theaters and if you don't like the Broadway, you can cancel the booking contract and take your show someplace else."

That's exactly what Herman Levin did. The show ended up at the Hellinger Theatre, not part of the Shubert chain, where it ran for many years and became a theatrical landmark.

Pat and I went to the third performance of *My Fair Lady*. During the course of the evening, I introduced myself to Herman Levin and told him how marvelous the show was. His reply was to the point: "You can tell that son of a bitch J. J. that I'm going to make more money for Anthony Brady Farrell"—the owner of the Hellinger, which had not housed many hits—"than he ever made in the theater in his life."

That turned out to be true, but you wouldn't have known it from J. J. He never referred to the show, or to the Hellinger. As far as J. J. was concerned, *My Fair Lady* never happened.

Later that spring, Adolph had an ulcer operation and was out of the office for several weeks. During his absence, I dealt with J. J. and John. The mere thought of crossing the street filled me with anxiety, which was not allayed by Adolph's frequent warning: "You're entering a lion's den. Be prepared for the worst."

I was at J. J.'s beck and call from about eleven in the morning, when he came down to his sixth-floor office from his eleventh-floor apartment, until around seven in the evening, when he went back upstairs. Saturdays were workdays until two in the afternoon. A free Saturday afternoon didn't mean a thing to J. J. Nor did a free Sunday. No matter what the time or where I was, J. J. felt free to summon me back to Forty-Fourth Street.

To my surprise, during the six weeks Adolph was away, J. J. and I got along fairly well, although my opinion of him didn't change. I kept him and John up to date on litigation and for the first time had the chance to meet many company executives. I also began to recognize the names, if not the faces, of the ever-changing ranks of producers. When Adolph returned, I told him I couldn't understand why he found J. J. so impossible to work with.

"You'll learn," he warned, "that with the Shuberts, familiarity breeds contempt."

Adolph's return eased my workload, but the calm didn't last long. J. J.'s nephew Milton Shubert and niece Sylvia Wolf Golde filed a lawsuit that would, once again, seriously threaten the Shuberts. In their petition, they claimed that they were entitled to an accounting of the value of their uncle Lee's partnership with J. J. as of December 25, 1953, the date of Lee's death. They were demanding that they receive payment of half of Lee's interest in the business, in cash, with interest.

A twelve-year headache was about to begin.

Because of the matter's complexity, Adolph felt it imperative to retain an estate-law expert. With J. J.'s permission, Adolph arranged a meeting with then–recently retired judge James A. Delehanty, a man of great integrity and brilliance. I accompanied Adolph to Delehanty's office in lower Manhattan. Delehanty was tall, with an ice-cold, aloof manner. During our meeting, the phone rang continuously, interrupting his comments in mid-sentence. His powers of concentration were so great, however, that no matter the duration of the call, he would pick up our conversation with the next word of his unfinished sentence. At the end of our discussion, Delehanty agreed to accept the case and join our defense team.

Also attending that meeting was a lawyer some ten years older than Adolph named James N. Vaughan. A pleasant-looking man with gray hair who seemed perennially consumed by a quest for knowledge, Vaughan had been Delehanty's law assistant. Vaughan would later become my savior.

Vaughan was actively engaged in the case from the beginning, and later took over when Delehanty was forced to retire for health reasons. That was fine with us. Vaughan was recognized as the outstanding trusts and estates lawyer in the state of New York, and was a worthy successor to Delehanty. More importantly, J. J. liked and respected Vaughan. In particular, J. J. was pleased that Vaughan was not Jewish, convinced as he was that every Jewish lawyer he had ever met invariably wanted to be his business partner.

Our first step in developing a strategy to protect J. J. was to file a motion that Milton and Sylvia's complaint be dismissed. The court denied our motion and granted their request to conduct an accounting. We appealed the decision and lost. It was now necessary to delve back into the Shubert brothers' financial records from the inception of their partnership in 1905. We had to ascertain all outstanding assets and liabilities and set forth their book values in the accounting. It was a major undertaking that took more than a year to prepare.

From the start, we knew that Milton and Sylvia's goal was to get the court to award them a cash payment, including interest, of a sum so large that J. J. couldn't possibly pay it. They hoped that, unable to come up with the funds, J. J. would simply turn over his share of the business to them. Adolph explained their strategy to J. J., outlining how a cash payment would force J. J. to sell off an enormous number of theaters and other properties. That could effectively put Shubert out of business.

J. J.'s reply was, "Give them half the stock."

But they didn't want half the stock, because that still left J. J. in control.

We now ordered a full appraisal of the business as an ongoing concern. The other side had already decided it was worth $53.2 million. It took two years, but our accounting firm decided that the amount was somewhere between $13.8 and $14.4 million.

An interesting sideshow took place during the course of the valuation. The accountants stumbled across an outstanding debt of $64,490.79

due from lawyer William Klein. J. J. demanded that Klein pay his debt. Klein had no recollection of the debt, which dated from 1928, more than a quarter of a century earlier. That didn't matter to J. J., of course, who continued to press Klein for payment. Finally, Klein made the fatal error of telling J. J. that the debt was barred by the statute of limitations. Enraged, J. J. called Klein a thief and expelled him from his office. The next day, J. J. warned Adolph that if Klein was not immediately removed from the offices and the firm, Adolph would no longer be his lawyer. He, too, would have to leave.

Adolph had no idea how to handle this sudden turn of events. Klein was his former employer. He simply could not tell him to leave. For his part, Klein was badly shaken by J. J.'s outburst. I offered to go to Klein and explain Adolph's predicament.

My relationship with Klein was cordial. I told him about J. J.'s demand. I mentioned Adolph's devotion to him and described as gently as I could the impossible position that Adolph was in. Klein did not react emotionally. To my surprise, he simply said he understood and left.

His departure ended nearly fifty-five years of Klein's dedicated and devoted service to the three Shubert brothers.

Placated, J. J. never mentioned the name William Klein again.

SIX

FRENETIC TIMES

The most difficult part of complying with the consent decree was the requirement that Shubert end its partnerships with theaters in Detroit and Philadelphia.

Shubert's partner in Detroit's Cass Theatre was E. D. Stair, the instigator of the government's antitrust case against us. His partner in Detroit's Shubert-Lafayette Theatre was David T. Nederlander, who had nursed a long-standing hatred of J. J., which, of course, was reciprocated.

To divest himself of the Cass, J. J. compiled a file on the theater and instructed me to meet with Stair's lawyer, Paul Marco. After meeting with Marco in New York, I reported back to J. J., expecting him to be pleased about the meeting. Instead he went into a fury, insisting that I had no right whatsoever to speak with Marco. I reminded J. J. that I had simply been following his instructions.

Further enraged, he screamed, "You're fired."

I didn't know what to make of it.

The next day J. J. summoned me to his office and told me again to meet with Marco. "Find out how much they'll pay for the Cass."

Obviously, he'd overlooked the fact that he had fired me.

After the second meeting, I returned to J. J.'s office. The temper tantrum I witnessed exceeded his earlier outburst. The next day, he called me to his office again, showed me the file on his desk, and told me to meet with Marco.

I soon deduced that the Cass file on his desk was a constant reminder to him that we needed to divest the theater, which then triggered the instructions for me to meet with Marco. To avoid falling into the same trap, I dictated a memo stating that J. J. had asked me to meet with Marco. His secretary, Belle Jeffers, typed it up. I then asked J. J. to initial the memo, which he did.

The following day, when J. J. became furious at me again, I showed him the signed memo. I thought that would appease him. Instead, he denied that it was his signature. At the end of the meeting, the Cass folder on J. J.'s desk surreptitiously followed me out the door. I consummated the transaction under John's guidance. J. J. never mentioned it again.

Divestiture of the Shubert-Lafayette Theatre should have been an easy deal, because the lease was expiring. But the matter got complicated when J. J. discovered that David Nederlander, one of his partners in the theater, was writing off the furniture, valued on the books at $75,000. The truth is that the furniture was old and practically worthless. But that didn't stop J. J. from calling Nederlander a thief and insisting that I get him his half of the furniture's value, as if it were new.

I met with Nederlander's son, Jimmy, and told him that despite the feud between his father and J. J., there was no reason why he and I shouldn't get along and resolve the problem. Jimmy was reasonable but only agreed to pay $2,500 for the furniture.

John Shubert accepted the offer, and I thought the matter was resolved. Yet every time the Nederlanders or the furniture was mentioned, J. J. would throw a fit. To his dying day, J. J. despised the Nederlanders. Perhaps not surprisingly, they felt the same way about him. It took forty years before Jimmy and I were able to bury the hatchet.

In Philadelphia, Shubert's partner in the Erlanger Theatre was a motion-picture exhibitor named William Goldman. His alliance was through Lawrence Shubert Lawrence Sr.—Fannie's son and Lee's nephew—whom Lee had made general manager of the family's theaters there. Goldman, who ran something like eighteen movie houses, had once sued the motion-picture companies for antitrust violations, claiming they had prevented him from obtaining first-run films. He had won and, I believe, had been awarded well over $1 million. We should have seen him coming.

Because the consent decree stipulated that no company employee could hold an interest in a legitimate theater, Lawrence Sr. had to make a choice: give up his association with Goldman, which meant giving up his interest in the Erlanger, or keep it and resign from the Shubert business. He decided to separate from Goldman. Accordingly, in June 1956 Lawrence Sr. sold out to Goldman for $2,500. Upon closing, Goldman handed Lawrence Sr. a check, and Lawrence Sr. gave Goldman a general release. But Lawrence Sr., a heavy drinker who knocked back brandies before eleven o'clock every morning and then disappeared for the day, acted without legal advice and failed to get a reciprocal release from Goldman.

That was a critical mistake. Picking up where the government left off, Goldman immediately filed a civil antitrust suit against us. He alleged that Shubert had conspired to prevent the Erlanger from getting first-class legitimate attractions. Goldman was playing the same game he'd played, successfully, with the motion-picture companies.

Adolph informed me that the case was my sole responsibility, and I brought in Jim Vaughan to help. That Jim was a man of unmatched brilliance meant little to J. J. That he was probably the most significant person in my career, a man who came to love me like a son and who taught me a tremendous amount, meant everything to me.

Antitrust cases are about documents, and once again, the amount of documentary evidence was enormous. In theory, even though the law said otherwise, if the consent decree could be used by Goldman as a basis for demonstrating the Shuberts' antitrust violations, then all the documents in the government case could be brought into play, which could hurt us. We settled in for a long battle.

J. J., still complaining about lawyers' bills, insisted on being kept informed about the Goldman case. One Saturday afternoon, Jim and I were in J. J.'s office, briefing him, when he looked at Jim Vaughan and said, as if I weren't in the room, "I think we should fire Schoenfeld."

Jim answered, "I don't think that would be a good idea, because Mr. Schoenfeld knows more about your business than anyone else. He's invaluable to you."

J. J. said, "All right," and that was the end of that.

Goldman's antitrust action could not have come at a worse time— right in the middle of our attempt to settle claims brought by Milton Shubert and Sylvia Wolf Golde against their uncle Lee's estate. I always tried to be cordial with Milton and Sylvia, but they never hid the fact that they detested J. J.

We would gladly have settled either of these cases quickly. Instead, the Goldman case went on for another four years, while the battle for Lee's estate would last nine years and consist of eighty-five days of testimony and 4,485 pages of transcripts.

During these frenetic times, Pat and I remained childless while our married friends were all starting families. It was not a happy time for us. Pat underwent two major operations to help her conceive, but to no avail. We started considering adopting a baby and moving to a larger apartment in Peter Cooper Village. With Pat's income and my increasing salary we could manage the higher rent. But I was overwhelmed by the possibility that Pat would have to stop working to care for the baby and that I would be their sole provider. It was a major decision.

Finding a two-bedroom apartment was the easy part, although it was located below us on the second floor, meaning we lost our river view. But the decision was eased by the prospect of a baby occupying the second bedroom.

The adoption process was difficult and consumed almost two years. We applied to a reputable adoption agency and went through a number of conferences with our caseworker. I resented my role as a supplicant, but Pat assured me that the procedure was part of the standard adoption process.

At one point, the caseworker asked me to describe the type of baby I envisioned. Pat wasn't specific, but I had once seen a cover of *Good Housekeeping* magazine featuring a gorgeous baby girl and had fallen in love. I answered, "I want a *Good Housekeeping* baby girl." Pat thought I'd just killed our chances. But the caseworker found my specific response significant, more so than someone simply saying they wanted a baby.

We waited, and kept attending difficult sessions with the caseworker. Pat had just started a new job as a guidance counselor in the public school system when, on a Wednesday at the end of October, the caseworker called to say they had a baby girl for us. She told us we could pick her up that Friday.

Needless to say, I was thrilled with the news, but it also worried me. We were not prepared. We had no crib, no diapers, nothing. We hadn't even told our parents that we were considering adoption. So imagine their reaction when Pat called them to say that we would have a daughter on Friday.

On Thursday, Pat and her mom ran out to Best and Company, where baby things like cribs and layettes were bought in those days. Pat's mother literally dragged a couple of young boys off the street to help them schlep everything back to Peter Cooper Village.

The next morning, we went to pick up our four-month-old daughter, whom we thought we'd name Abigail. But Pat's mother said, "Abigail Schoenfeld? She won't be able to write that name on one line. She's going to flunk out of first grade."

My mother wanted us to name her after my grandmother, Rose, and Pat's mother suggested we name her after my mother's father, Charles, and from there we somehow got to Carrie Rose. She was born on June 3, but it was on October 26, 1956, that I first saw my beautiful baby girl. I was so overwhelmed that I started to cry.

That same fall, Adolph began complaining of stomach pains. Pat and I never realized that this could be anything more serious than, say, ulcers. Adolph's wife, Esther, now came into the office with him every day, dutifully sitting close by, telling us that she was there because Adolph "isn't that well." His condition did not interfere with his regular routine of seeing J. J. many times a day and working with me. Nor did the constant pain and extreme fatigue stop him from accompanying J. J. to Boston on business the last week of December 1956.

When Adolph returned that New Year's Eve, he was admitted to Mount Sinai Hospital. The next morning, January 1, 1957, I went into the office. Pat, who was at home reading in the bedroom while Carrie crawled around the floor, received a phone call from Esther. Adolph had passed away that morning. The cause of death was colon cancer. Adolph was only forty-nine years old.

Pat was devastated, and I immediately fell into a state of despair. Adolph's death was the first major loss we had suffered. Our parents were still alive, as were three of Pat's four grandparents. My grandmother had passed away, but my grandfather was alive and living with my parents. We were new at this.

The Shuberts had lost a brilliant attorney. Adolph was an essential part of the business's survival. And I had lost my mentor and my best friend.

Once I'd pulled myself together, I phoned Esther and mourned Adolph's untimely death. After that, I phoned J. J. and broke the news as gently as I could. He began to weep. He told me to come to his office. But when I arrived, I found him completely composed. Without any ado, J. J. asked me if I would like to handle his affairs.

It took me a few minutes to absorb this. I was sick at heart that Adolph was dead. At the same time, here I was, at age thirty-two, being offered an unbelievable opportunity. Of course I said yes.

"Good," he said, "Because I don't want any old men handling our affairs. Old men have old ideas." This from a man of seventy-nine. "I want you to know we have a twenty-four-hour-a-day, seven-day-a-week business," he added. "I expect my lawyer to be on the grounds at all times."

At the end of my meeting with J. J., I called Jim Vaughan to get his advice. I told him my concerns about being able to cope with the job. As always, Jim gave me much needed encouragement.

The firm of Klein & Lund had effectively disappeared. I was now solely responsible for the entire operation, including paying all expenses. When I learned that J. J. had invited Jacob Klein, William's brother, into his office with an offer to stay as long as he wanted, I turned to Jacob for help. I had no savings to fund my office expenses. Jacob offered me a loan to pay a secretary's salary, telephone bills, and office supplies, with a little extra for myself. The loan, which amounted to $9,000, was to be repaid by the third week of March.

Picking up where Adolph had left off, I made the countless daily trips across Forty-Fourth Street. At the same time, I was working with the Philadelphia lawyers on the civil antitrust suit filed by William Goldman. I was also coping with the time-sensitive demands of the government antitrust consent decree, and trying to juggle time to work on the Lee estate case with Jim Vaughan.

After two weeks, I felt like I was trying to function in a madhouse. J. J. never brought up the subject of compensation. I knew that if I did, I'd be fired. When J. J. asked me to leave my work behind and go to Boston with him, I decided to quit. On a cold, wintry January night, I met Jim Vaughan, and we walked from my office to Fifth Avenue and Forty-Fourth Street, around the block to Forty-Fifth Street, and back to my office. Jim's advice was, "Do not quit." He said I had a great opportunity and assured me that I could handle the problems. He calmed me down.

Toward the end of February, Howard Milley, whom J. J. trusted enough to be head of Shubert's finance department, told me J. J. wanted an itemized list of my office expenses—the same thing he had demanded of Adolph. I prepared the list and sent it to Howard, and when he got back to me, he said, "Mr. J. J. will pay your expenses and give you an annual retainer of $18,980."

How he arrived at that figure, I have no idea.

Howard said the retainer would cover all my work, regardless of time spent and the degree of responsibility. The arrangement was retroactive to January 1.

This allowed me to repay Jacob Klein.

A few weeks later, J. J. summoned me to say he thought I might need some help and suggested I bring in another lawyer. He was only offering to pay three hundred dollars per week. He also warned me that I would be responsible for whomever I chose.

I spoke to two associates I had worked with at Cravath. After I explained the madhouse environment, both declined, and I couldn't blame them. Adolph Lund's admonition came to my mind: "With the Shuberts, familiarity breeds contempt."

Then I thought of Bernard Jacobs, my brother Irving's friend. During my law-school years, I would often discuss cases with him and ask his advice. When I started practicing law, I began to see Bernie more frequently. And after Pat and I were married, we often visited Bernie and Betty at their home in Roslyn, Long Island. Even though we were not contemporaries, the difference in our ages had become less significant.

Bernie was heavyset, of medium height, and not particularly concerned about his appearance. He was practicing law with his brother, representing small-business clients, mainly in the jewelry and shoe trades. He was also a partner in the Patio, a beach club in Atlantic Beach, Long Island, where Pat, Carrie, and I were his guests on many occasions. I invited him to lunch, told him I needed another lawyer to help me, and confessed that others had rejected my offers. Bernie never would have asked me directly, but I could see in his eyes that he wanted me to offer him the job. So I did. He immediately said yes.

I explained that J. J. had only authorized me to pay three hundred dollars a week. I also spelled out the perils that awaited him. The next morning Bernie arrived with all his files and took to his new surroundings as if he'd been there for years.

In many ways, Bernie and I were opposites. Cases that didn't interest me interested him. People I didn't enjoy dealing with were often people he didn't mind, and vice versa. One thing that truly set us apart was his hypochondria. In his younger years, Bernie carried a thermometer and took his temperature every hour. If he noticed someone popping a pill, he would ask for one, no matter what it was. If someone had offered him a Midol for menstrual cramps, he would have taken it. And whenever you asked Bernie about his health, his standard answer was, "I-N-L-F-T-W," meaning "I'm not long for this world," or more to the point, "Not good." Except that he was the healthiest sick man I ever met.

Extremely insecure, Bernie covered up his lack of confidence with a larger-than-life presence. In a meeting with Bernie, you could never get a word in edgewise. On matters of opinion, he would speak with great authority. He might not know much about a particular topic, but others who knew less thought he was a genius. While not overly modest, he was a generous man who, underneath all the bravado, was a very sweet guy.

He and I never had any serious problems. We would compromise, or if one of us was adamant, the other would relent. He never second-guessed me; I never second-guessed him. If he thought I was wrong, he told me. If I thought he was wrong, I told him—and I might have been the only one who could get away with that.

Early in our partnership, I briefed Bernie thoroughly on the provisions of the consent decree, the Lee Shubert estate litigation, and the Goldman antitrust case. I also often had Bernie accompany me across the street when I was summoned. That way J. J. became accustomed to seeing us together as well as separately. I also wanted to dispel any thoughts on the part of J. J. and John that I was their sole lawyer. And I wanted Bernie and me to be interchangeable, so that either of us could respond to J. J. when he called for his lawyer. Before long, our footprints were also embedded in Forty-Fourth Street.

Feeling guilty that I was making sixty-five dollars a week more than Bernie, I told him I would divide the extra sixty-five equally between us. I swore him to secrecy lest J. J. find out.

Early on, J. J. ordered Bernie to fire me for some reason or other. Whether J. J. meant it or whether he was just testing Bernie, I never found out. My suspicion is that he simply wanted to be sure that neither of us ever regarded ourselves as permanent fixtures in the Shubert business. Bernie met the challenge by telling J. J., "Jerry's indispensable to the company." I'm sure that if Bernie hadn't responded that way, I would have been fired. I'm equally sure that Bernie knew he could encounter a similar fate in the near future.

On another occasion, J. J. fired both of us and ordered the locks changed on our office doors so we couldn't get back in.

The frequency of J. J.'s firing me—and soon the frequency of his firing Bernie and me together—gradually subsided. Though we never could rest easy. One Sunday in July 1957, Bernie and I were ordered from Atlantic Beach to J. J.'s office. It was 104 degrees and a perfect day to be at the seashore. But we drove to the city fully expecting to be fired. When we arrived, J. J. was nowhere to be found. He was off with his wife and chauffeur, inspecting his many properties, one of his favorite activities. The next day, J. J. behaved as if the call had never happened.

Almost as a last resort, we turned to John Shubert for reason, sanity, and help in coping with his father's tyranny. Fortunately, Bernie and I were protected both by John and by J. J.'s secretary, Belle Jeffers. Every morning, Miss Jeffers received copious notes written by J. J. during the course of the night. Some of the notes that referred to "the lawyers" she took upon herself not to transcribe. Maybe she realized that if she sent them to us, they would have led to more firings. J. J.'s notes never carried any praise or appreciation for what Bernie and I were doing for Shubert or, for that matter, for what anyone else in the company had ever achieved.

Paradoxically, this behavior did not lessen anyone's loyalty to the business. Low salaries, continuous fear, and total insecurity were never, amazingly, reflected in anyone's job performance.

I would go home and tell Pat about J. J. and she would ask, "Why do you put up with it? Why don't you quit?" I never had a good answer.

She would say, "You should quit."

I'd say, "I don't know…"

She knew me very well by now, and she asked, "You think you'll never get another job?"

Such was the opinion I had of my own qualifications.

SEVEN

MORE UPHILL BATTLES WITH J. J.

No one was safe from J. J.'s maniacal behavior. Even when it was directed at someone else, you still had to worry about the fallout.

Many years earlier, the Shuberts had retained an insurance firm called Theatrical Brokerage Inc., with offices in the Sardi Building. The head of the company was Walter G. Keyser.

In 1957, Keyser decided, with J. J.'s tacit acquiescence, that he would be J. J.'s authorized representative in selling a number of Boston properties that were consistent money-losers. At the end of every day, Keyser waited outside J. J.'s office for the privilege of carrying J. J.'s "out file" up to his apartment. Confident that J. J. liked him, Keyser told Bernie that my days at Shubert were numbered and that he and Bernie should become the company's senior executives. It obviously made little difference to Keyser that John Shubert was alive and assuming ever greater responsibilities.

There's no telling how far Keyser might have gone had he been dealing with anyone but J. J. Unfortunately for him, while selling some properties he ran afoul of a real-estate broker who claimed he was owed a fee. The broker filed a lawsuit, and the complaint was served on J. J.

J. J. told Keyser in his typically loud and furious way that he had no right to deal with his properties or to get him involved in a lawsuit that was not of his making. Keyser responded that he'd had J. J.'s permission to sell those properties. That, of course, carried no weight with J. J., who finished his tirade with "you're fired."

The moral of the story was obvious. No matter what you did, it meant nothing to J. J. Appreciation, gratitude, loyalty were not in his nature.

My strategy of involving Bernie in meetings with J. J. and John continued to work so well that it inadvertently revealed that J. J. had a sense of humor. Behind our backs he began referring to Bernie and me as the Hall-Room Boys, a reference to two characters in a comic strip from the early 1900s. He also called us Itzik and Pitzik, a Jewish comedy team. But I can't for the life of me remember if I ever saw a smile cross J. J.'s face.

On rare occasions, J. J. invited us to his apartment for lunch. As soon as we crossed the threshold, he was a changed man. He became the consummate host, congenial and gracious, almost to the point of normalcy. But it was just a brief truce. The moment we took the elevator back down to the sixth floor, war resumed.

During the late 1950s, the shift of power from J. J. to John became more evident. We reported to John about pending litigation. J. J. even began to mellow a bit. One day as he and I were walking across Forty-Fourth Street, I reached out to hold his arm in the middle of the street.

"I know you mean well," he admonished, "but don't ever hold my arm in public."

At the time, neither Bernie nor I knew much about theater ownership and operation, or the production of plays and musicals. But our daily visits to J. J.'s and John's offices put us on a steep learning curve. We participated in meetings of all kinds, reviewed documents, prepared leases, litigated actively, and were as "inside" as any "outside" counsel could be.

Not just during regular business hours, but evenings and weekends too, we spent an inordinate amount of time with J. J. and John. A big difference between them was that with John, at least, Bernie and I never felt as if we were on top of a volcano that could erupt at any minute.

One day, J. J. asked Bernie and me where we lived. I told him I had an apartment on Twentieth Street between First Avenue and the East River.

Bernie replied, "Oh, Mr. Shubert, I live way, way out on Long Island."

From that time on, night and weekend calls were made to me.

Before long, Pat and I devised a system. After we'd been out for an evening, leaving Carrie with a babysitter, I'd wait outside the apartment until Pat checked the message board in the kitchen to see if J. J. had phoned. On nights when he had, we stood there wondering what to do. It was a real dilemma. Should I go meet him at the office? Should I pretend I had come home too late?

Most times I would run back uptown. On many occasions, though, when I did go back to the office, J. J. was nowhere to be found.

⸺•⬦•⸺

The more Bernie and I were exposed to the theatrical side of the business, the more people we met: booking handlers, finance-department managers, theater managers, and their staff. There were senior executives in the Shubert business, but they had no authority whatsoever. J. J. made the decisions, and everybody knew what he said was law. All these employees got to know us as "the Shubert lawyers." In their eyes, we were important enough to be courted. After all, we spoke for Shubert, and we provided a sounding board and an entrée to the Shuberts. We might have had J. J.'s ear, but—equally as important—we had John's trust and confidence.

What I didn't yet know was that J. J. had already warned John about me. In a typed memo dated August 7, 1957, from father to son, formally addressed to Mr. John Shubert and with "J. J. Shubert" typed as a signature, the old man wrote, "I do not think this man, Schoenfeld, is any good whatsoever. I do not trust him. I do not like his methods. I do not care for that kind of people..."

That kind of people being a reference, of course, to Jews.

He went on: "I could not trust this man whatsoever and I think it is very wrong of you to entertain these people in any way whatsoever, if I do not like them. I do not care for that type of individual to handle our business in any way."

This didn't stop John from letting Bernie and me handle business when he wanted us to do so. But when John suggested to his father that Bernie and I move our offices to the south side of Forty-Fourth Street, into J. J.'s offices, J. J. sent a scathing letter back. Dated May 2, 1958, it says, "I received your letter today regarding our lawyers, bringing Mr. Schoenfeld and Mr. Jacobs over here into the Sardi Building. They spread themselves all over the place across the street. We never see them. We don't know what they do and besides they run up a weekly expense of $1,030. I don't know why they need three girls: two stenographers and a messenger—telephone girl...I think it would be a bad proposition to have them here. To keep them out of our business the way we are doing now is much better, but at the same time I think the place over there has made them feel they are big shots."

The way J. J. saw it, having lawyers nearby was a good thing. But lawyers in his own office was another matter. "We don't need them," he wrote; "once they get a foothold, they assume a different position and half of the things we should know never reach our ears.... It is just as well to keep them out of our offices. The moment they come into our office and know all about our business is not a very good proposition."

I found that memo several years after it was written. I have kept it in the top drawer of my desk ever since, to remind myself of what I was once up against.

EIGHT

JOHN SHUBERT'S SECRET LIFE

As the years passed, it was increasingly noticeable that J. J.'s temper, concentration, and interests were lagging. That didn't mean he wasn't still capable of tantrums, but John gradually took on more and more responsibilities. As he watched his father slowly drift away from the business, he confided to Bernie and me that if anything happened to J. J., he would sell the business. That bothered me. Whether he really meant it I don't know, but I did know that John was capable of making that impetuous move. I liked him, nonetheless, and he must have liked me, because he made me executor of his will, along with his wife, Eckie.

Bernie and I knew very little about John's personal life, even though Eckie was always cordial to Pat and me, especially after Carrie was born. Slightly overweight, with a sweet face and curly blond hair, Eckie had no children; she showered our little girl, Carrie, with gifts. John often confided to Bernie and me of his love for Eckie. We had no reason not to believe him.

In the late 1950s, a new face began making regular appearances around John's office: Howard Teichmann. A professor at Barnard College, Teichmann had collaborated with George S. Kaufman on the 1953 comedy hit *The Solid Gold Cadillac*. Teichmann quickly became a strong influence on John, so much so that he convinced John to produce his ill-fated comedy *Julia, Jake and Uncle Joe*, which was set in New York and Moscow in 1946. Pat and I went to see a preview, and just before the intermission she whispered to me, "This is terrible. I am not sitting through the rest of this. Let's leave."

Under normal circumstances, it would be unthinkable for anyone associated with the Shuberts to walk out of a Shubert play. But this play was so awful that I agreed to sneak out at intermission. As the curtain came down, we headed for the exit and suddenly bumped into the general manager. We couldn't tell him how appalling the play was, so I said Pat had a terrible headache and we were going nearby to buy aspirin. The general manager sympathetically volunteered to wait with Pat while I went to the drugstore. I came back with the aspirin, and we suffered through the rest of the evening.

An unmitigated disaster, the play opened and closed after one performance, even though it starred Claudette Colbert, who—aside from being a wonderful actress—could curse more proficiently than a long-shoreman. It was the only Shubert-produced play between 1952 and 1973, a time when the business, for a number of reasons, refrained from investing in or producing new shows.

I don't believe J. J. ever knew about Teichmann or his friendship with John, which, consequently, kept Teichmann out of the line of fire. But no sooner had Teichmann appeared on the scene than John's life took a stunning and unbelievable turn, climaxing in one of the most bizarre lawsuits that Bernie and I ever had to handle. The case proved more difficult and had more far-reaching consequences to the business's future than any of the other pending Shubert lawsuits.

J. J. and John both loathed flying. Whenever possible, they would travel by train or ship. On September 6, 1958, John, J. J., and J. J.'s second wife, Muriel, a former showgirl, set sail for Europe. They did their "grand tour" and sailed back to the States from Le Havre, France. But while on the tender going to the ship for the sail home, John met a young woman named Nancy Eyerman. Their instantaneous attraction resulted that evening in the start of a tortuous love affair.

When Nancy became pregnant, her family put pressure on John to marry her, at which point John confided in Bernie and me. He never told J. J. about the affair, nor did anyone else. After Nancy gave birth, John leased an apartment in someone else's name for her and their child. All this time, he also maintained his marital home in Connecticut with Eckie.

Leading a secret double life eventually became too much for John, and he confessed to Eckie. Nancy's family, meanwhile, retained a lawyer to pressure John into divorcing Eckie. With his life unraveling, John told me he wanted to ensure that Eckie was protected financially. He put all his property, including his life-insurance policies, in Eckie's name. I completed the arrangements, which left John dependent solely on his salary from the business.

Eckie did not end her marriage to John. Nor did John end his extramarital relationship with Nancy. Throughout it all, John tried to maintain a business-as-usual attitude.

—————•◦•—————

But with the Shuberts, nothing was ever usual.

In 1957, *The Music Man*, starring Robert Preston, was in our Majestic Theatre. The show's producer, Kermit Bloomgarden, decided that the Majestic was unsafe, unsanitary, and otherwise appalling. He was incensed to the point that he stated publicly, "I could kill the owner of this theater."

He was right about the theater's condition. However, threatening to murder a Shubert wasn't one of Bloomgarden's better ideas. John sent me to the Majestic to make things right with the cast. I promised them we would do whatever was necessary to clean up the place and make it safer. In the end, Bloomgarden did not attempt assassination.

Next we had a problem with a naked lady.

A dance company was performing at our 54th Street Theater, which had been the Adelphi and later became the George Abbott. During the performance, a young woman appeared in a washtub, nude from the waist up. I received an angry call from the license commissioner (in those days, theaters were licensed) saying that if the woman did not put on clothes, they would shut down the theater. It was an era when people were terribly concerned about nudity and about what constituted obscenity. I knew that if we lost our license, we'd probably have to go to the U.S. Supreme Court to get it back. John sent me to the theater to make certain that from then on the naked lady in the washtub was clothed.

No sooner did I arrive at the theater than the woman running the dance troupe demanded to know, "What's all this shit about nudity?" I tried to explain our concern, but she wouldn't hear of it. For her, the performance was art, and anyone who tried to censor an artist's free expression deserved her irate response.

Hoping to bring some common sense into the debate, I appealed to the producer. He seemed less concerned with art than with his bottom line and suggested, "Why don't you let her go on and then ring down the curtain?"

I said, "Because that's a publicity stunt, and it will only get me into more trouble." I put my foot down, "She can't go on."

They weren't happy, but the naked lady did not go on.

Before long, it was Richard Burton who would pick up where Kermit Bloomgarden had left off and also threaten to murder John Shubert.

When *The Music Man* moved to the Broadway Theatre, the Alan Jay Lerner and Frederick Loewe musical *Camelot*, starring Richard Burton and Julie Andrews, moved into the Majestic. Burton was so unhappy about his dressing room, the backstage conditions, and everything else about the Majestic that during a dress rehearsal he declared, "I could kill the son of a bitch who owns this place."

Someone repeated that to John, who happened to have a license to carry a gun. Before I could stop him, John grabbed his pistol and stormed out of the office. He went down the block and charged into Burton's dressing room. "I'm the son of a bitch who owns this place," he announced, handing Burton the gun. "Go ahead, shoot me."

Burton decided John was crazy and passed on the opportunity.

By now, Bernie and I were close enough to John that he put us on the opening-night guest list, a rare privilege. Until then, we'd usually had to buy our own tickets to a preview. Pat and I attended the opening of *Camelot*. It was a big, glamorous night on Broadway—after all, the show starred Richard Burton. Just before the curtain went up, I turned to a gray-haired man sitting next to me and mentioned that he looked like Macdonald Carey, a prominent movie actor.

The man introduced himself as Irving Goldman. We chatted, and he told me that he'd known the Shuberts since he was seventeen, when he'd started selling scenery paint to J. J. I thought that was interesting, but didn't give it much thought. I certainly never dreamed that this paint salesman would emerge as a significant factor in the affairs of the business and in my life.

Several weeks after the *Camelot* opening, John said that he was considering going to Mexico to divorce Eckie. I couldn't believe it. I warned him that if he appeared before a court in Mexico without Eckie, or without her giving a power of attorney to a Mexican lawyer, the divorce would not be legal under New York law. I added that, ethically, I would have nothing to do with a Mexican divorce, and that I could not discuss it further. I insisted that he not go to Mexico under any circumstances.

My advice was not heeded. In early 1961, John obtained a Mexican divorce. Eckie did not appear in Mexico, nor did she retain a lawyer to appear for her. Four days later, while still in Mexico, John married Nancy, who was then pregnant with their second child.

By this time, J. J.'s visits to the office were less frequent and much shorter. Within a year he wouldn't come to the office at all. At eighty-two, he was bedridden in his Sardi Building apartment.

Aside from Howard Teichmann, another new face now starting coming to the office: John's cousin Lawrence Shubert Lawrence Jr., son of Lawrence Sr., the man at the heart of our still-ongoing antitrust lawsuit in Philadelphia. Junior was around forty-five, good-looking, with red hair and freckles. He regularly boasted that he'd been an English major at the University of Pennsylvania, even if the fact was irrelevant to the discussion. His sole theatrical accomplishment was that he had been company manager for two vaudeville shows before the war, and eventually house manager of the Majestic, a job that required no involvement in the Shubert business.

Now he spent his days sitting in a corner of John's office, quietly listening to discussions, trying to learn the business by osmosis.

Perhaps John didn't want to shoulder the business burdens alone. Perhaps he was too distracted by events in his personal life. But I never figured out what he saw in Lawrence Jr., or why he allowed him to become a fixture. Bernie and I knew little about Junior and had no idea that, like his old man, he had a drinking problem. But worse than his father, Junior turned out to be incompetent, bigoted, mean-spirited, vicious, and paranoid.

John's double life, which bore similarities to the old Alec Guinness role in *The Captain's Paradise*, soon got even more complicated as his mother, Catherine, intervened. John was simultaneously living with Eckie in Connecticut—despite the Mexican divorce—and with his new family in New York and Long Island. He began renovating an apartment for Nancy and the children in one of the old Shubert theaters and also bought a home for them in Florida. Greatly disturbed by the situation, Catherine wrote a series of letters to John demanding that he terminate his relationship with Nancy. She also warned Nancy, in writing, to leave her son alone.

Torn between his mother's admonishments and threats against Nancy and his love for Eckie, John told me he was going to Florida to end his relationship with Nancy. What finally drove him to this decision, I believe, was a phone call from a credit bureau saying that their records showed two women charging purchases in the name of Mrs. John Shubert. Not knowing how to respond to the bureau's inquiry, John handed the phone to Bernie. "Mr. Shubert will be responsible for both charge accounts," Bernie replied.

Afraid to fly, John left New York on Friday, November 16, 1962, on a train bound for Clearwater, Florida. At six forty in the evening on November 17, 1962, I received a call at home from a detective in Clearwater. He said there was a DOA on the train, and that he'd found a card among the dead man's effects listing my name as an emergency contact.

The dead man was John Shubert. He had apparently died of a heart attack.

NINE

THE BATTLE FOR JOHN'S ESTATE

I was dumbstruck. John was only fifty-three.

First, I called Bernie. Pat and I then went to the office, where Bernie and Betty met us. Together we found Lawrence Jr. After that, I promptly called a meeting of senior Shubert executives and announced John's death. I instructed someone to notify the banks where John had safe-deposit boxes so that they could be sealed. I also informed Jim Vaughan of the sad state of affairs.

The task of telling Eckie was delegated to Howard Teichmann. Bernie assumed the role of informing John's mother, Catherine. Supposedly, Catherine had a gun in her house, and I told Bernie to retrieve it. Given Catherine's hatred of Eckie and, in turn, Eckie's hatred of her mother-in-law, the last thing we wanted was some sort of incident.

As for J. J., confined to his bed and otherwise in another world, he had no knowledge of the last years of John's life, or of his death.

The following Monday, I went to Connecticut to see Eckie. I wanted to assure her that, as coexecutor with her of John's will, I would do everything possible to see that she received the totality of John's estate.

That same day, the manager of Bank of Manhattan's Forty-Third Street branch called me. John's mother, he said, had appeared at the bank early that morning and been given unauthorized access to a safe-deposit box that she and John had maintained there. The vault custodian, he added, noticed that the box was appreciably lighter when he returned it to its place. Catherine later swore she had not removed a thing from the box.

Before his death, John had prepared lengthy handwritten instructions. His wishes were extremely explicit, to say the least. The first two were: "One: Make sure I'm dead. Leave me un-embalmed as long as the laws allow. Two: Don't rush me into the ground. Take your time. Let the survivors suffer as long as possible."

He further stipulated that no autopsy be done, unless required by the police. Nor did he want any organs removed for transplanting to others or for hospital research. He instructed us to "take turns to remain with my body to see that it is unmolested."

Aware that embalming was a messy job, he wrote that, "for the few extra dollars," he wanted to be embalmed on the premises where he lived. "So somebody stick with the undertakers while some doctor gives me an intravenous anesthetic and while some mortician pumps in the formaldehyde, I believe there should be a faint glow of life after death, so if there is, let's play it safe."

Afterward, John asked that we let him "hang around where I've been embalmed for a day or two, then take me to Campbell's," a well-known funeral home on Madison Avenue. He was adamant about going there rather than to a place known for Jewish services. "Place me in a small room nearby, where the visitors"—and here he crossed out the words *if any*—"can kill a few minutes in a larger room alongside to talk normally, smoke, maybe take a drink, if liquor can be served. There's nothing like a happy wake without the corpse present."

He suggested saving money on the coffin: "The cheapest metal one will do." He wanted to wear a blue suit, white shirt, and black tie. He indicated who should ride to the cemetery in which car and described what should take place at the graveside. He stipulated no flowers, except perhaps at Campbell's: "Maybe we'd go for a bouquet of roses, cut in half."

The day after John died, Catherine phoned me, demanding her son be buried in the Shubert mausoleum at Salem Fields Cemetery in Brooklyn. I told her that John himself had chosen to be buried in Eckie's family plot in New Jersey, and that it was Eckie, as John's widow, who had the sole right to determine the burial place. We followed his instructions to the letter.

As for the memorial service, he wanted it to be held, with the coffin present, on the stage of any Shubert theater, but not on a matinee day. We held it at the Majestic. He stipulated that only Eckie be on the stage, sitting off to the side. And that's the way it was. John did not want his "other wife" present, so I posted Pat and Betty Jacobs at the doors to be sure Nancy did not get in. I'm not sure how they would have stopped her, but luckily, she didn't show.

Another of John's requests stated categorically, "There will be no clergymen of any faith. I don't want the hypocrisy of some hired stranger to preside."

A short passage he had written about himself, mainly about where he grew up and where he went to school, plus the Twenty-Third Psalm, a passage from Corinthians, and the Lord's Prayer were to be read by me, Bernie, and possibly Lawrence Shubert Lawrence Jr. For the readings, John admonished, "Read. Don't ad lib."

After John's coffin was taken to a hearse outside the theater, the procession of the hearse and limousines moved slowly down Forty-Fourth Street, past Shubert Alley to Broadway. Hundreds of Shubert employees lined the streets, many of them in tears.

For me, personally, it was a great loss. John was the only Shubert I had been able to get even slightly close to. With him gone, I felt insecure and unsure of my own future.

—•◆•—

John's premature death raised many questions about the future of the business. Who should book the theaters? Who should handle pending litigation, which—if lost—could mean the end of the business? Who should make financial decisions? Carry out complicated real-estate transactions? Oversee production activities? Conduct labor negotiations? In short, who should run the Shubert business?

In his meticulous handwritten wish list, John had expressed the desire to have Lawrence Jr. take his place. But, just as when Lee had wished for his nephew Milton to replace him, the instructions had no legal authority.

J. J. still owned the business, despite being too ill to run it. J. J.'s own will named John as executor. It also stipulated that if John did not survive his father, the executors would be J. J.'s wife Muriel, Eckie, and Morgan Guaranty Trust Company. It was therefore incumbent on me to speak to those three and determine whom they would ultimately approve as John's successor.

Since John had apparently been grooming Lawrence, I thought it politic to recommend him. Bernie felt that I should put myself forward to Muriel, Eckie, and the bank. He strongly urged me to do so, but I declined because I felt that my relationship with Muriel was not strong and I knew no one at the bank. When I said no, Bernie reluctantly went along with my choice of Lawrence Jr. We had no inkling at that time that Muriel Shubert disliked Lawrence and that Eckie detested him. Apparently, Eckie had never forgiven him for once throwing ice water on his pregnant wife, who was Eckie's friend. Making matters worse, the bank's people didn't know Lawrence at all.

Because of my own insecurities about my standing with the executors, I foolishly recommended Lawrence to them. Relying on my recommendation, they approved him to run the business, but only until J. J. died. They also approved that Bernie and I continue as the company's counsel, and they later retained me, along with Bernie and Jim Vaughan, to represent them as coexecutors of the estate.

Because John predeceased his father, J. J.'s estate, which would normally have gone to John, now had to be dealt with. J. J.'s wife, Muriel, had signed a prenuptial agreement, so she would not be affected. And J. J. had no obligation to provide for anyone else. Since he no longer had children, his estate would go to the Shubert Foundation.

Founded in 1945 by Lee and J. J., it was originally called the Sam. S. Shubert Foundation. A not-for-profit-corporation that owned the Shubert business, it is subject to oversight by the Charities Bureau of the State of New York.

When Lee had died, half of his estate was intended for the foundation and the other half was to be divided into trusts to benefit his nieces and nephews. Milton and Sylvia's suit was dragging out the final settlement of Lee's estate, and this time we hoped to avoid similar dilemmas. That is, until Nancy got into the picture. Nancy piped up with a suit claiming that she was John's rightful widow, and that she and her two children were entitled to John's estate.

We were still battling Milton and Sylvia for Lee's estate, and fighting those antitrust claims in Philadelphia. Nancy's suit opened a third front in what felt like a never-ending war to keep the Shubert business from exploding.

Nancy's claim was one we had to take seriously. The stakes were enormous. Everything hung on her status and that of her children. Was she John's legal wife? Were the children legitimately his? Did the children have legal status as grandchildren of J. J. Shubert? Even if only one was deemed to be legitimate, New York State law entitled that child to claim half of J. J.'s estate. The implications of losing the case were that if the Shubert enterprise survived, it would be an entirely different business.

The proceedings to establish Nancy's status and that of her children were set for trial. Depositions were taken before the trial date. Suddenly, I was made aware of a letter written by John to Eckie, in which John explained that his Mexican divorce would have no effect on her. He was going to Mexico so that the children would be legitimate there, at least. His explanation echoed Nancy's mother's written wishes that he marry Nancy in Mexico, even though the marriage would not be recognized in New York. John assured Eckie that his Mexican divorce and his subsequent Mexican marriage were void and that she should check with me to confirm that.

During the pretrial deposition of Nancy's mother, conducted in the Surrogate's Court, a telephone call came in from my former employer, Milton Weir. He was representing Nancy and John's mother, Catherine, who had suddenly switched over to Nancy's side. After admonishing John to get rid of Nancy, Catherine was now in cahoots with her to usurp Eckie's claim as John's widow.

You can imagine how uncomfortable it was to have Milton on the opposite side. This was more than just any two lawyers representing two clients—one of us was going to lose big. I hated to think that my old boss, who had given me my first job and whom I highly respected, might have a detrimental effect on my career. Or I on his.

Weir dropped a bombshell: the will we had offered for probate had been superseded by a later will. If true, it was devastating news. I sent one of John's former assistants to Weir's office to examine the document. She said it was a copy of an unwitnessed will that left John's estate to his mother and Nancy. But, she added, though it was signed John Shubert, in her opinion the signature was a forgery.

This was a stunning development. After all, as John's former assistant she had seen John's actual signature enough times to know the real thing. We then retained a noted handwriting expert, who had previously testified in the famous Lindbergh baby kidnapping case, to render his opinion. After examining the document, his opinion was that the signature was "a clear and unmistakable forgery."

We searched everywhere for the copy's original but found nothing. I asked Weir how it had come into his possession. John's mother, he said, had been told by a public stenographer at the Times Square Hotel that she had typed the will at John's behest. I asked if we could interview the stenographer. Weir replied that he had no objection.

The stenographer told us that on the evening of June 26, 1962, she had received a phone call at her workplace from John Shubert, who had asked her to come to his room at the Hotel Astor so that he could dictate his last will.

John was a meticulous note taker when it came to appointments. We checked his memo pad for that date, and it showed that he had dined at Sardi's Restaurant that evening with a group that included his secretary, Vi Fisch. We obtained a copy of the bill for the dinner, which indicated the number of people in the party and what they had ordered. We then asked Vi for verification. She confirmed that John was at the dinner and that he had not left Sardi's at any time.

The stenographer claimed she had delivered the document to John so that he could sign it and have it properly witnessed. We asked Vi if anyone had delivered anything to John during dinner, and she said no. The stenographer also insisted that, although they had once spoken on the phone, she had never met John's mother. We subpoenaed Catherine's phone records and found numerous calls between the stenographer in New York and Catherine in Connecticut.

I had to warn Weir, "If Catherine does not withdraw her objection to the probate, we will refer the matter of a forged will to the district attorney for prosecution." Just like that, Catherine withdrew her objection to the probate of the genuine will.

A hearing then took place in the Surrogate's Court, where Weir's cocounsel, Monroe Goldwater, a highly competent and politically well-connected lawyer, argued a motion on behalf of John's mother. He wanted the courts to order us to search for the original of the later will. I explained we'd already done so, and urged the court to have Mr. Goldwater inform me as to how I could search further for an original of a forged copy.

Goldwater shrewdly replied that my objection was not appropriate, because if this was a copy, there must be an original somewhere.

I argued that if Goldwater could tell me where to search, I'd be willing to do so.

The surrogate gave Goldwater thirty days to advise me where to search. That was the last we ever heard from Goldwater.

Next came the hearing on Nancy's status. Tensions were high on that first day, a sweltering August 5, 1963. Eckie attended, with Pat and Betty looking after her at my request. A few weeks earlier, Eckie had fallen and suffered a broken leg. She arrived in a wheelchair with a cast on her leg. It was, I think, the only time that Eckie and Nancy ever came face-to-face. Pat and Betty kept them far apart.

Jim Vaughan questioned Nancy, who admitted that she had met John on the tender going to the passenger ship from Le Havre, France, and that they had begun their affair the night they met.

At this point Nancy's father asked for a recess. He was a very wealthy man and announced, out of the blue, that he wanted to settle the matter. His overriding concern was his grandchildren. Setting aside personal emotions, Eckie agreed to settle the case.

Years later, a second suit involving John's estate was brought forward by Nancy's two children. In 1979 and 1980, when they each turned eighteen, they contested the settlement, partly on the grounds that they had been minors when it was made. Rather than try the case before a jury, who despite the evidence might be sympathetic to the children and give them the right to half of J. J.'s estate, we settled their claim.

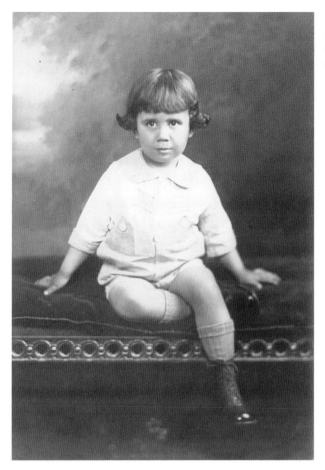

I had to include at least one baby picture! Me at two years old.

My parents, Sam and Fanny Schoenfeld.

The twelve-year-old who stole the show.

BOY, 12, 'STEALS SHOW' ON CHILD WELFARE DAY

Lad Wins Applause of 1,000 At Luncheon Here; Dr. Rice Warns of Low Birth Rate

To advance the cause of "health protection for every child," the Child Welfare League of America, co-operating with the Children's Bureau of the U. S., used May Day to plead for the nation's unfortunate youngsters.

At the Waldorf-Astoria and in Hollywood, Cal., speakers alternated over the radio, urging always that the care of the helpless children was the obligation of every citizen of the country. More than 1,000 persons attended the New York luncheon, over which Paul Cornel, of the board of the league, presided. Edwin C. Hill, radio news commentator, was master of ceremonies.

Persons prominent in the child health movement spoke, but the applause they received was nothing compared to that given Gerald Schoenfeld, 12, of P. S. 87 at Amsterdam ave. and W. 77th st., who stole the show. He was there as a representative of the Junior Welfare Council.

Safe Drivers Needed

He told the adults who crowded the ballroom that taking health precautions was all right, but what the youngsters of this city needed most of all was a world full of cautious automobile drivers. He said:

"We kids have done all we can to prevent accidents, and we are proud of the record that you and we have made since 1925. In that year there were 838 fatalities. In 1936 there were only 362.

"We boys and girls of New

In my Army Air Corps
uniform.

With Bernie Jacobs and my
brother, Irving Schoenfeld.

With Pat on our wedding day.

With Pat's parents, (*left to right*) Mabel and Peter, and my parents, Fanny and Sam.

"Our joy has arrived." Carrie, at four and a half months.

With Carrie.

The Founding Fathers, Lee and J. J. Shubert.
Courtesy of the Shubert Archive

J. J. Shubert with chorus girls, circa 1910. *Courtesy of the Shubert Archive*

J. J. Shubert with Al Jolson, circa 1920. *Courtesy of the Shubert Archive*

J. J. and John in J. J.'s office. *Courtesy of the Shubert Archive*

Esther and Adolph Lund.
Courtesy of the Lund Family

TEN

LAWRENCE AND
THE SYCOPHANTS

After we promoted Lawrence, a dinner was held for him at a nearby restaurant. Lawrence got drunker by the minute, and long before the meal was over, he claimed that he had no intention of being an interim booking. He was taking the job for life. Bernie said something, I don't recall what, and Howard Teichmann, who had now become Lawrence's best friend, took offense. An argument ensued, and in front of a number of people, Teichmann slapped Bernie in the face.

Teichmann's reaction was absolutely off the wall, but it set the tone for Lawrence's arrival. It also presaged a return to the dark ages. For the next nine years and seven months, there would be no peace. One clash after the other would start and run its course, only to end with another battle. If anything, the years with Lawrence were worse than those with J. J. It didn't take long for people in the business to learn that Lawrence was mean and nasty when drunk, and that he was best avoided.

Ironically, as the one responsible for Lawrence's overnight rise to the top of the company, I was also the one who would suffer the most at his hand.

Lawrence frequently had to sign documents pertaining to show bookings, real-estate transactions, financial and legal instruments, labor agreements, and such. But dealing with him was like walking through a minefield. Bernie or I had to allay his paranoia about signing a document by placing our own initials on it first before he would add his signature.

We tried our best to teach Lawrence the business and help him make important decisions. But it was very difficult. Lawrence began each day at home in New Jersey with stingers,—brandy and crème de menthe— and then showed up at Sardi's Restaurant, or some local hotel bar, and continued drinking. He got to the office anytime between noon and four in the afternoon, or sometimes not at all. He had arranged to have a telephone installed for himself in the second-floor bar of Sardi's, and for his trips to London he also had one installed for his use in the Savoy Hotel.

Lawrence couldn't live with us because he thought we were after his job, and he couldn't live without us because he didn't know anything about his job.

My decision to put him in charge was one of the worst I have ever made in my life.

It was also my mistake, although a minor one by comparison, to bring Alvin Cooperman into the business.

He had been employed by the Shuberts long before I got there and had left just after World War II to become a big shot in television in California. He was a smartly dressed man with a square face and reddish hair. Although I only knew Alvin slightly—he would stop by whenever he was in New York to say hello—I knew of his reputation. So in 1963 I recommended him to be the new booker.

Soon after he arrived, Alvin told Lawrence that, unlike lawyers, the two of them were creative people, and that lawyers should not be involved in creative matters. Before long, Lawrence's cousin Norman Light, a venal, insidious man who managed the Winter Garden Theatre and could match Lawrence drink for drink and then some, joined Alvin in convincing Lawrence that they were the reincarnation of Lee and J. J.

Before long, producers, managers, and creative people were coming to Alvin, Bernie, and me for advice and decisions because they found it impossible to talk to Lawrence. Lawrence never cultivated these businesspeople, nor did he ever meet with anyone on his own. Most of his time was spent at a neighborhood bar, surrounded by his drinking buddies, like Norman, who formed a group that Bernie and I referred to as the sycophants.

Alvin Cooperman, who had been an office boy for the Shuberts thirty years before, was still a newcomer to the bizarre happenings in the company, but he quickly joined the ranks of the sycophants, drinking regularly in Lawrence's company with Howard Teichmann, Murray Helwitz—who was the Shubert relative in charge of theater tickets— and others. Sadly for Alvin, he was blissfully unaware of the quicksand surrounding him. The idea of a friendship between Alvin and Lawrence was repugnant to the other sycophants, who regarded Lawrence as their private preserve. Alvin stood out from the group, and like others, including Bernie and me, he became their target.

One evening, Alvin made a mistake that made his position untenable. A group of the sycophants, together with Alvin, Bernie, and me, went to dinner at Sardi's. We were fourteen and had a long table on the second floor. When the check came and everyone prepared to pay their share, Alvin demurred, saying that he had only ordered soup and should only pay for the soup. After that, Norman Light passed up no opportunity to remind Lawrence and everyone else that Alvin was the cheapest SOB he'd ever met and didn't belong in the company. Alvin soon realized he was a marked man. His role as booker came to an abrupt end in 1965, when he left for an important position at NBC.

A new booker had to be hired, and at my suggestion Lawrence brought in Warren Caro, who at one point had been married to the screen actress Nancy Kelly. Caro was a distinguished and respected figure in the theater community. He had spent most of his career working at the Theater Guild–American Theater Society, the organization that controlled subscription sales in major American cities.

Warren was a consummate gentleman, who eagerly accepted the position. But it didn't take him long to realize he'd made a disastrous mistake. He was unable to cope with Lawrence, from whom he received neither respect nor courtesy. If Lawrence went out of town or abroad to see a show, Warren was ordered to go along on the trip. This was torture for him, since invariably his fellow escort was Norman Light. Warren didn't enjoy Norman's company, nor did he appreciate Lawrence's routine. Lawrence forced everyone to stay at hotels with the best bars, and whose bartenders could refer them to their counterparts in other cities on the itinerary. There was business to conduct and there were shows to be booked, but Lawrence and his sycophants were more interested in barhopping.

Warren's life with the company ultimately became so insufferable that he went to a psychiatrist to help him navigate the perilous waters threatening to drown him.

It was around this time that Irving Goldman, the paint salesman I'd met on the opening night of *Camelot*, the man who resembled Macdonald Carey, contacted me to say he wanted to meet Lawrence. We chatted, and he regaled me with stories about J. J. and other Shubert people. The stories sounded true—he seemed to know them well—so I arranged the appointment.

When Goldman arrived, Bernie and I were in Lawrence's office. Goldman looked like a successful New York businessman and seemed to be well connected politically. He reminisced about J. J. and asked about Howard Milley, the company comptroller. Lawrence summoned Milley, who was then in his seventies and probably the most trusted person in the entire organization. Milley came down to say hello, and basically authenticated Goldman. Milley told us that Goldman used to hang around the offices with J. J. late at night.

The story Goldman gave us was that he'd been an errand boy for a company that supplied the Shuberts with scenery paint, when in 1938 J. J. loaned him $5,000 to start his own paint company. It didn't sound like something J. J. would do, but we had no way to check that.

Goldman's company, called Gothic Color, continued to supply paint to the Shuberts. That wasn't his only business. He told us he had his fingers in a lot of different pies. He appeared to be a wealthy man. Lawrence liked him, and so Irving Goldman became a fixture in Lawrence's office.

To the sycophants, however, Goldman was an unwanted intruder. They did their best to convince Lawrence that he was an impostor, but Lawrence didn't buy it. He believed Goldman and his claim that he was closely connected to many prominent politicians and judges. One of his closest friends, he told us, was Manhattan surrogate S. Samuel DiFalco.

One day, to demonstrate his close ties to New York's governor, Goldman said he had to beg out of a morning meeting. "I'm having breakfast with the governor," he announced. It sounded important. But it turned out that the breakfast was being held by an organization of Jewish police officers. So yes, technically, Goldman was having breakfast with the governor. But so were three thousand other people. That was the sort of game he played.

The fiftieth anniversary of the opening of Shubert Alley was a milestone for Broadway and our company. In spring 1963, Howard Teichmann came up with the idea of celebrating the street, and put in his bid to organize the event and invite the dignitaries. When Goldman got wind of it, however, he told Lawrence that he could deliver the U.S. senator from New York, Kenneth Keating. With that, Lawrence put Goldman in charge.

Teichmann blew his stack. He'd already drawn up a long list of theater luminaries and his pals in the press. In Teichmann's eyes, Goldman was a carpetbagger, and from then on, Teichmann and Goldman were enemies. Teichmann was so furious about Goldman's interference that he never stopped campaigning against him, trying desperately to convince Lawrence to break ties with him. But as Teichmann's efforts to change Lawrence's mind failed, he started losing face with the other sycophants.

Lawrence was getting closer to Goldman, and even put him on the opening-night guest list. In return, Goldman hosted Shubert employees at his home, ingratiating himself with company executives.

To some extent, that group included Bernie and me. I assumed that Goldman's friendship was real, but I was naïve. I never imagined someone would want to be my friend just because I could do something for them. Looking back, I realize that at this point Bernie and I were so insecure about our position with the Shuberts that we opened the door to people who were trying to gain their way into our favor.

Teichmann was like that. He lived on Park Avenue, and we would sometimes go there to have dinner with his family. He was twelve years older than I was and lived in a privileged world that Pat and I had never known. When Irving Goldman came along, he played the same game, although I realize now that Goldman was hedging his bets. He spent time with Lawrence, and then without Lawrence's knowledge he walked across the street and spent time with Bernie and me.

On Christmas Eve, December 24, 1963, the United States government moved for a judgment to cover taxes on the Lee Shubert estate. They were seeking $15.7 million.

The next day marked the tenth anniversary of Lee's death.

The day after that, December 26, J. J. died in his penthouse apartment overlooking Shubert Alley. He was eighty-six. Almost as soon as I heard the news, I thought of something he had once told me: "There may be a lot of people who are smarter than me, more powerful than me, or even richer than me. But very few people have their own street."

J. J.'s death was truly the end of an era. The era had lasted for more than fifty-three years, and during that half century the three Shubert brothers had created a theatrical dynasty that has never been equaled.

J. J.'s will was quickly probated, and after executors were appointed, they approved Lawrence's continuation as president of the company. Bernie and I, regretfully, did not oppose this, believing that if we did, we couldn't be sure of the outcome.

1963 had been a terrible year for Shubert fortunes. The business was in one of its cyclical downturns. In the midst of it, Lawrence came up with the idea of redecorating the theaters. The first one on his list was the Shubert. He engaged a decorator and poured money into it for no real results. Lawrence's idea of redecorating wasn't restoration, as we would do now, so the little he did was wasted.

Howard Teichmann was also busy spending money we didn't have. He sold Lawrence on the idea that we give annual grants to universities in the form of Shubert playwriting fellowships. At one point we were sending $2,500 a year each to sixty-three schools. Teichmann administered the program, which resulted in absolutely no theatrical productions. As far as we could see, it served no purpose, except to make Teichmann a very welcome guest on college campuses across the country.

Years later, after Lawrence and Teichmann were gone, we found 1,500 scripts from the playwriting fellows sitting in office files. I sent them to George White, who ran the Eugene O'Neill Memorial Theater in Waterford, Connecticut, and asked for his opinion. He returned all 1,500, saying that not one was worthy of production anywhere, let alone on Broadway.

That was the kind of nonsense going on with Lawrence and the sycophants.

At the same time that Broadway was in a slump and money was scarce, Lawrence saw fit to follow Norman Light's advice that the company did not need to go out and attract shows, but rather that producers needed to come to Shubert. The strategy made things worse. Only six of Shubert's seventeen New York theaters were open during this period, and all Shubert road theaters were dark, as we waited for producers to come to us.

Attaining the top position at Shubert did not change Lawrence or make him feel more secure. If anything, it made him more paranoid, more susceptible to the sycophants' advice, and more fearful that Bernie and I wanted to take over his job. He would tell people that he was no fool, when in fact he was a man of limited intelligence. And being an alcoholic didn't help.

In order to get any business done, Bernie or I had to track Lawrence down in some bar and describe the transaction to him while the syco-phants milled around, listening. I particularly disliked it when Lawrence brought the sycophants into the discussions, inviting them to offer advice. I was uncomfortable with this manner of conducting business, and so was Bernie, although to a lesser degree. I think he partly saw it as just another challenge. Bernie was also better at the bar scene than I was and would sometimes even drink with them. He explained that he did so to ensure that neither one of us was being stabbed in the back.

One night, while driving home along the West Side Highway, Lawrence crashed into a light pole, knocked it over, and was arrested for drunken driving. The police booked him and locked him up. By the time I got the call to bail him out, it was the middle of the night. Well, in those days you couldn't get a bail bondsman at four in the morning, so I didn't get him out until maybe ten or eleven a.m. He was furious with me that he had been forced to languish in jail all night and kept repeating what it was like in there. Then he blamed me for the whole incident.

Lawrence distrusted me, perhaps because I don't drink. I distrusted him for many reasons, including the fact that he did drink. But by then Lawrence realized that no matter how many times he may have wanted to fire Bernie and me, he couldn't without the consent of J. J.'s executors, who now controlled the Shubert Foundation, which in turn owned Shubert. On the occasions when Lawrence had to attend a board meeting at Morgan Guaranty, the agenda was scripted for him by Bernie and me. Left to his own devices, he could never have conducted a meeting or reported on the company's activities.

I cursed the day I had recommended Lawrence. I constantly asked myself, "Why don't I just leave?" I had no rational answer. I simply believed I had to stick around at that point because I had invested so much of myself in the business. I couldn't just walk away and allow Lawrence to destroy it.

The Shubert reputation, partially rehabilitated under John, had quickly gone into reverse. I thought things could not get any worse.

I was wrong.

ELEVEN

THE ICE KICKBACK STORM

ICE, which stands for "incidental campaign expenses," is a corrupt theatrical practice that has never really died. The ticketing business and laws have changed tremendously, and while ICE is not the problem it once was, there are still issues that arise. But at the time, as far back as anyone could remember, not a single ticket that the Shuberts printed had gone to a ticket broker without a surcharge—the "incidental expense," sometimes as small as a quarter, which was then remitted to the box-office treasurer.

These were kickbacks, and the Shuberts weren't alone in the practice. Everybody was doing it. ICE was standard operating procedure. Producers collected a share of the money from their managers, who in turn had collected it from their box-office treasurers. Theater owners then received their share, as did their house managers and the rest of the box-office staff. It was a way of life, probably as ancient as the world's oldest profession, not only in the theater but anywhere that a reserved seat ticket was sold to a ticket broker. The fact that it was illegal did not deter anyone from paying it, or collecting it.

The moment Bernie and I found out about ICE, we went to John Shubert to warn him that the company was breaking the law.

He heeded our warning by coming up with what he described as "the answer to ICE." He set up a central ticket office in a room on the fifth floor of the Sardi Building, one floor below his office. There, all tickets for all Shubert theaters were kept under lock and key for distribution to theater-party agents, group-sales agents, mail-order patrons, and ticket brokers. Any remaining undistributed tickets were sent to box offices for sale to the public. The room was filled with wire cages to prevent unauthorized people from getting near the tickets. The number of the office was 504. And that's how the room became known.

To manage it, John put his cousin Murray Helwitz in charge. Helwitz installed a large safe with elaborate security devices that activated if anyone disturbed the strings he placed across the office at closing time. It was Helwitz who determined which brokers received tickets and in what quantities. It was Helwitz who determined how much ICE should be paid by the brokers. It was also Helwitz who collected ICE from the brokers. And, it was Helwitz who paid a share of the ICE to everyone in the distribution loop, in amounts he determined.

The result of this simple plan was that the treasurers working in the box offices could not set their own surcharges on broker tickets. Needless to say, brokers didn't like the system. Nor did the rest of the box-office personnel. I told John, "You should abort the plan. It's fraught with peril. ICE is illegal. It would be hard to deny illegal activities one floor below your own office."

John assured me, "This is the most efficient way of handling ticket distribution, and I will not stand for any illegal activity."

Little did I know.

Obviously, J. J. knew all about this, and if anyone could have stopped it, he was the one. But J. J. was hardly likely to do so. And, clearly, my advice to John didn't matter.

What worried me was what might happen to the Shuberts if, one day, law enforcers decided to crack down on ICE. Murray Helwitz, John, and maybe even J. J. could be held criminally liable. As it turned out, I was right to worry.

Sometime in 1963, New York's attorney general, a hard-nosed lawyer-turned-politician named Louis J. Lefkowitz, decided to open a full-scale investigation into ICE. Lefkowitz not only wanted to stop the practice, he wanted to put people in jail. Broadway was in a panic. And the attorney general's prime Shubert targets were Lawrence, who had succeeded John by then, and Helwitz.

Adopting a "see nothing, know nothing" defense, Lawrence insisted that because he was new on the job, he'd had no knowledge of what was going on behind his back. The owners of the business, J. J.'s executors, had little choice but to accept his denials. In truth, Lawrence never had attended any of the meetings, nor did he ever understand the inner workings of the business. His defense shifted Lefkowitz's inquiry to Helwitz, who in fact did know what was going on. Despite intense pressure, however, he never implicated Lawrence or anyone else.

The investigation rocked the industry. Broadway League meetings were held during which famous producers, such as Cy Feuer and Ernie Martin, Leland Hayward, and the Rodgers & Hammerstein Organization, expressed outrage at having their reputations tarnished. Box-office treasurers and brokers were subpoenaed by Lefkowitz to testify before a grand jury. They either asserted their Fifth Amendment privilege or received immunity from prosecution in exchange for their testimony. Everybody was holding their breath and walking on tiptoe.

Helwitz was arrested in 1964 and, the following year, pleaded guilty to ninety-one counts of collecting ICE from nine ticket brokers, for a total sum of more than $70,000. The judge who sentenced Helwitz to prison commented at the time, "I suspect somebody above you got some of the money." Eventually, some people thought Schoenfeld and Jacobs were on the take too. The fact is, Bernie and I could not help but know of ICE's existence, but we never saw one cent being exchanged, nor did we ever benefit from the practice.

Needless to say, after the Lefkowitz investigation concluded, a fundamental change occurred. For fear of prosecution, theater owners, producers, general managers, company managers, and other participants fell out of the distribution loop. On my recommendation, memoranda were posted in all box offices informing box-office treasurers that if they were found to exact or accept ICE they would be fired on the spot.

Of course, where there's a will there's a way, and in the wake of the ICE scandal, ticket brokers long entrenched in New York started an exodus to New Jersey, where there were no scalping laws, and where they received ICE from and paid ICE to New York box-office treasurers. Later government investigations found ICE to be still prevalent, not only in the theater, but wherever reserved-seat tickets were sold.

The often-amended laws regulating ticket scalping, which were diffi-cult to enforce, have since been repealed. With the advent of the Internet and computerized ticket sales, the public came to realize that tickets to desirable events could be resold at a premium. Now it's open season for all kinds of scalpers. Only a federal law prohibiting the resale of tickets over the Internet, similar to the prohibition on Internet gambling, can curtail this insidious practice.

Murray Helwitz was a long-time Shubert box-office treasurer and part of the Shubert family—Lee and J. J.'s mother was a Helwitz. There was a fear that, despite Lawrence's denials, Helwitz might try to implicate him, and others, after he had served his jail term. As a result, the co-executors faced the problem of what to do with Helwitz once he was free. The decision was made to rehire him in the real-estate department. For Helwitz, it was banishment to Siberia.

Attorney General Lefkowitz won this battle.

What I didn't know at the time was that, in Lefkowitz's mind, this was just the opening shot in what would become a full-blown war. The next time, the enemy would be Bernie and me.

TWELVE

TROUBLE IN PHILADELPHIA

While Irving Goldman, the paint salesman who would eventually become a serious problem, was ingratiating himself with Lawrence, the other Goldman—William, the theater owner from Philadelphia, and no relation to Irving—was already a problem. I was now traveling to Philadelphia several times a week on the antitrust case he had brought against us. The only pleasant thing about those trips was the candy store at Thirtieth Street Station, where I stopped regularly to bring home chocolate turtles for Pat and Carrie.

J. J. was still alive at the outset of the case in October 1956, when we made a motion that the Philadelphia court did not have jurisdiction. To thwart us, William Goldman's lawyer, an overly aggressive, disagreeable, yet very capable attorney named Harold Kohn, cleverly responded by asking that the court sever part of the case. We argued that the court had neither jurisdiction nor venue, and therefore no power to transfer the case. The suit went all the way to the United States Supreme Court, and we lost.

Kohn now served notice to take J. J.'s deposition.

That morning, I walked across the street to pick up J. J. in the Sardi Building, and as soon as he emerged from the elevator, I felt the full force of his temper.

"It's you!" he screamed. "You're the one who got me into this litigation. You're the one who got me deposed. I'm going to fire you. I'll never forgive you."

Adding insult to injury in J. J.'s mind was the fact that the accuser William Goldman, who was also being deposed, was present in our office, on Shubert property. It was more than J. J. could stand.

Whose fault was this? Mine, of course.

J. J.'s mood went from bad to worse, and the more Kohn pressed him, the more he boiled. When J. J. finally reached his limit, he snapped at Kohn, "Your client is a no-good, blackmailing kike."

Reacting immediately to this anti-Semitic slur, I requested that J. J.'s remark be stricken from the record.

Kohn replied, "In my cases, everything is on the record."

I warned him, "This case is like a rubber ball, and someday it will bounce back in my direction and you'll be asking me for a favor."

Being polite made no difference to Kohn. The case continued for another ten years.

A few years into the case, I discovered that Kohn was acting in a lawsuit *against* his client William Goldman. A man named Harry Sley, owner of a movie theater in Philadelphia, had hired Kohn to sue several distributors and exhibitors, including Goldman, for depriving him of first-run motion pictures. One of the defendants in that case was represented by Louis Nizer and Walter Beck, both famous and formidable lawyers. I arranged a meeting with them to point out that Kohn was acting for Goldman in the antitrust case against us, and also acting against Goldman as a violator in the Sley case. Not only was this highly irregular, it was a direct conflict of interest.

They didn't see it my way. At least, not at first. My argument must have grown on them, however, because later they invited me to attend a hearing on their motion to disqualify Kohn from the case. I couldn't get to Philadelphia fast enough.

Staring down from the bench, the judge told Kohn that he was going to refer his conduct to the board of judges of the federal court. Kohn immediately volunteered to resign from the Shubert case, since his other case was ready for trial. The judge said the offer was not satisfactory, and Kohn was compelled to resign from both. I was thrilled to see the back of him.

Kohn's replacement was Edwin Rome, a refined and congenial fellow. Right away he wanted to discuss a settlement. I offered $50,000. He laughed. "This case is worth well over $1 million."

That was the end of that. So now it was my turn to depose William Goldman. He was a member of the school board and relatively important in Philadelphia. But that didn't stop me from putting him on the spot. I said, "You've alleged the existence of a conspiracy. How did you know of the existence of this conspiracy?"

Goldman must have had J. J.'s blood in his veins, because he answered, "I'm not going to tell you."

I said, "You can't or you won't?"

He said, "I won't."

I turned to Rome. "Would you mind instructing your client to answer the question?"

Rome told Goldman he had to answer, and when he finally did, he said, "When there's a nigger in the woodpile, you can smell it."

Immediately, Rome jumped up. "Please strike that from the record."

"I would love to accommodate you," I said; "however, your predecessor, Mr. Kohn, long ago laid down the ground rules in this case. The ground rules are that everything is on the record."

Waltzing out of that deposition, I spent the next several weeks trying to figure out how to get Goldman's racial slur before a jury. It was an unacceptable comment by any standard, but coming from a school-board member in a city where nearly half the population was African-American—this would be fatal for him.

The next thing I knew, we received a notice from Rome, who had earlier demanded a jury trial, waiving Goldman's right to a jury trial.

We started lining up witnesses, and a three-month non-jury trial followed.

During those months, I would take the early-morning train down to Philadelphia, spend the day in court, then catch an early-evening train back to New York so that I could be in my office by seven p.m. I worked there until ten or eleven p.m., went home to sleep, and was back at Penn Station in time for the early-morning train to Philly.

Among the people I put on the stand were the producer Robert Whitehead; Philip Langner of the Theater Guild; Carl Fisher, who was manager to the legendary George Abbott; and Victor Samrock, manager of the Playwrights' Company. Each swore that they played at Shubert's Forrest Theatre in Philadelphia rather than Goldman's Erlanger because the Forrest was a superior theater. But the best witness of all was the legendary David Merrick.

Dark-haired with a black mustache, and always smartly dressed, Merrick was a difficult man at the best of times. By then he was the most important producer on Broadway. Year after year, he won Tonys for bringing hits to Broadway such as *Gypsy, Look Back in Anger, La Plume de Ma Tante, Becket, Irma La Douce, Carnival, Oliver!, Stop the*

World—I Want to Get Off, and in 1964 the hugely successful *Hello, Dolly!* starring Carol Channing.

The show was originally called *Dolly: A Damned Exasperating Woman,* but then its main song, "Hello, Dolly!" was recorded by Louis "Satchmo" Armstrong and hit number one on the charts. At that point, Merrick changed the name of the show to match the song. *Hello, Dolly!* opened on January 16, 1964, at the St. James Theatre, and ran for 2,844 performances. When Channing left the cast, David brought in several leading ladies to fill the role, but in 1967 he had the brilliant idea of keeping the show alive with an all-black cast that featured Pearl Bailey, Cab Calloway, and a very young Morgan Freeman making his Broadway debut.

During this period, I spent a lot of time preparing David for his testimony. As ornery as he was influential, he kept snapping at me: "Do you think I'm an idiot? I know what to say."

In mid-November, his all-black *Hello, Dolly!* opened on Broadway to rave reviews, which was great for David. Except that he was set to testify in Philadelphia the morning after the opening. He and I were supposed to meet at Penn Station for the seven o'clock train, but I knew he would be up late, since opening-night parties famously go on into the small hours of the morning. I didn't sleep all night, worrying that David would miss the train.

By the time he got there, a few minutes before the train was about to leave, I was a wreck, pacing back and forth on the platform. He just looked at me and said, "What did you think? I told you I'd be here."

David was himself a lawyer, and his testimony was wonderful. Not only did he reiterate and emphasize what the other producers were saying—that ours was a better theater than Goldman's—but David took it a step further. He said he didn't like doing business with people who sued other people. Goldman, he said, was a *suer*—using the word to be understood as *s-e-w-e-r.*

A few days later, the court rendered its decision, which was totally in our favor. I immediately called J. J.'s widow and told her we had won. She said in her deep voice, "Mr. J. J. would have been very pleased."

Next I phoned Eckie, who was overjoyed.

Then I called the third executor of J. J.'s estate, Frith Pickslay of Morgan Guaranty Trust Company, and gave him the news. He was especially pleased.

Finally, Bernie and I debated about whether to call Lawrence. Had we lost, we would have had to pay treble damages and possibly suffer more divestiture. In my mind, I had not only saved the day, I had saved Shubert.

Lawrence was in London at the Savoy Hotel, so we sent a telegram. It was delivered to him in the hotel's American Bar, where he and Warren Caro were drinking. Warren opened it, read it to Lawrence, and added, "This is great news."

Lawrence's response was, "Fuck 'em. That's what they get paid for."

THIRTEEN

ALL-OUT WAR WITH LAWRENCE

Lawrence was equally unimpressed when we finally settled Lee Shubert's estate.

The report of the legal referees came out in June 1965. To get to that point had required eighty-five hearings to value every Shubert property. The conclusion was that Lee's half interest in the partnership at the time of his death was $16.79 million, without interest. Since nearly thirteen years had elapsed since Lee's death, the other side was claiming that they were entitled to approximately $30 million.

We went through extensive contested proceedings to confirm the referee's report and determine the appropriate interest rate to impose. The final settlement came in at $18 million, payable to Milton and Sylvia over a period of many years. The door to yet another dire threat to the Shubert business was finally shut.

Lawrence hardly noticed the end of a long and hard-fought battle.

———•◦•———

As the mid to late 1960s wore on, no thanks to Lawrence and his incompetent stewardship, a spate of highly successful plays and musicals with top stars ran in Shubert theaters. Among them were *Dylan*, with Alec Guinness; *Funny Girl*, with Barbra Streisand; *Luv*, directed by Mike Nichols; the blockbuster *Fiddler on the Roof*, with Zero Mostel; Neil Simon's masterpiece *The Odd Couple*, with Art Carney and Walter Matthau; *Mame*, which ran for nearly four years and starred Angela Lansbury and Bea Arthur; *Cabaret*, with Joel Grey; *Wait Until Dark*, with Lee Remick and Robert Duvall; Burt Bacharach and Hal David's musical *Promises, Promises*; and Abe Burrows's comedy *Cactus Flower*, with Lauren Bacall and Barry Nelson.

But those successes couldn't mask the many serious problems that Shubert, Broadway, and the entire American theater community faced.

Lawrence never showed any sign of being aware of them.

Critically, the industry was conducting business in substantially the same way as in the earliest days of American theater. On top of that, our Broadway audience was getting older every year. In fact, it was dying of old age. Younger patrons were going to rock concerts, dance clubs, and other venues. Older patrons did not want to venture, either as couples or with families, to midtown's sex-driven, hooker-infested, crime-riddled Times Square. Morale in the business was low and heading lower.

In 1969, Warren Caro introduced us to Paul Levin, who was in charge of American Broadcasting Company's real-estate department. In a meeting with Bernie, Lawrence, Warren, and me, Levin said he was looking for someone to sublease a new legitimate theater to be built in an undeveloped area near Beverly Hills, Los Angeles. The theater would be part of a major development consisting of office buildings, movie theaters, restaurants, shops, and a hotel. It was to be named the ABC Entertainment Center at Century City.

We later negotiated a sublease for the theater, plus an adjacent office building with some fifty thousand square feet of rentable space. Our thinking was that rent from the office building would provide an income stream that would insulate our new theater from the vicissitudes of show business.

The decision proved to be near fatal for the company. Completing the construction of the Shubert Theatre in Los Angeles took years, until fall 1972. And while we waited, costs kept rising. This at a time when the real-estate market nationally was falling through the floor. Our theaters should have been very valuable properties, but most were nearly worthless, and we couldn't borrow on them. These were dire years for us.

It seemed obvious to me, first of all, that Times Square and the theater district needed cleaning up. But that would not be enough. We also needed to attract younger audiences, but getting shows that appealed to them cost money. Although the Shubert business was losing considerable sums, it still had some resources, and we had to put those resources to work.

We needed to reinvent ourselves. We needed newer, more innovative marketing techniques. But Bernie and I knew that nothing would happen as long as Lawrence Shubert Lawrence Jr. was still around.

In early March 1970, Norman Light passed away unexpectedly. His death meant that there was one less sycophant. Light was not a religious person, and I don't believe he attended a synagogue. Nevertheless, in the tradition of Lee and J. J., funeral arrangements were made for him at New York's premiere Reform synagogue, Temple Emanu-El. There was no great outpouring of mourners, and I don't believe the rabbi who delivered the eulogy had ever met him, although that didn't diminish his generous comments about Norman.

On the way out of the synagogue, I bumped into Irving Kessler, whose company held the contract to furnish housekeeping personnel for the theaters. He turned to me and said, "I thought I was attending Norman Light's funeral, but obviously I was in the wrong place—I didn't know who the rabbi was speaking about."

Later on, and for years afterward, when the name Norman Light came up, it was followed by the stentorian reply, briefly stated, with a rising inflection: "L-I-G-H-T-S . . ." followed by a short, breathless "OUT!"

Just about three weeks after Norman died, J. J.'s widow, Muriel, passed away. She was not well known to many company employees or the theater community, despite being a Shubert Foundation board member. Muriel's passing meant the old regime was dying off. The only two surviving Shubert Foundation board members were Lawrence and Eckie. And their relationship was increasingly hostile.

Jim Vaughan, who was advising Eckie, suggested to her that left unchecked, Lawrence was all too powerful, and that the board should be enlarged. Eckie agreed. To Lawrence, this was a declaration of war. Jim then sent a letter on Eckie's behalf to Louis Lefkowitz, who as attorney general of New York State supervised the activities of all foundations and charities, requesting that the board of the Shubert Foundation be enlarged.

By then, Lawrence had another lawyer for his personal affairs, not Bernie and me.

Apparently it was Irving Goldman, the paint salesman, who convinced Lawrence that if he and Eckie each appointed two new board members, there would still be a deadlock and he would still retain control. So, facing the possibility of otherwise losing it, Lawrence agreed. Eckie selected Bernie and me. Lawrence nominated Irving Wall, a lawyer who had once represented Lawrence's girlfriend, and his second nominee was Irving Goldman.

We were shocked that he named Goldman, not Teichmann. After all, Teichmann was his best friend. But there were no restrictions on whom Lawrence could name. To reach a compromise with Eckie, he could have picked Mao Tse-tung and the pope. I can only speculate that Teichmann didn't get the appointment because Goldman wouldn't stand for it. At the same time, Goldman had enough influence to put his own name forward.

Immediately following the election in August 1971, Lawrence retained new counsel to represent the foundation. At Goldman's suggestion, the prestigious firm of Shea, Gould, Climenko & Kramer was engaged. Milton Gould was among the most eminent lawyers in America, and his partner Bill Shea, equally distinguished, was the man most responsible for bringing baseball back to New York. A few years after the Brooklyn Dodgers left for Los Angeles, Shea helped create the New York Mets, and the stadium they played in was named after him.

The partner at Shea Gould in charge of the matter, Theodore Jaffe, was not yet actively involved. J. J.'s executors were in control of the business until J. J.'s estate was administered and its assets distributed to the foundation. The executors fixed June 30, 1972, as the date for distribution of those assets.

I saw the handwriting on the wall. Once the matter of J. J.'s estate was settled, Lawrence would make his move, and Bernie and I would be gone. Our relationship with Goldman was cordial, as was our relationship with Wall, and our relationship with Eckie was perfect. Our relationship with Lawrence, however, was increasingly difficult.

Nine months after we were elected to the board, Theodore Jaffe died. This was now May 1972, just five or six weeks before the expected turnover of the assets to the foundation. A few days later, Goldman walked across the street to tell us that he had taken Lawrence to Shea Gould, this time to meet with Bill Shea.

I'd never set foot in Shea Gould, nor had Bernie. Nor did we know why Goldman was telling us about Lawrence meeting Shea. Either he was trying to ride the fence by being nice to Bernie and me at the same time that he was chummy with Lawrence, or he was having second thoughts about having taken Lawrence to Shea Gould without informing us. After all, as board members, we had a right to know what was going on.

So I said I wanted to meet Shea. Goldman set it up, and the three of us went to his office. After a cordial greeting, I said to Shea, "I have only one question. Are you representing Lawrence or the Shubert Foundation?"

Shea answered, "The foundation."

Satisfied that he was not acting on Lawrence's part alone, I said, "That's all I needed to know," and that ended the meeting.

A few weeks later Goldman told me, "I think Lawrence knows that I took you to see Bill Shea."

I wondered if it was supposed to have been a secret. But Lawrence was so paranoid about everything that Goldman was right to worry. After the Shea incident, every time I saw Lawrence, I could tell he was furious. He looked at me with more than just anger.

On Memorial Day weekend that year, Pat and I were in Westhampton, Long Island—with Alvin Cooperman, the former Shubert booker, and his wife, Marilyn—when I received a call from the Shubert office. The operator said Irving Goldman was urgently trying to reach me and needed to talk privately. There was only one telephone in the house, and I didn't want Alvin to overhear my conversation, so I excused myself, walked down the beach to a public phone, and placed a call to Goldman.

"Nobody can talk to me that way," Goldman said, quivering with rage. He'd just gotten off a two-hour phone conversation with Lawrence. "He spoke to me in a way that no man will ever speak to me. Called me a Judas. He said he's going to get me, and Judge DiFalco, and everybody I'm friends with."

As he ranted on, I thought back to Milton Weir's confrontation with J. J. This was life with the Shuberts. Goldman was learning, as I had all those years before, that with the Shuberts, familiarity indeed bred contempt.

Now Goldman said, "I realize what kind of person he is. I won't have him running this business if I have anything to say about it."

"Are you serious?" I asked.

"Absolutely," he said. "He's a disgrace. I've never been so insulted in my life."

I told Goldman we would have to meet to discuss the matter.

Once back in the city, Bernie and I met Goldman at a steakhouse on the West Side. We listened to him vent. He was insisting that Lawrence be ousted at the upcoming board meeting on June 30.

This was big news, which Bernie and I had to communicate immediately to Eckie, so off we went to Byram, Connecticut. Eckie said she also wanted to get rid of Lawrence and would vote for his ouster. With Goldman and Eckie on our side, a majority of the board thus became united in their resolve to terminate Lawrence.

During the interval between Memorial Day and June 30, Bernie and I prepared the meeting agenda. Apparently, Lawrence had spoken to Irving Wall, the fifth director, and told him about his altercation with Goldman. Wall quickly realized the consequences—that Lawrence would be gone—and phoned me several times, urging me to forgive Lawrence and give him another chance.

I promised to discuss it with Bernie but didn't give him any reason to be encouraged. To be honest, we had never thought about how to get rid of Lawrence. We had never planned a palace coup. We had simply never thought we could get rid of him. But with Goldman we now had the votes.

The big day arrived. It was obvious that Lawrence knew something momentous was about to happen. This was confirmed by looks that could kill directed at Bernie and me. He was sober and unusually well dressed in a dark blue suit.

Following the meeting's agenda, we announced that the Shubert Foundation was now the rightful owner of the Shubert Corporation. We then prepared to elect new directors for the foundation. I nominated myself, Bernard Jacobs, Irving Wall, Irving Goldman, Eckie, and Lawrence, all of whom were elected. Lawrence was then named chairman, but he was stripped of any authority and would have only ceremonial duties. Even Wall voted with us, so it was five to one. Lawrence rose in a fury and stormed out.

The corporation would now be run by three executive directors: Bernie, Goldman, and me as chairman. Since Bernie and I were really not title conscious, we thanked Goldman for his swing vote by naming him president. No one in the theatrical community knew Goldman. And they only knew Bernie and me as lawyers. That outcome created a flurry of activity in the press to the effect that relative strangers were now running the Shubert business. They would soon refer to us as the triumvirate.

At the end of that meeting, I invited senior company executives into the board room and notified them of the change. All but two were delighted. Only one of the sycophants voiced his objections. His employment was terminated.

Lawrence spent days and nights trying to get back at us. He fed other people questions, and they demanded that we respond. One asked, "Why don't you and Jacobs pay rent?" His argument was that while we'd worked there as lawyers, we had not been Shubert employees and we should have paid for our office space. But that had been our arrangement with J. J. So my answer was, "That's none of your business."

Lawrence also fed the press whatever delusions he could get them to print. For instance, he complained that Bernie and I had objected to his nominees for the board. They supposedly were the long-retired producer Max Gordon and the composer Richard Rodgers—I'm not convinced that Lawrence knew either man—as well as the syndicated gossip columnist Earl Wilson, and Louis Lotito, who operated five theaters and was our competitor. We couldn't have objected to them, because he had never mentioned them to us. In fact, Lawrence had never had any intention of putting any of them on the board.

Sycophant in chief Howard Teichmann, who'd become Irving Goldman's bête noire, was on an annual retainer to write Lawrence's speeches and press releases, and also to ghostwrite a few articles for papers like *Variety* with Lawrence's byline. Teichmann's employment was terminated.

The board agreed that Bernie would be responsible for the booking and for negotiating certain union contracts. I would be responsible for the financial and real-estate side, for theater and property maintenance and restoration, for negotiating certain other union contracts, and for government relations and insurance matters.

Despite these divisions of responsibilities, Bernie and I agreed that we both would be involved in all decisions, and that if one of us objected strongly to any matter, it would not be pursued.

June 30, 1972, was Liberation Day.

I was free at last from twenty-two years, eleven months, and nineteen days of saving Lee, J. J., John, and Lawrence from every type of difficulty imaginable: the clutches of the Antitrust Division of the U.S. Department of Justice; internecine family warfare over Lee's estate and J. J.'s estate; the private antitrust suit brought by a vicious competitor; and the trap of John's bizarre matrimonial controversy with potentially disastrous consequences. All had threatened the existence of the business. Losing any of the cases would have marked the end of our careers with the Shuberts, upon whom Bernie and I had become totally dependent, and with whom we were personally involved.

Now that Lawrence no longer ran the business, also gone were the sycophants and the barhopping and running to Sardi's to conduct business. Litigation seemed a thing of the past, although one more would be lurking in the wings.

For the moment, however, hanging oppressively over us was a company on the verge of insolvency. We had experienced years of increasing losses. The new theater in Los Angeles required year-round employees, and the expenses were draining us. Public relations could not have been worse: hatred of anything Shubert was at a peak in the industry. Further, the theater district and Times Square were in dire straits, and the theater business was in one of its cyclical lows. Shubert's production of plays and investing in them in order to help fill theaters had long ceased. And the city's economy was also in a downturn.

Goldman had expressed a desire to play an active role in the company, but his knowledge of the theater, and its creative talent and literature, was deficient. We realized, though, that had it not been for Goldman's swing vote, the Lawrence era would have continued and Shubert's fortunes would have been totally bleak. We felt we owed him more than a figurehead title, so we put him in charge of theater maintenance.

A few weeks after Goldman started coming to the office every day, he suggested we retain Meade Esposito, then Brooklyn's political leader, to handle our insurance business. We were already adequately represented and would not agree to a change under any circumstance. Goldman didn't pursue the matter, but that should have been a warning to us that Goldman had his own agenda.

Lawrence, fighting desperately to get the company back, now accused Goldman of sticking his nose in the John Shubert litigation, along with his "crooked friend" Judge Sam DiFalco. Of course, Goldman was absolutely not involved in John's case—this was Lawrence's vendetta, pure and simple.

"I have done nothing to be ashamed of," Lawrence told the press. "My life is an open book. I have been betrayed."

At the same time, Teichmann publicly accused Bernie and me of being "money men," claiming that Lawrence was, in contrast to us, "an educated man who knows and loves the theater."

While Teichmann was willing to admit that Lawrence was "sometimes wild" and "liked to drink," he insisted that we money men had secret plans to sell off several Broadway theaters, and that Goldman had been appointed to the board solely because his friend DiFalco had the power to fix anything.

Irving Goldman's appointment to the board had had nothing to do with DiFalco. Besides, Goldman had been appointed by Lawrence. In the face of Lawrence's disparaging remarks, DiFalco felt the need to put him and Teichmann in their place. "If I had this much power in the Shubert business, I would quit my job as judge and take Irving Goldman's job with the Shuberts," he said.

As for our secret plan to sell off theaters, that was a blatant lie on Teichmann's part. Selling real estate was never on the agenda. Even if we had wanted to consider it, which we hadn't, New York City was going through the worst economic crisis in memory, and real-estate values had plunged. Selling into that market would have been suicide. What's more, if we'd been so hungry for money, we could have rented several theaters to porno-house operators for plenty.

By mid-July 1972, Bernie and I had completed a reorganization of the business, bringing twenty-three various Shubert companies under one umbrella. We renamed the business the Shubert Organization and amended the bylaws accordingly.

Goldman was out as president, although he remained on the board and as head of the maintenance department. The board elected me chairman and named Bernie president.

FOURTEEN

LEFKOWITZ ATTACKS, AGAIN

One afternoon in August 1972, our friend Ted Cott was walking home along Madison Avenue when he found himself right behind Lawrence Shubert, Lawrence Jr. and Howard Teichmann.

"No, that is not the way to do it," he overheard Teichmann say to Lawrence, "We must have a plan."

Pat and I had known Ted and his wife, Sue, for some time. He'd once been the boy genius of NBC radio, but despite being creative, he had not been able to make a successful switch to television. Sue was smart and gorgeous, taking a PhD at Columbia in Russian studies, and also appearing occasionally as a panelist on television shows like *What's My Line?*

When Ted told me what he'd heard, I worried. I had no idea what it meant, but it didn't sound good.

Anyway, I had a lot of other things to worry about.

The Shubert Theatre in Los Angeles was finally ready to open, after several years of cost overruns. Bernie and I had already decided that it was essential to inaugurate the theater with a prestigious show, so we booked the national touring production of *Follies*.

Directed by Hal Prince, choreographed by Michael Bennett, with music and lyrics by Stephen Sondheim, it had a glamorous opening followed by a glamorous party. Excitement was in the air, and although the engagement was to last only ten weeks, we were a happy group that night. Our fingers were crossed that the show would be a hit in Los Angeles. We needed *Follies* to help stop the tremendous financial drain on the company as a result of the theater's cost and the poor theater business in general.

Sadly, *Follies* wasn't a hit. The rest of the engagement did not live up to our expectations. In fact, the show generated a loss for us, due both to inordinately high operating costs and disappointing box-office receipts. It was, however, a financial success for its producers, thanks to favorable booking terms and to our granting a reduction in booking-contract terms to Hal Prince.

In those days, the prevailing custom for theaters that lost money presenting profitable touring shows was to renegotiate financial terms. Since we had presented a number of Hal Prince shows in New York and on the road, including *West Side Story*, *Fiddler on the Roof*, *Zorba*, *Company*, and *Cabaret*, we thought our relationship with Hal would help us renegotiate the booking contract. But Hal rejected our plea, saying that obligations to his investors precluded him from giving us any relief.

Whatever money we were making in New York had to be diverted to Los Angeles. After such an inauspicious start at the L.A. Shubert, things did not improve. Subsequent successful productions at the new theater were few and far between. What's more, the office rental market was so depressed that we could not lease space in the building, space that cost us $200,000 a year, not counting our share of taxes, security, maintenance, utilities, and additional charges. With twenty-seven years remaining on the lease, we had no alternative but to approach ABC and ask what we would have to pay to surrender it. We settled for $250,000 and, frankly, were hard-pressed to raise the amount.

In my mind, things couldn't get worse. Still lingering in the back of my mind, however, was the conversation Ted Cott had overheard on Madison Avenue. It was Christmas when I found out that, once again, I was right to worry.

During the holidays, Bernie and Irving Goldman, who was then still heading the maintenance department and a member of the Shubert board, were attending a press conference in Los Angeles about the theater in Century City. I was alone in our New York offices when a messenger with a hand truck emerged from the elevator. On the hand truck were identical volumes, each about three inches thick, containing a summons from the courts to answer a complaint by Lawrence to oust Bernie, Goldman, and me, and to reinstate himself in his former position.

Lawrence had filed his complaint with the state attorney general, our old nemesis Louis Lefkowitz. He charged that we had stolen the company from him. He alleged that Irving Goldman, together with Judge DiFalco, Bernie, and me, had conspired to remove him as head of the company and had also conspired to fix the settlement of the John Shubert litigation. Lawrence said that Goldman and DiFalco were crooks, and that Jim Vaughan, who was a coexecutor of the estate, was also a crook.

Taking the charges seriously, Lefkowitz announced that he would conduct an investigation into the allegations and pursue criminal proceedings, if necessary. Couched in those terms, Lefkowitz was saying publicly that Bernie and I were also crooks.

I phoned Bernie in Los Angeles and asked him and Goldman to return to New York. Then I went into a tailspin. I'm someone who doesn't even park illegally for five minutes. Furthermore, I have never invested in any play for my own account. I have always believed that doing so would be taking away from the organization and would constitute a conflict of interest.

No sooner was Lawrence's suit filed, and Lefkowitz's intentions apparent, than I received a call from Leo Shull, publisher of the trade paper *Show Business*, who said he had something important to discuss. So he came to my apartment on New Year's Day. "You don't understand what's going on here," Leo told me. "Lefkowitz is determined to throw you out and put you in jail."

Leo knew a lot of politicians, so I presumed he had some sort of inside track. But this was the first time anyone had actually said that word: *jail*.

I blurted out, "Are you serious?"

He insisted, "Of course, I'm serious."

That rocked me. It rocked Bernie, too, but he didn't show it.

Lefkowitz invited Milton Gould, representing the Shubert Foundation, to join him in the fight against us. Gould categorically refused. Lefkowitz then demanded that the directors of the Shubert Organization and Shubert Foundation step down until his investigation was completed. Gould replied that the boards would not step down, that they would fight his allegations.

Not surprisingly, Lawrence thought restructuring the board was a great idea, imagining that Lefkowitz would put him back on it. Lawrence announced, "I always favored, in principle, a representative board, including prominent members within the theatrical field." But even Lawrence's buddy Irving Wall knew better and told the press, "No way."

Undeterred, Lefkowitz demanded to see the books. He said he intended to conduct a full-scale audit and retained the noted accounting firm Seidman and Seidman.

On the day the auditors arrived, they told our financial department staff that Lefkowitz had instructed them to find any incriminating evidence they could about Bernie and me. One of the Seidman accountants actually said, "Our instructions are, 'You've got to give us something to hang our hat on.'"

The accountants spent months and months reviewing the books, and introduced something like sixty-six objections to the J. J. Shubert accounting proceeding, some of which were directed at Bernie and me. Based on their reports, Lefkowitz made allegations about our fees, about the executors' commissions—even though I was not an executor—and a host of other things. He came at us with guns blazing.

I was frozen. I couldn't make any decisions. I was more frightened than I had ever been in my life. I told Pat, "I want to jump out the window, but I'm afraid if I do, I'll hurt myself."

With the audit heavy on my mind, there was still day-to-day business to conduct. The pressure was enormous, and my preoccupation with the situation drove me to a psychiatrist's office. I was told I was suffering from a mild depression. But I simply couldn't function. To me, it was a depression of major proportions.

My first visit to the psychiatrist lasted fifty minutes. When he told me to return the following week, I couldn't believe it. I wanted to yell, "I'm sick and you're telling me I should wait a week for my next visit?" Instead, I filled his prescription for a red liquid, perhaps a barbiturate, which I kept in my office desk drawer and took whenever I felt anxiety overwhelming me.

As a congenital worrier, I drove Pat crazy. At one point, she asked Carrie if she was worried about her father. Carrie replied, "No, because I know he would never do anything wrong."

Not even that brought much solace.

What Pat didn't tell me was that Carrie came home from school one day and announced, "My friends say Daddy is going to jail." Similarly, Bernie's daughter, Sally, asked him, "Daddy, are you a crook?" He broke down.

It took me nearly two years to return to normalcy. Bernie didn't believe in psychiatrists and eventually returned to normalcy on his own. For me, the depression was deep and would, unfortunately, resurface later in my life.

————•·•·•————

The press was relentless.

Bernie and I, along with Jim Vaughan, had been the attorneys for J. J.'s estate at the same time that we'd been the attorneys for the Shubert business. We were paid a fee from the estate. Bernie and I also got our regular fee for our work for the business. Lefkowitz was claiming that, since J. J.'s estate had been left to charity, it had been inappropriate for us to take a fee from the business as well.

The press picked up on this, and headlines read, "Lawyers Accused of Illegally Taking Money from Charity."

Not only was it the most outrageous allegation, but Lefkowitz knew it was untrue. He knew that the matter of J. J.'s estate and the daily workings of the Shubert business were separate and different.

I didn't necessarily mind that Lefkowitz chastised Lawrence and demanded that he repay, with interest, $84,000 in travel expenses, nearly $16,000 for limousines and chauffeurs, and another $84,000 in restaurant bills. But Lefkowitz was wrong when he decided, out of the blue, that Bernie and I were self-dealing because—he must have heard this from Lawrence—we didn't pay rent for our offices.

He proclaimed, "Rent-free space constitutes self-dealing and a conflict of interest." Again, there was no truth to that statement. The office arrangement we had was part of our working relationship with J. J., and was perfectly aboveboard.

The press then reported, as if revealing a huge secret, that we were also the attorneys for producers, clients, and suppliers, as well as pension-fund members.

There was nothing secretive or wrong about this practice. We represented a few friends who went into the theater business, and in every instance we made it clear that we would not take part in any negotiations relating to a show's booking terms.

Here, too, Lefkowitz claimed a conflict of interest. Yet, if a conflict is disclosed and accepted by both parties, the usual presumptions that might flow from such a circumstance do not exist.

As far as the pension funds were concerned, we had represented them since their inception, obviously with the full knowledge of the League of American Theatres and Producers. Indeed, we had done so at their request and on behalf of all the employers in the industry. And, of course, it had been done with the consent of people running the Shubert business at that time.

Lefkowitz objected to our fees, our work, everything imaginable. Lefkowitz had an agenda. I believe he had contrived a scheme that would force us to resign and, ultimately, allow his cronies to take control of the Shubert business. He had said he wanted us to step aside while he conducted his investigation. He had also announced that he wanted to replace the board with seven new people, at least three of whom he would personally select. One of his choices would have been Sam Housman, a confidant of then-governor Nelson Rockefeller. Housman was a political sycophant who had some charities of his own.

I found it all highly suspicious and was convinced that Lefkowitz and his cronies intended to get inside our business and perhaps liquidate it. Lefkowitz's timing was dubious enough: the run-up to an election year in which he was again on the ballot for attorney general. But the basis of my suspicion was that he'd already pulled similar stunts a few times. I believe that Lefkowitz might have been acting on behalf of powerful friends who supposedly wanted the Shubert properties.

Interestingly enough, in December 1973 Rockefeller was appointed by President Gerald Ford to be his vice president, and left his position as governor. When Hugh Carey became governor, with the matter against us still pending, he appointed me to a panel studying casino gambling in New York State. Clearly, Carey didn't believe I had done anything wrong or he would never have considered me.

The starting point of Carey's panel was to assume that casino gambling would become legal in New York and then to ask, "How should it operate?" As it turned out, my appointment on the panel would shed further light on our nemesis Lefkowitz.

One member of the panel was assistant district attorney Al Scotti, then head of the New York district attorney's Rackets Bureau. Scotti and I were talking one day about the need to license vendors who do business with casinos, when Scotti said, "The most important ones are the liquor vendors. I know what I am talking about because I put L. Judson Morhouse away."

Morhouse was a former Republican state chairman who had been in cahoots with a man named Martin Epstein, then head of the State Liquor Authority. When the Playboy Club in New York was denied a liquor license, Morhouse and Epstein had arranged to get them one, in exchange for a $40,000 bribe. They had told the club to contact a lawyer named Hyman Siegel, who was then also indicted by Scotti for bribing officials. Siegel was one of the most important "liquor lawyers" in the state, a man who could produce a license when everyone else failed. His firm, which he ran with his partner of twenty-seven years, was probably the busiest of all "liquor lawyer" firms.

Hyman Siegel's partner was Louis Lefkowitz.

So I leaned over to Scotti and said, "But you let the big guy get away."

He knew I meant Lefkowitz and said, "I got his partner, didn't I? I had Lefkowitz in the palm of my hand, but the statute of limitations ran out."

FIFTEEN

LAWRENCE TEAMS UP WITH LEFKOWITZ

As the battle with Lefkowitz was heating up, Lawrence filed a civil suit against us.

In a seventy-seven-page brief, supported by more than three pounds of documents, Lawrence contended that Bernie and I were guilty of "unlawful self-aggrandizement" for illegally and unjustly reducing Lawrence to a $139,000-a-year figurehead. He claimed that during his ten-year term as president and chief executive officer of his family's business, he had been powerless to cope with the "manipulations" of his enemies—that would be Bernie and me—and ignorant of what we were doing. Lawrence wanted the world to believe that we had stolen the company from him.

"In retrospect," he swore in the affidavit, "everything they did fit in. So it is natural to ask why I didn't act. I didn't act because I didn't know and couldn't have done anything had I known."

To that he added, "I, my family, the Shubert business and charitable beneficiaries have all been betrayed. Regardless of what I did or did not do, or knew or did not know, Schoenfeld, Jacobs and Goldman are using this public interest for their private interest." As an example, Lawrence said that Goldman had used his position to pressure someone into a million-dollar deal with a paint company. He didn't name names and conceded that there was no evidence that Goldman had profited from the deal.

We didn't know it at the time, but this was an allegation that would come back to haunt us.

While all this was going on, Pat was in poor health. As a child, she had had some serious health issues. Unfortunately, just as the problems with Louis Lefkowitz started, Pat's doctor said she needed to have surgery. The thought of Pat being away from home and my being on my own during this stressful time terrified me. I went to my therapist and asked, "What's going to happen to me if she goes into the hospital and I'm left alone?"

The therapist said, "I don't know. It might be very difficult for you."

Pat felt that if she didn't have the surgery, she would blame me for her health problems and the pain. She believed that she needed to get well and strong so that she could be a support for me. But I felt as if I couldn't cope with her absence. Thoughtfully, Pat arranged for her sister Cynthia to stay with me and Carrie during her hospital stay.

Each morning, I would visit Pat in her hospital room and sit there until she forced me to go to the office. In some ways, I believe Pat herself was trying to run away from me and our problems. We had financial concerns. We had rent and school bills. Yet with all the turmoil in the Shubert business, I wasn't even sure I would get my next paycheck. The stress was overwhelming us both. I needed Pat to be strong, she needed me to be strong, and neither of us could be.

I couldn't sleep. I took sleeping pills to no avail. In the office, I couldn't function. I couldn't dictate a letter, not even a line. The press was all over us. I hid under my desk, figuratively. I felt that everyone was looking at me, talking about me. That was nonsense, of course, because most people were too immersed in their own problems. Nevertheless, the pressure seemed relentless.

This was one of the most agonizing times of our lives.

We suffered for months, until Lawrence's suit demanding our ouster and his reinstatement was mercifully dismissed. That was one less thing to worry about. Except that in the wake of Lawrence and Lefkowitz, not surprisingly, new areas of concern arose.

Bob Brustein, then dean of the Yale School of Drama and someone I'd known since I was seven years old, inexplicably announced publicly that I had once put certain conditions on a Shubert Foundation grant to the school. He claimed that our grant required the school to purchase paint from Irving Goldman. The school subsequently ordered $107 worth of paint, according to Brustein, but was dissatisfied with the product and returned it. Afterward, they ordered only $25 worth. Brustein now claimed that, as a result, I had reduced the size of their grant.

It was outlandish. I mean, I'd have had to be a moron to do that. Not just for $107 worth, but for any amount. It had simply never happened. I didn't talk to Bob after that for many years.

Once again, the papers were blowing everything wildly out of proportion. The press was convinced that we were bad guys and never let up. They were shooting at us at every opportunity. Especially the *New York Post*, which had a field day. One story they reported, fed to them by Lefkowitz, said I had given $31,083 of Shubert's money to my mother-in-law, Mabel. Lefkowitz said the money was "unwarranted and unjustified."

What Lefkowitz didn't say and what the papers didn't report was the truth. When Pat's father had died in 1975 at age sixty-nine, he hadn't left her mother very much, and Mabel had had to get a job. I had never had the authority to hire, and I hadn't hired her. I had asked Lawrence if there was a job for her, and he had said yes. She worked in the Majestic Theatre box office. So while it's true that she was paid $31,083, what was not mentioned was the fact that this was her total salary over a period of more than seven years.

In those days, Pat was working at the International Center of Photography and was getting calls there from a *New York Post* reporter trying to corroborate that her mother had made that amount. The *New York Times* also came after us. Teichmann had contacts there and used them to paint an evil portrait of Bernie and me. He was very well connected with the paper's deputy managing editor, Arthur Gelb, who had once been a theater critic. Teichmann also knew Abe Rosenthal, the *Times*'s managing editor.

Years later, we became friendly with Abe. One night he came to dinner, during a period when he was being criticized publicly for an article he'd written. He was telling Pat how upset he was about being publicly chastised. Pat looked him straight in the eye and said, "Now you know what it's like." Abe had had no idea of the misery that the *New York Times* had caused us.

A ray of sunshine in all this gloom was the overwhelming support we received from the theater community. The first person to speak up for us was producer Gene Wolsk. He and fellow producer Alex Cohen, who actually flew back from his vacation home in France to help out, enlisted the support of everyone they knew, including the unions and guilds. Gene invited Bernie and me to breakfast at the City Club on

Fifty-Fifth Street, where he showed up with John Wharton, a highly respected New York lawyer.

Right away, Wharton said, "You can have the services of my firm gratis if you need it. I will not tolerate anybody like Lefkowitz getting involved in the theater business." Wharton made a few other choice comments about Lefkowitz, all negative. But his kindness to us was touching and comforting.

Gene Wolsk organized a group to meet face-to-face with Lefkowitz. Ten producers were there, including Alex Cohen, David Merrick, and Hal Prince, as well as the head of the local musicians' union and the heads of the local stagehands' union, the Society of Stage Directors and Choreographers, the International Alliance of Theatrical Stage Employees, and the Theater Development Fund. Tagging along, too, were a few theatrical lawyers.

After the meeting, Merrick told the *New York Times* that in his nineteen-year career, it was the first time he had ever seen leaders of the theatrical community in one room standing together in total unanimity. Referring to Bernie and me, he said, "Their conduct has always been absolutely impeccable and honest."

Alex Cohen insisted, "This is the best management of the Shuberts... We have no complaint with the board."

Lefkowitz refused to comment.

With so many people supporting us against Lefkowitz, we finally got some good publicity. What effect that may have had, I don't really know. Lefkowitz's influence was perfidious.

I never thought that in my lifetime I would ever be involved in a cause célèbre. But that show of support felt terrific. It did not, however, significantly diminish the pressures we faced.

———•◦•———

Bernie and I had been obscure unknowns outside the theater business. We had had no public profile. But the Lefkowitz case changed all that. Ironically, the man who did have a high public profile, Irving Goldman, had to this point pretty much emerged unscathed. One day Goldman called Bernie and me into his office in the conference room and announced that the mayor, Abe Beame, intended to appoint him as cultural-arts commissioner for the city of New York. Goldman asked, "What do you think?"

I knew he was close to Beame and had raised funds for him. If Beame was rewarding him with this position, I figured Goldman must have been a major fundraiser. "I think you should accept it. But do you know what the job is all about?"

He admitted he didn't, adding, "But I can do it as good as anybody else." So without any understanding of the job, he took it.

Well, my God, the cultural minions of the city rose up in high dudgeon. No one could understand how a Neanderthal like Goldman could represent the city's cultural institutions. The *New York Times* described his appointment as an absolute sacrilege.

I'd always thought Abe Beame was a lovely guy, but he was oblivious to Goldman.

Before long, complaints started coming in to Lefkowitz, and to us, that Goldman had used his position with the Shubert Organization to demand that certain parties buy more paint. Bob Brustein's false allegations against me were coming back to haunt Goldman and the Shubert board.

Goldman's paint company, Gothic Color, had an association with another company, Campbell Painting Corporation, which Lefkowitz now alleged had received more than $1 million from the Shubert Organization, money that he called "unexplained, unjustified, and excessive."

Further doubts about Goldman surfaced when Walter Keyser, who for forty-five years had handled Shubert's insurance, insisted that—contrary to what Goldman had told us—"J. J. never saw Goldman. J. J. never heard of him."

Goldman, in his role as overseer of bids for Shubert contracts, had conducted a deal in our name with Campbell. But then he'd suspiciously had someone placed on our payroll, probably to oversee the Campbell kickbacks to himself. Some recipients of Shubert Foundation grants now said that Goldman had made it known that because they hadn't bought any paint that year, the following year's grants would be reduced.

From there, things deteriorated further. The newspapers dug up the fact that Goldman controlled a vending-machine company that did business with the city—the machines were located in the subways. Goldman had failed to disclose that business interest to the mayor's staff during the vetting process for cultural commissioner. The revelation prompted a federal investigation into his financial dealings.

Suddenly the government was talking about grand larceny. Goldman resigned from the Shubert Organization, and as cultural commissioner.

He was eventually arrested and indicted on fifteen felony charges. There were also charges of conspiracy, bribery, and witness tampering. Many of those charges were eventually dropped, and the ones that weren't, he subsequently beat. His association with Judge DiFalco was also closely scrutinized, especially when DiFalco was indicted on official misconduct charges, which were later dismissed. DiFalco was also indicted for criminal contempt, but he died of a heart attack before the case went to trial.

Goldman never spoke to us again, but before he left in disgrace he did two important things. He somehow put the bug in Abe Beame's ear that I was a good guy, and Beame appointed me chairman of the Mayor's Midtown Citizens Committee. For years I had been determined to clean up Times Square and the theater district. Beame now put me officially in charge of the task. Goldman also recommended a potential board member, John Kluge, who would become highly influential in my life.

In fact, we appointed three new members at that time. Irving Wall nominated Helen McVey Hollerith. I don't know how he came to know her, but she was a member of the Pew family, which controlled Sun Oil. She was a woman of great wealth, had a great reputation, and loved the theater. Her husband, Charles, was a producer, whose father had invented the punch card for IBM. We welcomed her to the board. Bernie and I suggested Lee Seidler, a young professor at NYU and an expert in accounting and taxes. We also welcomed him to the board.

I didn't know John Kluge, and we pondered long and hard over whether, since he was Goldman's nominee, we should accept him. We really wanted independent board members. But then we decided that a man who ran radio and television stations licensed by the FCC and who was founder and chairman of a large company, Metromedia, had to be a man of good character. So we welcomed him.

It was a wise decision. As I got to know John Kluge, I found him to be an incredible man, quiet, generous, unassuming, and appreciative of a job well done. His basic measuring rod was if you did well, you got paid well. If you didn't do well, I guess, he moved you out.

When he came onto the board, it was not a prosperous period in his life, although years later he would be named the richest man in America. But John was a visionary. He could see around the corner, and beyond the horizon, and he saw it before anyone else. He first saw the importance of radio stations, then television, and then outdoor advertising. He saw cellular telephones and telephone paging early on. He was also among the first to see the potential of fiber technology.

I can say, without reservation, that John Kluge is one of the greatest men I ever met in my life, and my best friend.

I can also say without reservation that Louis Lefkowitz was one of the worst men I have ever met.

That he showed up with guns blazing and disrupted our lives, hurt the business deliberately and without just cause, hurt Pat, hurt me, hurt Bernie, hurt our families, and ruined other people's lives is beyond disgraceful. Then, one day, just like that, Lefkowitz announced that he was dropping all the charges and allegations. Without apologies, and apparently without regrets, he simply walked away from us.

It wasn't that we were found not guilty—we'd never been guilty of anything to begin with. The charges and allegations he dropped were false and baseless. They were vindictive and, I insist, were prompted by a hidden agenda.

That Louis Lefkowitz could have been elected attorney general of the state of New York, that he was allowed to behave so despicably and yet wind up with an office building in downtown Manhattan named in his honor—I still can't believe it.

Sixteen

STRUGGLING TO KEEP SHUBERT AFLOAT

In the early 1970s, we embarked on a plan to present shows that would appeal to young as well as minority audiences, shows such as *Grease, Zoot Suit, The Magic Show, Candide, The Rocky Horror Show, The Wiz, I Have a Dream,* and *Your Arms Too Short to Box with God.*

Then, in October 1972, we opened a new musical, *Pippin,* starring Ben Vereen and John Rubinstein, at our Imperial Theatre. It was directed and choreographed by Bob Fosse. The show's producer, Stuart Ostrow, told us he was $50,000 short of the capital needed to produce the show, and he implored us to invest. In light of our circumstances, $50,000 was a fortune. Yet we agreed to take the risk.

It frightened us, not just because it was a hefty sum at the time, but also because this was Bernie's and my first decision to have Shubert invest in a show.

Mindful that Shubert had not produced a show since Howard Teichmann's ill-fated *Julia, Jake and Uncle Joe* in 1958, we decided to sell off $40,000 to other investors and to the show's general manager and its press agent. Ostrow accused us of having no confidence in the show, but we were glad not to have so much money riding on its success.

As it turned out, *Pippin* was a tremendous hit and played for four and a half years.

We had also begun highlighting brave new works by the South African playwright Athol Fugard, the young African-American playwright August Wilson, and the always wonderful actor, director, screenwriter, novelist, composer, and playwright Melvin Van Peebles.

I had first met Melvin in 1971, when he'd come to a meeting in Lawrence's office about his new musical *Ain't Supposed to Die a Natural*

Death. Melvin was a hip character, self-confident, very intelligent, very much a product of the 1960s. The musical was about the black experience in America, and Melvin had written the book, music, and lyrics. Our booker, Warren Caro, was having a hard time convincing Lawrence to take it, and he hoped Bernie and I could change Lawrence's mind.

When we told Lawrence we thought it was a good idea, he went into a harangue about shows with controversial black themes. We waited for him to calm down and started to reason with him. Reluctantly, he agreed to book the play, which went on to win seven Tony Award nominations, including for Best Book, Best Score, and Best Musical.

A year later, Melvin was back with a new play called *Don't Play Us Cheap*. When a late-afternoon SOS came from Warren Caro, we went across the street to find Lawrence three sheets to the wind. This time he was angry at Warren for bringing two of the same kind of play to Shubert theaters. After some cajoling, Lawrence relented. The play opened at our Barrymore Theatre on May 16, 1972, and, although it ran for only 164 performances, it received a Tony nomination for Best Book of a Musical, and Avon Long was nominated for Best Featured Actor in a Musical.

By now, Bernie and I were madly in love with the theater. Surrounded by successful producers, we decided to try our hand at producing for Shubert. Unfortunately, our first attempt gave birth to a bomb. And not a small bomb. A great big bomb. With Shubert's meager resources, we embarked on the production of *Truckload*, an original musical set on an open road. Believe me, it was a truckload. To borrow the phrase that David Merrick once said about one of his plays, *Truckload* got off to "a flying stop."

The theatrical highway is littered with disasters, some of which are Shubert-produced disasters. But our first show's demise was so quick that it never even got a mention on Broadway's list of most memorable flops. It never had an official Broadway opening. It closed after six preview performances on September 11, 1975.

Ever since that first foray, I have been asked repeatedly how we know which plays to invest in. How do we determine to produce a show? And, how do we decide to book a show? Booking theaters is a juggling act. We invest in a show because we think it may be a hit, of course, but also because we may have a theater we want to fill. By investing, we're encouraging the producers to bring the show to us. Or even if we don't think we have a hit show on our hands, we might invest because we need to fill a theater temporarily as we wait for a show we really want to arrive. It's never wise to leave the house dark.

For plays, we read the script and perhaps attend a performance or a staged reading at some out-of-town venue. For musicals, we read the script, listen to the score, and attend a showcase, workshop, or backers' audition in which the cast performs. We seldom commission the writing of a musical. The author's agent generally solicits us to produce a musical.

Selecting shows we wish to book is not a scientific process. We evaluate the producer, script, general manager, cast, and press agent and assure ourselves that the necessary financing is in place to produce it. We follow a show through the rehearsal process, out-of-town engagements if any, and previews in New York, often conferring with the producer and director. We evaluate the creative team's skills and the track records of the producer, the director, and the designers. Each show we book is a multimillion-dollar investment. If it's a hit, we might earn that amount. If it's a flop, we need to book another show as soon as possible.

The more Bernie and I did this, the better we became at it. He and I even used to make bets on how long a show would last. By now, as soon as the curtain comes down on opening night, I can tell how long the show will last. I can look at ticket sales, see how much we have in the pot, and calculate how long it'll take for the pot to run dry.

In cases of potential flops, I tell producers, "You're throwing good money after bad." But they never listen. They don't want to hear it. That has been especially true during the last decade, when Wall Street money has poured into Broadway and "angel" investors, who are now called producers, back shows for the pleasure of going to the Tony Awards and of announcing at dinner parties, "Did you know we're producing a Broadway show?"

The sixth sense that Bernie and I developed was pretty sharp. Still, investing in Broadway is not an exact science; it's more like a roll of the dice. One factor that can't be predicted is the critics' reviews. As George S. Kaufman, a great director and playwright, once said about a succès d'estime, "It is a success that has run out of steam."

———◆•◆———

Back in the mid-fifties, a seminal change occurred in American theater. America's not-for-profit theaters expanded rapidly after their inception as a result of the Internal Revenue Act of 1954. Originally, their ranks were filled by people who, like Joe Papp, disdained the commercial world of Broadway, by dissidents who could not find steady employment in the relatively small world of Broadway and its counterparts in other American cities, and by new, young talent who saw greater opportunities for their work.

Not-for-profit theaters came in all stripes. Some were restored or converted burlesque houses, motion-picture theaters, garages, stores, open-air theaters, or other imaginative spaces. Some were newly constructed, modern, state-of-the-art theaters in complexes like Lincoln Center, the Kennedy Center, the Los Angeles Music Center, and Denver Center for the Performing Arts. Some were on university campuses. Some were funded privately, and some by the government or charitable contributions, including grants from the Shubert Foundation. Many were dedicated to producing new plays and revivals of Broadway successes. Their audiences consisted of subscription-series ticket buyers. Their productions were mounted with limited budgets and little union involvement.

Few not-for-profit theaters had the physical space required to present large-scale Broadway musicals. They lacked gridirons from which scenery could be hung. They did not have proscenium stages, orchestra pits, dressing-room blocks, adequate seats, wing spaces, and other necessary amenities. Typically, the not-for-profit world did not understand the financial implications of a major Broadway hit.

But everything changed in 1975—for the not-for-profit theaters and for Shubert—when along came *A Chorus Line*. Joe Papp and Michael Bennett's massive success altered the landscape of the American theater. The not-for-profit theater community suddenly embraced the fact that the Broadway musical was a truly American artistic creation that could produce an annuity to create other successful musicals. Gradually, all over America, not-for-profit theaters began originating Broadway-bound musicals—unfortunately, most with disastrous financial and critical results.

As an alternative, some opened their doors to Broadway producers, offering them a place to try out their musicals at the not-for-profit theater's expense. For the privilege of presenting the musical, they negotiated a share of the show's profits and a royalty if the musical moved to Broadway, to other domestic theaters, or abroad.

Some theater people, like Robert Brustein, stood firm. Brustein, who

The Smiling Days, with (*left to right*) Irving Goldman,
Bernie Jacobs, and Eckie Shubert.

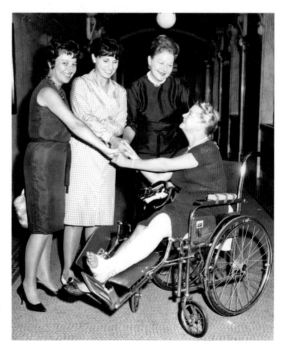

At the trial for John's will, (*left to right*) Betty Jacobs, Pat, Shannon Dean, and Eckie Shubert (in wheelchair.) *Courtesy of the Shubert Archive*

Pat and I with the Stevensons in the South of France.

Pat and I with Marilyn and Alvin Cooperman.

Michael Bennett and Bernie Jacobs: "Bernie treated Michael like a son."
Courtesy of Betty Jacobs

With Bernie Jacobs: "I loved Bernie like a brother."
© *Steve Friedman*

With (*left to right*) Larry Gelbart, Jack Gilford, and Arthur Penn.

With Bob Fosse at the rehearsal for *Big Deal*, 1986.
Martha Swope

Zero Mostel in *The Merchant of Venice*.
Courtesy of the Shubert Archive

Liza Minnelli in *The Act*, 1977.
Courtesy of the Shubert Archive

The Playbill for *Richard III*, starring Al Pacino. *Photofest, used by permission of Playbill*®

Ian McKellen in a scene from *Amadeus. Courtesy of the Shubert Archive*

With Jane Seymour during the run of *Amadeus.*

The Playbill from *Lettice and Lovage*, featuring Maggie Smith. *Photofest, used by permission of Playbill®*

Betty Jacobs and Cameron Mackintosh.

Sir Andrew Lloyd Webber and Pat.

With Sir Andrew Lloyd Webber.

ran the Yale Repertory Theatre in New Haven, Connecticut, and then the American Repertory Theater in Cambridge, Massachusetts—and who had once falsely accused me of putting conditions on a Shubert Foundation grant—argued that not-for-profit theaters were being corrupted by presenting Broadway-bound musicals instead of their own original productions.

I have my own opinion of not-for-profit theater. It begins with the adage, "There's no profit like nonprofit." I've found that no expense is too great for a nonprofit theater, and that there is no greater wrath than a nonprofit theater scorned. There is no greater irony than a nonprofit theater finding success on Broadway. Nor is there any greater avarice than a nonprofit theater negotiating terms for a move to Broadway.

For Joe Papp, success and salvation on Broadway was a slightly bitter pill to swallow. Here was a man who had spent his entire career deliberately staying away from Broadway. He even admitted to me that he suffered the irony of gaining recognition, not for his altruistic not-for-profit activities, but from a commercial Broadway hit.

A Chorus Line will go down in history as one of the greatest Broadway musicals of all time. It signaled the beginning of a symbiotic relationship between the not-for-profit and for-profit communities. It cemented Joe's reputation and Michael's status as a genius. And it helped us save the Shubert Organization.

SEVENTEEN

THE GENIUS OF
MICHAEL BENNETT

M ichael Bennett and Joe Papp were both small in stature, with dark, piercing eyes and dark hair. Joe, as founder of the New York Shakespeare Festival and the Public Theater, a place for new dramatists, will be remembered as the man who made Shakespeare more accessible to the general public by staging free plays on summer nights in Central Park. Michael Bennett DiFiglia, who never used his last name, will be remembered as one of the greatest, most brilliant talents in American theater.

Born in Buffalo, New York, in 1943, Michael studied dance as a young boy, dropped out of high school to join a touring company of *West Side Story*, then came to New York to try his luck on Broadway. He made his debut as a dancer in the 1961 musical comedy *Subways Are for Sleeping*, followed by a seven-day run in 1962 on *Nowhere to Go But Up*, for which he got billing as assistant to the choreographer. Michael returned to performing in the 1964 musical *Bajour*, and at one point was lead dancer in, and choreographer of, the then-popular television series *Hullabaloo*.

His first full-fledged Broadway choreographer credit came in 1966 with the short-lived musical *A Joyful Noise*. Although it ran for only four previews and a dozen shows, Michael's work was good enough to earn a 1967 Tony Awards nomination for Best Choreography.

He was nominated again the following year for his choreography in *Henry, Sweet Henry*, which ran for eighty performances, and yet again in 1969 for choreographing *Promises, Promises*, the Hal David–Burt Bacharach musical written by Neil Simon. Produced by David Merrick and starring Jerry Orbach, the show ran for 1,281 performances. It was Michael's first real hit.

In 1970 he received his fourth Best Choreography Tony nomination for *Coco*, the Alan J. Lerner and André Previn musical based on the life of Coco Chanel. The show stared the inimitable Katharine Hepburn. One day in rehearsal, Hepburn remarked, "Who is that little son of a bitch Michael Bennett?"

Everyone looked at her.

She quickly answered her own question. "You know, though, he is a genius."

Clearly he was, and he proved it, convincingly, with his next two shows, both Stephen Sondheim hits: *Company*, which got him another Best Choreography nomination, and *Follies*, which Michael choreographed and codirected with Hal Prince. For *Follies*, he shared the Drama Desk Award for Outstanding Director of a Musical with Prince, and won that award for Outstanding Choreography. He and Prince also shared the Tony for Best Direction of a Musical, and, finally, *Follies* brought Michael his first Tony for Best Choreography.

I met Michael just after that, when he was directing George Furth's series of one-act plays, *Twigs*, at our Broadhurst Theatre. Sporting a black beard and mustache, he had a bounce when he walked. By now, no one could deny that he was a Broadway star.

The producers of the Cy Coleman–Dorothy Fields musical *Seesaw* clearly thought so in 1973 when they begged him to rescue their show, which was in serious trouble. Michael agreed, on the condition that he had absolute control as director, choreographer, and book writer. He wound up with Tony nominations for Best Book of a Musical and Best Direction of a Musical, and won his second Tony for Best Choreography.

Bette Midler then hired Michael to help her stage her three-week Broadway concert, a terrific success. After that, he directed the Neil Simon comedy *God's Favorite*, which apparently wasn't. Even Michael couldn't save the show, which ran for only four months.

He and Joe Papp then teamed up for *A Chorus Line*. By this time, Pat and I had been close to Michael for several years and had spent a lot of time together. He was also friendly with Bernie, and with *A Chorus Line*, their friendship deepened into a father-son relationship.

In fact, Bernie quickly became one of the most significant people in Michael's life. He indulged Michael, pampered him, and catered to his capriciousness. Michael would phone Bernie at three or four in the morning, and say, "I need to talk to you," and Bernie would run over to meet him. Michael was involved in drugs and the gay party scene, and Bernie became very protective of him. Bernie also became very proprietary about Michael. Not wishing to compete with Bernie, Pat and I stepped back.

And Bernie could be very competitive. Once, he accompanied me as I shopped for a gift for Pat's birthday. I bought her a little mink shrug. Right away Bernie decided to buy his wife, Betty, a sable shrug. Another time, after Pat took courses at the French Fashion Academy and started to design clothes, I got her a good sewing machine. Betty didn't sew, but Bernie bought her a top-of-the-line machine nonetheless. It sewed so fast that the needle once went right through her finger.

Pat used to tell Bernie, "Just pray that Jerry doesn't get a Rolls-Royce."

I don't know why Bernie felt compelled to one-up me. We loved each other like brothers. I could not have cared less about matching him, or anyone on that level. But that's how Bernie was, and I suspect it drove him crazy that his competitiveness had no effect on me.

———————

A Chorus Line was a natural to take to Los Angeles. We decided the show should have an open-ended run, rather than be limited to a specific number of weeks as was customary for shows in Los Angeles. When we announced the show, it was big news. When we opened it on July 1, 1976, it was even bigger news. *A Chorus Line* ran there until December 31, 1977.

But two weeks after the opening, we hit a bump in the road. Excerpts from a number of letters to the editor appeared in the *Los Angeles Times*, all to the effect that *A Chorus Line* was an exercise in profanity and a disgrace to the community.

Without thinking twice, I sent a letter to Dan Sullivan, the paper's theater critic, voicing my dismay. It was a shame, I said, that the paper hadn't run any letters that praised the Shubert Organization for building the theater in the first place, for helping establish Century City, and for bringing the Pulitzer Prize–winning, universally heralded musical to Los Angeles.

The following week, my remarks were printed on the Letters to the Editor page. A week later, a number of letters appeared praising the Shubert Organization, *A Chorus Line*, and the fact that a magnificent new theater had been erected in Beverly Hills, the most desirable part of Los Angeles. I felt vindicated.

But another week went by and more letters appeared, including vitriolic remarks suggesting that "those carpetbaggers from New York" take their theater and their show back to New York, the "city of sin," where it belonged.

I resolved never again to write another letter to the editor. It was increasingly clear to me that the West Coast media looked differently on us New Yorkers.

As it turned out, everybody out there did. That became blatantly evident later when our landlord decided not to renew our lease on the Shubert Theatre, despite the fact that we had built, renovated, and operated the theater for nearly three decades. The news was especially bitter for us because the landlord who refused to renew the lease was Morgan Guaranty Trust Company, the banker for the Shubert Organization.

The explanation they gave was that as trustee to certain pension funds, Morgan Guaranty was required to maximize returns of the funds' assets. To do so, they were replacing the theater with an office building, which they believed would be the most profitable use of the Century City property. When I pointed out that they had had a fiduciary obligation not to place the property in the trust in the first place, as it resulted in a conflict of interest, the bank admitted I was right. But that was small consolation.

Probably one of the finest theaters ever built in America without any government support or subsidy, the Los Angeles Shubert was demolished in 2002. A magnificent 2,100-seat house, less than thirty years old, located in the best part of Los Angeles, was razed to accommodate a new office building. Not one voice was raised in protest. Not from the city of Los Angeles. Not from the L.A. media.

No one saw fit to mention that without the Shubert Theatre, Century City, an important business center that was once an old movie back lot, might never have been put on the map.

<hr />

Our relationship with Michael remained strong through the years, and it was thanks to him that Bernie and I met David Geffen, a major figure in the record and entertainment business.

David started his career in the mailroom at the William Morris Agency, became an agent, and later left to become a personal manager for the musical group Crosby, Stills & Nash, for singer Laura Nyro, and for a youngster just starting out named Jackson Browne. While trying to get Browne a record deal, David met the famous producer Ahmet Ertegün, who told David that the easiest way for him to get anyone a record deal was to start his own label.

Taking Ahmet's advice, David created Asylum Records and was soon recording such artists as the Eagles, Joni Mitchell, Bob Dylan, and Linda Ronstadt. He merged that company into Elektra Records, which brought him into the Warner Brothers organization, where he became vice chairman. David retired from the job and was told that he had a serious illness. A few years later, he found out he'd been misdiagnosed, and he went back into the music business, eventually forming a partnership with Steven Spielberg and Jeffrey Katzenberg to create DreamWorks.

Meanwhile, Michael Bennett asked David to record the original cast album of his next musical, *Dreamgirls*, an exciting story with great dancing and music based loosely on Diana Ross and the Supremes. David loved it, and that was the start of a successful collaboration. David became our coproducer of and investor in *Dreamgirls*, as well as coproducer of and investor in Athol Fugard's *Master Harold and the Boys*; *Cats*; *Good*; and our Off-Broadway production of *Little Shop of Horrors*. Later, in March 1986, David joined us in *Social Security*.

To help finance *Dreamgirls*, Michael invited a select group of backers and theater people to hear the show. He put actors on chairs on the stage of the Shubert Theater and performed the show with just the accompaniment of a piano. It was thrilling, and we immediately agreed to produce it. The show went into a workshop, and among the people we invited along to see it was our friend Roger Berlind.

Roger is a 1954 Princeton graduate who made a lot of money on Wall Street and, in 1976, decided to pump some of it into theatrical productions. Over the years, he produced or coproduced many wonderful original plays and revivals. In addition to *Amadeus*, he was involved with *Long Day's Journey Into Night*, *Ain't Misbehavin'*, *Guys and Dolls*, *A Funny Thing Happened on the Way to the Forum*, *Copenhagen*, *Kiss Me, Kate*, *Anna in the Tropics*, and *Wonderful Town*. Today, the McCarter Theatre Center at his alma mater, Princeton, houses the 360-seat Roger S. Berlind Theatre.

Right after the *Dreamgirls* workshop performance, Roger called me to say, "I don't understand the show." I told him to speak to Michael, which he promptly did. Bu in the end, Roger passed on the show.

Throbbing with energy and excitement, *Dreamgirls* opened at our Imperial Theatre on December 20, 1981. With his second original musical, Michael confirmed his *Chorus Line* reputation. Using a scenic concept by Robin Wagner, the production featured metal towers with embedded lights that moved up, down, and across the stage, essentially creating many stages on one. The effect was electrifying. But then, everything about *Dreamgirls* was electrifying. All of us were convinced that we were Tony-bound. However, shortly before the cutoff date for eligibility, a musical called *Nine*, based on Federico Fellini's semiautobiographical film *8½*, opened at Nederlander's 46th Street Theater. Unbelievably, *Nine* won the 1982 Tony Award for Best Musical.

We were distraught. I like to think, however, that history vindicated us. *Nine* ran for 729 performances. *Dreamgirls* ran for 1,521. Both are considered terrific musicals, but *Dreamgirls* is generally regarded as one of America's truly great musicals, and has been memorialized on film to critical and popular acclaim.

Four years later, Bernie and Betty attended a London concert version of the musical *Chess*. It was written by Tim Rice, working with Benny Andersson and Björn Ulvaeus of the group ABBA. In the world of pop music, ABBA was a juggernaut. Bernie's idea was to engage Michael Bennett as the director and choreographer for a full-blown London stage production of *Chess*, to be followed by a Broadway production.

Michael did not immediately respond to Bernie's enthusiasm for the show, but finally relented. We agreed to coproduce *Chess* in London with Benny and Björn and Tim Rice as 50-percent partners, and Robert Fox and Shubert each as 25-percent partners. Michael proceeded to cast *Chess*. However, in early January 1986, a somber Michael walked into our office. After a few minutes of innocuous conversation, Michael asked to speak to Bernie privately. When they returned to my office, Bernie told me that Michael could not proceed with the show. I was dumbfounded but didn't ask why. It was only after Michael left that Bernie confided that Michael had AIDS. Because he didn't want his illness to become a public matter, Michael later announced that he had had to withdraw because of a heart condition.

Bernie, playing the role of surrogate father, tried to do whatever he could for Michael. But the following summer, 1987, when Michael went to Arizona hoping to find a cure, he told Bernie not to come. Bernie was deeply hurt by that rejection. But then, Bernie's friendships with difficult people like Michael almost always ended in tears. Michael died that summer at age forty-four. In his will, he left Bernie and Betty the *Chorus Line* silver top hat.

EIGHTEEN

SUPER-AGENT SAM COHN
AND FRIENDS

Michael Bennett was trying at times, especially for Bernie, who was so close to him. But now, fresh off the success of *A Chorus Line*, and suddenly feeling much better about the future of Shubert than we had for a very long time, we were about to discover that in show business, *trying* can really mean "relatively easy."

Every show and every negotiation is an uphill battle—even with the very people we assumed were on our side. Having been baptized under fire with the Shuberts, the courts, the protracted lawsuits, and Louis Lefkowitz, we soon found ourselves in constant combat with directors, agents, stars, the unions, and even the politicians who ran the city of New York. Some of our more difficult moments came in dealing with the ubiquitous Sam Cohn and his stable of stars.

In the summer of 1975, Bernie and I were invited to the home of Charles Strouse to hear him play songs from his new musical, *Annie*. The show's co-producers, Stephen Friedman and Irwin Meyer, were there when we arrived. So were director Mike Nichols and his agent, Sam Cohn.

Five years my junior, Sam was born in Pennsylvania, where his family was in the oil business. So Sam was never poor. He was a lawyer by profession, and started in show business working as an in-house counsel at CBS. From there he joined Mark Goodson–Bill Todman Productions, producers of game shows like *What's My Line?*, *The Price Is Right*, and *Concentration*. After that, he went to work for a small talent agency, General Artists Corporation, as their lawyer. Through a series of mergers and acquisitions, he helped grow GAC into a larger agency, Creative Management Associates, and then into the giant International Creative Management. By the mid-1970s, as a founding partner of ICM, Sam Cohn was the first of the "super-agents."

Sam was a short man who always wore white socks, penny loafers, and sweaters with visible holes. He was famous for preferring to work in New York instead of Hollywood. He never hid the fact that he hated Southern California and openly avoided going there whenever possible—this at a time when other agents felt that if they weren't in L.A., they were nowhere.

Almost every day, Sam ate lunch at the Russian Tea Room on Fifty-Seventh Street. At every meeting, Sam ate paper. Seriously, he was constantly chewing paper. Concerned friends brought napkins for him to munch on so that he wouldn't chew on hard matchbook covers. He was also legendary for being nearly impossible to reach on the phone. That trait was the source of the famous joke that his tombstone would read "Here lies Sam Cohn. He'll get back to you."

He was never afraid to ask for what he wanted, and he usually got it. At this point he was at the height of his powers, with a client list of Hollywood and Broadway superstars that included Paul Newman, Meryl Streep, Liza Minnelli, Woody Allen, and Whoopi Goldberg, to name a few—and director Mike Nichols.

Mike and his family came to America in 1939 to escape Germany under Hitler. Seven years my junior, Mike attended P.S. 87, my elementary school, and began his show-business career as a comedian, doing nightclub and television routines with the actress Elaine May. Before long, he was directing plays, including Neil Simon's *Barefoot in the Park*, and films such as *Who's Afraid of Virginia Woolf?* and *The Graduate*. Only a handful of talented people have won an EGOT, the acronym for all of America's major show-business awards: the Emmy, the Grammy, the Oscar, and the Tony. Mike is one of them.

While we all sat around, Charles Strouse played the score of *Annie* for us, after which Friedman and Meyer left. No sooner were they were out the door than Mike quipped, "I'm glad that I'll have nothing more to do with them."

I replied, "I wonder what you'll say about Bernie and me when we leave."

Sam explained that Mike was going to be involved with *Annie*, which added interest for us, although he was not going to direct it. Martin Charnin was directing. Instead, Sam said, Mike would be there to advise the director during the preproduction activities.

To this day, Mike's exact role in the success of *Annie* is still unknown to me.

Sam told us that in order to get the show to Broadway, they needed an additional $300,000 in cash. He wanted Shubert to make the investment. That was a large amount for us at that time, especially since we had just recently seen our first profitable year after six years of losses. So I asked if we could have until Monday to reply. Sam and Charles agreed.

Over that weekend, Bernie and I talked about it and, given the track record of all the people behind the show—not just Mike, but especially Strouse, who had written *Bye Bye Birdie* and *Applause*—we decided to get involved. But before we could tell Sam our intentions, he announced that Mike had been looking for other funding sources and that, over that same weekend, Roger Stevens, a noted producer and head of the Kennedy Center, had teamed up with our competitor, Jimmy Nederlander, and agreed to cover the needed $300,000. In other words, Sam and Mike had gone behind our backs to hedge their bet in case we couldn't raise the money. This is not atypical in our business.

What's more, the deal they made with them wasn't the same deal they'd offered us. Theirs included a waiver of the usual deposits at the Kennedy Center and the Nederlander's Alvin Theatre, plus guarantees of all union bonds. This reduced the cash part to $80,000. In exchange, Stevens and Nederlander received an equivalent percentage of the producers' share of net profits, corresponding to their share of profits based on a $300,000 investment.

I was angry that we hadn't been offered the same terms, nor the opportunity to discuss the matter before Stevens and Nederlander took the offer. I told Sam Cohn exactly what I thought. As a consolation, *Annie* was booked into the Shubert Theatre in L.A. the year after *A Chorus Line* appeared there.

Annie, like *A Chorus Line*, had been presented first at a not-for-profit theater. *Annie* played at the Goodspeed Opera House in East Haddam, Connecticut, before opening on Broadway at the Alvin on April 21, 1977. It came to Los Angeles, as the Shubert's second-ever open-ended run, on December 3, 1978, and played for a year.

———•◦•———

A year later, in 1976, Sam Cohn was back in our office with a new play, *Sly Fox*. This time he was with Martin Starger, the senior executive in charge of programming at ABC, and the acclaimed director Arthur Penn, whose film credits included *The Miracle Worker*, *Bonnie and*

Clyde, *Little Big Man*, and the then recently released *Missouri Breaks*, with Marlon Brando and Jack Nicholson. Penn's Broadway stage credits included *Two for the Seesaw*; *The Miracle Worker*; the Pulitzer Prize–winning *All the Way Home*; *Golden Boy*, starring Sammy Davis Jr.; and *Wait Until Dark*.

They brought along the script of *Sly Fox*, written by Larry Gelbart, creator of *M*A*S*H*. It was a modern adaptation of Ben Jonson's 1606 comedy *Volpone*. George C. Scott would star in *Sly Fox*, with a cast that included Trish Van Devere, who happened to be Scott's wife at the time. We agreed to coproduce the play with Starger and the legendary British impresario Sir Lew Grade. It was an instant success upon its opening at our Broadhurst Theatre on December 14, 1976.

This time, it wasn't Sam's client who was difficult; it was our star. George C. Scott, who had a resounding reputation as a tournament drinker, was a loner. He would remain in his dressing room until curtain time, totally content with a chessboard and a television set for watching sporting events. The extent of my conversations with George was limited to, "Hello," "Are you okay?" and "Good-bye."

Onstage, if the audience laughed, George gave gracious bows and a smile at the curtain call. If they didn't, George gave a perfunctory nod and a look of disdain. When George's contract was up, we were fortunate enough to engage Robert Preston, of *Music Man* fame, for the main role. After George's last performance, we gave a "Good-bye, George; hello, Robert Party" at Windows on the World atop the World Trade Center. I found myself alone with George and told him, "This is the only time you and I have had a conversation."

Towering over me, he placed his hands on my shoulders, stared into my eyes, and said in a soft voice, "Jerry, you must really like actors, and I want you to know that I'm not a son of a bitch."

I replied, "George, you must really like producers, and I want you to know I'm not a prick."

After the Broadway run, George appeared in *Sly Fox* at the Shubert in Los Angeles in 1978. When I went to his dressing room to say hello, he announced, "I don't drink anymore."

I said, "How about an occasional snort?"

He said, "Absolutely not."

I said, "How about a few glasses of wine?"

He replied, "No."

To cover all bases, I asked "How about a couple of beers?"

He said, "I'm finished."

That's when his wife, Trish, walked in. I asked her, "How's life with George now?"

She rolled her eyes and said, "It is different."

But it wasn't long before George reverted to his old ways, and with a vengeance. In spring 1996, he starred in a revival of *Inherit the Wind*. I'd go looking for him after a Wednesday matinee, only to find him sitting on a bar stool in a theatrical hangout across the street. There were two shots of vodka and a beer in front of him.

Occasionally, I was called to the theater when George was acting up. The company manager told me I was the only one George would allow into his dressing room. Our talks were always cordial. Once George told me he had an aneurysm but was afraid to undergo surgery. Had he done so, it would not have been the cause of his untimely death in 1999, on my birthday, September 22.

<hr/>

Next, Sam Cohn came to ask us if we would produce Arnold Wesker's play *The Merchant*. Wesker was an English playwright who'd written one of my favorite plays, *Chips with Everything*. This time he had adapted Shakespeare's *The Merchant of Venice*. It was to star Zero Mostel as Shylock. Not by coincidence, Sam also represented Zero. We agreed to coproduce the play with the Kennedy Center for the Performing Arts in Washington, D.C., and Roger Berlind. It was to be directed by the great English director John Dexter.

A run-through was held before opening at our Forrest Theatre in Philadelphia in September 1977. It was electrifying. Zero was extraordinary. But the play was much too long. We were confident that the necessary cuts could be made to shorten it, so after the reading I went to visit Zero in his dressing room. He'd been playing on Broadway since the mid-1940s and had won a string of Tonys, including a Best Actor in a Play award for *Rhinoceros*, and another for *Ulysses in Nighttown*, plus two awards for Best Actor in a Musical, for *A Funny Thing Happened on the Way to the Forum* and *Fiddler on the Roof*.

Zero was chatting with the legendary old comic actor Sam Levene, the man who had created the role of Nathan Detroit in the original 1950 Broadway production of *Guys and Dolls*. Zero was telling Sam what a great director John Dexter was. Sam, who had an acerbic personality, replied, "Fock 'em." Zero repeated his praise of Dexter several times, and each time Sam gave the same reply. Finally, Zero said to me, "Isn't Sam incredible? Anybody else would say, 'Fuck him,' but not Sam. He says, 'Fock 'em.'"

The first and only preview of *The Merchant* took place in Philadelphia on the Friday before Labor Day. I went, convinced that it would be a hit even though it was still too long. The next day Pat and I left to visit friends in New Jersey for the weekend. On Sunday, I received a phone call that Zero had been hospitalized for tests and that the show would not resume until his doctors allowed him to go on.

Bernie and I followed Zero's progress daily, and on Wednesday we went to Philadelphia to visit him in the hospital. He was sitting in a chair with the play in his lap. It was a very pleasant visit, and as we were ready to leave, he said, "Don't worry about that little son of a bitch Wesker. I'll cut his play down to size."

The following day, Zero died from a ruptured aneurysm. There was no funeral service. He disappeared from the face of the earth. To this day I don't know if he was buried or cremated or simply vanished into thin air.

That Friday, I received a call from John Dexter. John had a mean, nasty streak. Not bothering to say hello, he snarled at me, "You've got to tell me what you want to do with your fucking show, because I can direct *Eugene Onegin* at the Metropolitan Opera or I can direct your fucking show."

I suggested he come to my office at ten thirty the next morning to talk about it.

He again said, "I can direct *Eugene Onegin* or I can direct your fucking show."

I said, "We can talk about this tomorrow," and hung up.

At ten thirty Saturday morning, Dexter arrived at my office. He danced out of the elevator saying, "We've all made up our little lists of replacements, and I want you to know that Larry Olivier is not available."

We discussed suitable replacements, went through everyone we could think of, and got absolutely nowhere. By then we had used up most of the production money, and we were now undecided about whether to go ahead with the show. I called Roger Stevens, chairman of the Kennedy Center, who said he would guarantee the show against loss for the Washington, D.C., engagement. With that we made up our minds and agreed to Dexter's suggestion to get Zero's understudy to take over. Berlind and Stevens concurred. Dexter's parting remark to us was, "Don't worry, I'll trim the show."

It opened in Washington. Just before the curtain went up, Dexter handed us a postcard that he had received from Wesker. Not only did Wesker not approve of shortening the show, but he also insisted that no changes at all be made to the script. Dexter cut the show nonetheless.

Unfortunately, Zero's understudy was not a box-office star, and the play was poorly received. After a week of previews, *The Merchant* opened at our Plymouth Theatre in New York on November 16, 1977, and closed four days later.

Sam Cohn also represented Hume Cronyn and his wife, Jessica Tandy, Broadway stars who often performed together. Jessica, who would later win an Oscar for her role in *Driving Miss Daisy*, had already won a Tony Award for her performance as Blanche DuBois in the original 1947 Broadway production of *A Streetcar Named Desire*.

Reenter Mike Nichols. In the summer of 1977, Sam met with us to say that Hume and Jessie had agreed to star in *The Gin Game*, a first play by a then-unknown playwright, Donald L. Coburn, and that Mike Nichols had agreed to direct it. We agreed to be partners and coproducers of the play with Mike, Hume, and Jessie. Our deal with Mike, negotiated through Sam, was that he would get his usual 7 percent of the gross box-office receipts. In addition, Sam demanded that Coburn pay Mike an additional 2 percent as a collaborating author.

At the time, Mike was living in Connecticut but also had an apartment at the exclusive Carlyle Hotel at Madison Avenue and Seventy-Sixth Street. When Sam also requested that Mike be paid a per diem when he worked in New York rehearsing the show, I pointed out that Mike had an apartment at the Carlyle and that, therefore, a per diem was inappropriate.

Sam's response was, "Are you doing a bed check on my client?"

I let the matter pass, and Mike was paid a per diem.

The Gin Game opened on October 6, 1977, and we had another hit. But Sam and Mike wanted to be sure Shubert was pulling its weight. There was no automated ticket system at that time; all tickets were purchased at the box office. So Sam and Mike got on the phone and called the box office every two to three minutes to see how quickly the staff responded to incoming ticket requests. They were counting the number of phone rings. If it was more than two, they complained to Bernie or me about the slow service.

The games didn't stop there. The day after an opening, producers generally meet with their advertising-agency representatives to agree on the layout for a post-opening ad in the *New York Times*. After the *Gin Game* opening, we spread our agency's proposed ad on our office floor, got on our hands and knees, and discussed how it should be revised. That was life before computers and the Internet. On the following Monday, when the revised ad arrived, it bore no resemblance to what we had agreed on. I called the agency and asked why it had been changed. I was told that Mike Nichols had said he had veto power, and he had changed the ad. I informed them that changes required the approval of all the producers and that Mike did not have veto power.

I soon learned that Mike was making disparaging remarks about us to everyone, saying that he would never again play in a Shubert theater. I finally couldn't take any more and told Sam to meet with me and to bring Mike. I also invited the advertising agency's representatives and our managers, Liz McCann and Nelle Nugent.

As Liz McCann was walking down the corridor to Bernie's office, where the meeting would be held, she said, "I hope one day that I have enough fuck-you money that I don't have to listen to Mike anymore."

At the meeting, I related the story about the ad. Mike denied having had anything to do with the changes. I became so angry that I told everyone to leave except Sam and Mike. I then warned Mike, "If I ever hear you make one more remark denigrating me, Bernie, or the Shubert Organization, I will close more doors in your face in this business than you ever knew could open."

The next day, I told the story to the producer Alex Cohen, who asked me what I would really do if Mike continued to bad-mouth us. I replied that I didn't know, but I thought what I had told him sounded great. As with most show-business disagreements, once the show gets going, and especially if it's a hit, the arguments recede and the mutual respect remains. So it was with Mike.

The final episode of the *Gin Game* story occurred when playwright Don Coburn's agent, Flora Roberts, called me, outraged. She said Sam had sent her a bill, for thirty-five dollars, which Mike had received from the Dramatists Guild. The bill represented dues for Mike's royalty share as Don's collaborator. Flora had phoned Sam and told him that he had some nerve sending her the bill. After all, Mike hadn't made any contribution to the script, and the bill was for a piddling thirty-five dollars.

Sam quickly closed off Flora's objections. To Mike, he said, thirty-five dollars was a lot of money.

NINETEEN

THE DIFFICULT BOB FOSSE

Bob Fosse was yet another client of Sam Cohn's.

Fosse had been around Broadway for a very long time, having made his distinctive choreographic debut in *The Pajama Game* in 1954. He followed that with *Damn Yankees*, *Bells Are Ringing*, and *How to Succeed in Business without Really Trying*. In 1959, Bob debuted as a director-choreographer for *Redhead*, and successfully repeated himself in *Little Me*, *Sweet Charity*, *Pippin*, and *Chicago*.

Fosse's name in lights was magic, so when Sam Cohn asked us in the fall of 1977 if we would produce a musical without a book but with a score comprised of existing songs, and said that Bob Fosse would direct and choreograph it, we immediately agreed. We didn't know anything about the project, except that it was called *Dancin'*. But what we did know was that Fosse was a grumpy, dark, and difficult man. He was married to Gwen Verdon, who, even after they divorced, stood by him no matter what. She was sweet and lovely and always connected to him. But he was hard work.

What made him special was that he had his own distinct signature choreography, and it was brilliant. *Dancin'* had no plot, but it throbbed with energy and excitement. We tried it out in Boston, where the show underwent considerable change.

Sex was a predominant feature in Fosse's choreography, and "The Dream Barre," a number in which Ann Reinking and Charles Ward were in particularly graphic sexual positions, bothered me. I mentioned this to Fosse, who dismissed me, saying, "The matinee ladies are going to love it."

At the following Sunday matinee preview, I met Fosse backstage and asked, "Are you cutting the 'Dream Barre' number?"

He replied, "I told you, the matinee ladies are going to eat it up."

I put my hand on his shoulder. "I hope you're right, but yours is a minority view."

With typical disdain, he threw my hand off his shoulder. "This is a lousy thing to say to me with the opening night a few days away."

Dancin' opened at our Broadhurst Theatre and thereafter continued at our Ambassador Theatre. It ran for 1,774 performances and won numerous awards and nominations.

Despite his early enthusiasm for the "Dream Barre" number, Fosse omitted it when we produced the road company of *Dancin'*. He never said anything to me about the cut.

———•◦•———

Eight years later, Sam asked if we would produce *Big Deal*, a new musical written, directed, and choreographed by Fosse. It did not contain any original music, so Fosse had no creative collaborators. Naturally, we said yes, and it opened in Boston the following spring. But problems arose that we had never envisioned, and the show had to go through substantial revisions. To begin with, I couldn't see the show.

I told Sam, "It's too dark. Nobody can see what's happening on stage."

Sam answered, "He wants it to look like a Reginald Marsh painting." Marsh, an early-twentieth-century American artist, was part of the "social realism" movement. He painted New York scenes that captured actors in vaudeville and burlesque theaters, vagrants looking for work on the Bowery, crowds filling Coney Island. His colors were often drab and dark. Fosse was trying to recreate that feeling.

"That's fine," I said, "but the audience has to be able to see it. He's got to give it more light."

He didn't.

We also had sound problems. I suggested that we engage a new sound designer. This time Fosse agreed, and the new sound man worked the latter part of the Boston engagement and then the rehearsal period in New York.

Once the cast was onstage, Fosse began complaining about the color scheme of our newly restored Broadway Theatre. "It should be black instead of red." Then he complained again about the sound. "It's not working. The sound stinks." He and the music arranger, Ralph Burns, kept running back and forth from the orchestra pit to the sound console at the rear of the orchestra.

I admired Bob's enormous talent, but he was being impossible, so I told him, jokingly, "You're wearing out the new carpet running back and forth like that."

He gave me a nasty look.

Big Deal opened on April 10, 1986. To help sales along, our coproducers and I decided we needed a television commercial. We all put in some extra money to pay for it and asked Sam to ask Fosse to direct it.

Sam asked, "How much will you pay Fosse?

I answered "Nothing."

Sam said okay, and Fosse said okay.

As Fosse was shooting the commercial in the theater, I sat down to watch with Nancy Coyne from our advertising agency.

She told me, "Bob's shooting every fucking minute of the show."

I said, "Then we'll have a great commercial."

Later in the afternoon, we received word from our manager that Fosse had given instructions to have the shoot go until midnight. Normally he should have wrapped up for the day at eight p.m. Filming beyond the agreed hour would add a substantial amount to our budget. I suggested a compromise, that the shoot should go only until ten p.m. Fosse didn't like that. I told our theater manager, "Shut off the lights at ten."

He did. And Fosse didn't like that, either. But Fosse did a wonderful job. The commercial was outstanding. Unfortunately, it did not stimulate ticket sales and wasn't enough to overcome *Big Deal*'s poor notices. When the curtain came down on opening night, April 10, 1986, I asked one of the weekly-magazine reviewers what he thought.

He insisted, "This is really a loser."

Big Deal closed on June 8, after only sixty-nine performances, and Bob stayed angry with me because of it.

The following year, Fosse directed a revival of *Sweet Charity*, which played at the Minskoff for nearly a year. At the opening-night party, Fosse was seated at Sam Cohn's table, which was right next to where I was sitting. When Fosse spotted me, he turned his chair around so his back was to me. I decided not to react.

Sam came over to me and whispered, "Make nice with him." I got up, went over to Bob, said hello, and reminded him, "That commercial was fabulous."

He practically spit in my eye. "You're so damned cheap you had to cut it short." He went on to tell me how I'd ruined everything. He snapped, "You threw me out of the fucking theater."

I didn't want to get into a fight, but I wanted him to know: "We didn't stint a nickel on the show. And if you think that going from ten p.m. to midnight would have made any difference, you're wrong."

I returned to my table, fuming, sat down, and did a lot of mumbling. After a short while, Sam came over and said, "I want you to know Fosse was way out of line." It was the last time Bob and I ever spoke. Gwen Verdon, whom I always adored, blamed me for years for the problems Bob claimed he'd had with me. Gwen and I eventually made up many years later, but it had been a very unpleasant time.

Fosse had health issues that, I suspect, overshadowed much of what he did and the way he lived his life. Sadly, he suffered a fatal heart attack outside our National Theatre in Washington, D.C., on September 23, 1987, where he was working with the road company of *Sweet Charity*.

He was just sixty years old.

TWENTY

THE IMPOSSIBLE JERRY ROBBINS

If Bob Fosse was difficult, Jerry Robbins was downright impossible. Born Jerome Rabinowitz on the Lower East Side of Manhattan in 1918, he was universally recognized as the theater's greatest musical director-choreographer. His successes include blockbusters like *On the Town*, *West Side Story*, *Gypsy*, *Peter Pan*, *Fiddler on the Roof*, *Funny Girl*, *A Funny Thing Happened on the Way to the Forum*, *The King and I*, *Wonderful Town*, *Bells Are Ringing*, *Silk Stockings*, *High Button Shoes*, and *The Pajama Game*—and on and on and on.

Michael Bennett once said to me, "I am the greatest director-choreographer there is," and then insisted, "but don't put me in the same class with Jerry Robbins, because he's in a class by himself."

Bernie and I produced Jerry's 1976 revival of *Fiddler on the Roof*, starring Zero Mostel.

Zero had originated the great character role of Tevye in the original *Fiddler*, which Robbins had directed in 1964. They had also worked together when Zero had starred in Robbins's *A Funny Thing Happened on the Way to the Forum*. So Zero and Jerry had history. And yet when the film version of *Fiddler* was cast, Zero didn't get to play Tevye. The role went to the Israeli actor Topol. Zero was bitter about that and blamed Robbins. As a result, when the *Fiddler* revival opened in Boston and Robbins came to see it, Zero didn't hide his animosity.

Zero told me, "I hated that little son of a bitch, but was absolutely delighted that he came to see the show. I talked to him, but I never shook his hand."

The original production of *Fiddler* had played at our Imperial Theatre, and so had Jerry's *On the Town*. *Gypsy* had played at our Broadway Theatre. But that was before Bernie and I were running the Shubert business. And while we had overseen a revival of the Rogers and Hammerstein smash hit *The King and I*, which Jerry had choreo-graphed, we had never produced a Jerome Robbins original musical.

That changed when Floria Lasky, Jerry's lawyer, came to see us in early 1986. She told us Jerry wanted to do a reconstruction of some dance numbers from a few of his shows. He was asking for total carte blanche—the freedom to do whatever he wanted, at his own time and pace. We immediately agreed to his terms, even though Jerry was not promising that his work would eventually materialize into a Broadway show. We engaged all the necessary personnel and arranged for him to have full access to the videotapes of his shows so that he could reconstruct his dances precisely.

At this point, I received a phone call from a representative of Suntory International Corporation, Japan's largest distillery, saying that the company wanted to be our partner in our forthcoming production of Jerry's show. I suggested we meet in person in New York. Five Suntory representatives soon showed up. I explained that I could not give them an interest in a single show but that if they wished to invest in all our shows, as ABC did, I would entertain their request. In other words, there would be no cherry-picking. They would get a package of shows, of our choosing, not theirs. They replied that they would decide if they wanted this kind of relationship after partnering with us on Jerry's show. I told them this was not acceptable, and they left.

A short time afterward, Suntory requested another meeting. Five new representatives came to my office, and we pretty much replayed our first meeting. Not long after that, I received yet another call from Suntory. This time, it was to say that the chairman, Keizo Saji, was in New York and wanted to meet with me. We had previously met when Suntory had produced *Dancin'* in Japan, and I said I'd be honored to see him again. I was informed that Mr. Saji would come to my office, which I understood to be a great honor.

When he arrived, he warmly embraced me, much to the amazement of his staff. We discussed my two previous meetings with his representa-tives. I reconstructed what had taken place, after which he asked for twenty-four hours to consider my proposed arrangement. Early the next day, I received word from Mr. Saji that he would be honored to be our partner. And I must say he turned out to be a wonderful partner. Not only with *Jerome Robbins*, but in subsequent Broadway shows like *The Heidi Chronicles, A Few Good Men, The Circle, City of Angels, Tru,*

The Grapes of Wrath, Once on This Island, and *A Streetcar Named Desire.* Mr. Saji was one of the most memorable men I have ever met.

But several problems remained. One was Jerry Robbins's demand for, as his collaborators put it, "his egregious compensation."

To say that Jerry was not well liked by his collaborators is a gross understatement. As Stephen Sondheim succinctly put it, "He is the worst son of a bitch that I ever worked for." He quickly added, "And if I was in Borneo and I got a call to work with him, I'd be on the next plane."

Actually, Jerry's financial terms were simple. He wanted 50 percent of the total royalties. Everyone else—the writers of the various books he was using in the compilation, the composers, the lyricists, the designers, etc.—would have to get their compensation from the remaining 50 percent.

That was only the beginning. We needed to resolve how much of the royalties would be allocated to each show from which he took material. We suggested that each segment of each show receive a share of the writers' royalties in proportion to the minutes each segment bore of the show's total length. The designers, as a group, would then receive a fixed percentage of the 50 percent of the writers' royalties. Further refinement had to be made for segments originally included and then replaced by new segments. It was a nightmare. And since negotiations were not going anywhere quickly, I arranged a meeting with Sam Cohn, who represented some of the writers, asking that all the creative people's representatives also attend.

Fourteen representatives came to the meeting at Sam's office. They represented the forty-two different people whose works were to be included. By this time we had expended over $1 million on the reconstruction idea and had received Jerry's approval to proceed with a Broadway production.

I opened the meeting by telling the group that they had to arrive at some decisions or we would abandon the production. What I didn't know was that before the meeting, Leonard Bernstein, who was present at the meeting and whom everyone respected and loved, had told the group that it was their obligation to cater to Jerry's genius and to arrive at an agreement. In the end, it was his approach, rather than my threat to abandon the production, that carried the day. Thus began part two of a three-year journey with Jerry.

Keeping in mind that we were involved with a Jerome Robbins show, we kept our creative input to a minimum. Jerry did the casting and informed us that he wanted to rehearse for twenty-three weeks—sixteen weeks longer than the usual rehearsal period for a musical. The cost for the additional rehearsal weeks was of little concern to Jerry.

We knew that if we raised any issues with Jerry, he would immediately become aggressive. In fact, we couldn't say a word to him. The mere assumption that we were going to comment caused him to become belligerent. But watching him work with the dancers in the rehearsal studio dispelled all the angst. Jerry was then in his late sixties, yet his leaps, pirouettes, and grand jetés were like those of the young dancers. He was never satisfied, and his criticism of the dancers' performances would often drive them to tears. But as unrelenting and demanding as he was, if he complimented the dancers, they swooned with delight at receiving praise from the master.

After we recovered from the demand for a twenty-three-week rehearsal period, Jerry told us he wanted a one-week vacation right in the middle of the rehearsals. That meant having to pay everyone else for that vacation week as well. Jerry had two assistants, who served primarily as his slaves, and Jerry decided to reward them. He owned a house on the beach in Bridgehampton, Long Island. It was not an imposing house; in fact, it was an unimposing small house with an unkempt appearance. Jerry told his two assistants that they could stay at the house while he went to Lucca, Italy, for his vacation. They were ecstatic, until Jerry qualified the invitation by saying that there were cans of white paint at the house and that they should paint the exterior while they were there. The assistants agreed, but not too happily. Then he added that they should also pay half the cost of having a maid come to the house a few times that week. That was the last straw, and the assistants found another way to spend their week off.

During one of the later weeks in the rehearsal period, I was in East Hampton, Long Island, when I got a call from Jerry. I had no idea how he had tracked me down. He simply said he wanted to see me. I said I'd go to his house, but he insisted he would come to meet me. I gave him directions, and soon afterward he drove into the driveway in a beat-up old Mini convertible. Without any preliminaries, he said, "I have a proposition for you. I will reduce the number of rehearsal weeks to twenty-two, provided you give me an extra week of previews." That was easy to agree to, since it meant that we would have a paying audience for the additional preview week.

The show moved into the Imperial Theatre and completed its technical rehearsals. Jerry then scheduled a few run-throughs. At the first one, where the Jets and the Sharks in the *West Side Story* segment came leaping out of the wings, he stopped the action and told the cast he didn't want them to leap; he wanted them to reach for the stars. With that, they took off as if they were about to fly. That evoked a few words of praise from Jerry, which was enough to carry the dancers for the next few days.

During the last of the run-throughs, I summoned up enough courage to ask Jerry if I could make a comment. He said I could, and I told him I wasn't crazy about the second number in the show, which was the conga sequence from *On the Town*. It takes place in a restaurant where two sailors are trying to cheer up a despondent buddy. As part of the therapy, they start to dance the conga.

Jerry said, "I'm not happy with the number either. Tell me what I should put in its place."

I replied, "If you don't know, I certainly don't."

When the show commenced its preview performances, the conga number got loud applause. Jerry came over to me and said, "I told you that number would be great."

During the rehearsal period, we had to agree on the name and artwork for the show. We suggested it be called *Broadway*, but Jerry insisted that it be called *Jerome Robbins' Broadway*. He also wanted his name to be larger than the *Broadway* portion of the title. The artist created a *J* for the first name that was about twice as large as the rest of Jerry's name. It passed muster not just because of its size, but because the *J* resembled a dancer. Months later, Jerry confided to me that maybe if his name had not been not as prominent as it was in the artwork, the show might have fared better.

We had trouble with the rest of the artwork too, because we really didn't know how to describe the show. We didn't want to call it an anthology of Jerry's dances and had difficulty describing each of the segments. The reviews for the show were very good, but even the reviewers seemed to have trouble describing the show accurately.

The next question was whether the show would qualify for a Tony Award in the Best Musical category. To be eligible, the music had to be at least 50 percent new material or it would be included in the Best Revival category. I told Jerry he had to submit a letter to the nominating committee describing all his new work in the show. So Jerry wrote a letter, which met the new-show test. In retrospect, maybe we should have originally defined the show as a new musical. It went on to win the Best Musical Tony and ran for 633 performances. After it closed in New York, we moved it to the Shubert Theatre in Los Angeles for a limited engagement. It featured Jason Alexander and a cast of sixty-two. Unfortunately, it did not recoup the production costs.

At the end of the Los Angeles engagement, Suntory took the show to Japan, where it opened in Tokyo, moved to Osaka, and then went back to Tokyo. The cost of the intercity moves and the limited playing time of eleven weeks in Japan precluded Suntory from earning a profit. Nevertheless, they were ecstatic with the show, and to commemorate the occasion, Mr. Saji invited Jerry to a luncheon in his honor at his Tokyo apartment.

When I told Jerry about the invitation, he refused to go. I got angry and reminded him that Suntory was meeting all the demands he had made to go to Japan: a two-bedroom suite for him in the Okura Hotel, the finest in Tokyo; a car and chauffeur at his disposal; a visit to the Kabuki and Noh theaters; and transportation to Kyoto, with one of their executives acting as his guide. They had also arranged a one-week stay for him and his companion at the Tarawaya, a *ryokan*—a typical Japanese inn—the poshest in Kyoto.

I said, "I can't understand how unappreciative you could be to decline the invitation."

He reluctantly agreed. When he arrived, he was overwhelmed by Mr. Saji's generous gift of a silk screen that could be mounted like a painting on the wall of his townhouse.

The next big event was Suntory's opening-night party, where Jerry would be the guest of honor. Again, he told me he wasn't going. I said, "I'm disgusted with you. How can you possibly justify this behavior?" I don't know if I had any effect, but he showed up for the opening-night party and was paid the obeisance usually reserved for the emperor.

I was also on that visit to Japan, and I saw another side of Jerry. During his stay, I saw Jerry shower tender, loving care on his friend and travel companion, who was suffering from AIDS. His warmth and solicitude toward his partner was beautiful, and I told him so. By the time we flew back together to New York, I felt that Jerry and I had achieved some common ground. This was confirmed whenever we would meet, usually in a theater. I'd sneak up behind him and rub his bald head. He'd turn to see who it was, benevolently smile, and say, "Hello, baby." To him it was the equivalent of love.

These encounters went on for several years, and then I saw him less and less frequently. One evening, Jerry was at an event honoring Kitty Carlisle Hart, a beloved woman of the theater. When I saw him, I repeated my usual greeting, and he again said, "Hello, baby." Afterward, a group of us went to Orso, a local restaurant. I was told Jerry was seated in another part of the restaurant, so I went over and asked if we could give him a lift home. He was alone and said he appreciated the offer and would meet me at my table. A little while later, I saw him shuffling over to us. He couldn't lift his feet off the floor. My heart sank. I knew he'd been ill, but I hadn't known how incapacitated he had become. It was not very long thereafter, in 1998, that he suffered a stroke and died.

Despite all the angst in dealing with Jerry, he was worth it. I have never seen anyone merely glance at the stage and absorb it all in a few seconds. Everything was in his grasp. He more than confirmed Michael Bennett's appraisal of him: he was definitely in a class by himself.

Living with Jerome Robbins for several years was not one of life's easiest experiences. But then, we were dealing with an absolute genius. At one point, after he and I had started to talk to each other as colleagues, I asked him why he had left the theater after *Fiddler on the Roof* in 1964 and gone to work almost exclusively for the New York City Ballet.

His answer was short and to the point: "No collaborators."

TWENTY-ONE

THE BRITISH INVASION: JESUS CHRIST, EVITA, AND AMADEUS

When I became chairman of the company in 1972, Shubert had not had a presence in London for more than fifty years. In the early part of the twentieth century, Shubert owned and/or operated seven theaters in London. Over the years, leases for theaters expired, and the rest were sold. Indeed, few people in London knew anything about the Shuberts. For years, we were too preoccupied with stabilizing the company and attending to litigation to tear ourselves away and go to London. Now Bernie and I started traveling there two, three, and sometimes four times a year. Producers seeking American productions of their plays opened their doors to us. We also met with leading London agents and with theater owners who were active producers.

Our first coproduction of a London-originated play came to us, surprisingly, through our competitor James M. Nederlander. Jimmy needed a theater and asked us to work with him and the Royal Shakespeare Company on *Sherlock Holmes*. We needed a booking and agreed to collaborate. The hit show opened at our Broadhurst on November 12, 1974, and ran for 471 performances. This was the precursor to our coproductions years later of many London-originated plays and musicals.

During the latter half of the 1970s, we realized we needed a presence in London, and we sent *The Gin Game* and *Ain't Misbehavin'* there. Although the shows had only brief runs, they served a valuable purpose: the name Shubert was no longer unknown in the U.K. However, crossing the Atlantic is a difficult trip for a play or musical in either direction.

Great musical directors and choreographers had flourished on Broadway in the mid 1950s and 1960s. Playwrights who nourished the theater during that era, such as Arthur Miller and Tennessee Williams, for the most part wrote plays that were not based on America's social problems but that focused more intently on interpersonal relationships and universal themes in a timeless setting. Their plays, unlike most of their predecessors' work, can still be seen today, even occasionally on Broadway. But by the end of the 1960s, successful American musicals and plays were relatively scarce.

The British dramatic theater was entering a golden age, with an abundance of world-class directors. With a few exceptions, however, musical performing talent in England did not compare with Broadway. It was to Broadway that the audience looked for the best of musical theater. But Broadway was rapidly losing its director-choreographers and its well known musical directors, such as Morton DaCosta, Joshua Logan, and Abe Burrows, to the movies.

One show that appeared to have made a successful crossing from London was the Andrew Lloyd Webber and Tim Rice rock opera *Jesus Christ Superstar*, which debuted on Broadway in 1971.

Except that the show really started in America. Originally produced as an album in the U.K., it was first staged by a high-school group in Long Island. Soon, hundreds of unauthorized productions were happening all over the country, forcing Andrew and Tim to file lawsuits to shut them down. When the show finally opened on Broadway at the Mark Hellinger Theatre, the reviews were mixed. Some critics found it overhyped. Various religious organizations found it blasphemous. Still, it ran for 711 performances and won five Tonys, including Best Original Score for Andrew and Tim, and Best Featured Actor in a Musical for Ben Vereen.

From Broadway it went, bizarrely, to Lithuania, where it was banned by the Soviets, then to Hungary before going to Paris. It finally opened in London in 1972, where it stayed in the West End for eight years and became, at the time, Britain's longest-running musical.

While *Jesus Christ Superstar* introduced American audiences to Andrew and Tim, it wasn't until they brought *Evita* to Broadway that everything changed. Based on the life of Argentina's legendary first lady Eva Peron, *Evita* too began as an album, with the song "Don't Cry for Me, Argentina" hitting the top of the British pop charts. One year later the musical opened in London, where it played for eight years and some 2,900 performances.

Evita debuted at our Shubert Theatre in Los Angeles, and it ran for seven weeks. That's where I first saw it and was overwhelmed by Mandy

Patinkin's performance. I had never met Mandy, and after the curtain came down, I went to his dressing room and introduced myself. I told him he would win the Tony Award for Best Actor in a Musical, which he did. Patti LuPone was a marvelous Evita, and she too would win a Tony Award, for Best Actress in a Musical. We brought the play to our Broadway Theatre, and the awards rolled in: it was nominated for eleven Tonys and won seven, including Best Musical, Best Original Score, Best Book of a Musical, Best Lighting, and Best Direction, which went to Hal Prince.

On opening night at the Broadway Theatre, September 25, 1979, Bernie and I bumped into Bill Honan, the cultural critic of the *New York Times*, who asked if we could introduce him to Hal Prince. After the two met, Hal turned to leave and asked us, "Why do you guys kiss the ass of the *New York Times*?"

I answered, "So you don't have to."

Evita still reverberates today as a landmark musical. It ran on Broadway for four years and 1,567 performances. Later, following *Annie*, it returned to the Shubert in Los Angeles, where it ran for another two years.

The British had landed.

And a full-scale invasion soon followed. Enter here Robbie Lantz, one of the leading agents in the business.

After fleeing his native Berlin in 1935, Robbie lived in London for more than ten years and, with the war over, made his way to New York. He brought with him a heavy accent and a wonderfully tuned ear to British talent. Among others, he represented the Liverpool-born dramatist Peter Shaffer.

One of the theater's most respected playwrights, Peter's successes up to that point included *Five Finger Exercise*; *The Private Ear* and *The Public Eye*; *The Royal Hunt of the Sun*; *Black Comedy* and *White Lies*; and *Equus*.

Around the same time that *Evita* was enjoying its huge success, Robbie contacted me about Peter's new play, based on the life of Mozart, which he wanted to submit for our consideration. It was called *Amadeus*. It was marvelous, and we immediately agreed to produce it.

But Peter had a strong desire to open his play at the National Theatre in London. Therefore, we agreed to forego the London production rights provided we could have the U.S. and Canadian touring rights, plus an interest in the subsidiary rights, which included motion pictures, television, radio, stock and amateur productions, and foreign-language productions.

Peter's director of choice was John Dexter. However, when Dexter demanded that he receive a share of Peter's subsidiary rights, Peter rejected him out of hand and turned to Peter Hall, who was then artistic director of the National Theatre. Their contract with Hall required us to negotiate a new deal with him, which meant we had to go to Hall's London agent, Larry Evans, who also represented Sir John Gielgud, Sir Laurence Olivier and Sir Ralph Richardson.

To prepare ourselves for the negotiation, Bernie and I spoke with Robert Whitehead, who had recently engaged Hall to direct his New York production of *No Man's Land*. Whitehead told us what he had paid Hall, and we resolved to offer him the same terms for *Amadeus*.

We sat down with Evans in London, and everything was cordial until we presented our offer, the same terms Hall had previously accepted from Whitehead. Evans demurred, insisting that it was not the same offer and claiming that Whitehead's offer had provided better terms than our offer. He even opened his desk drawer to retrieve the file containing Hall's *No Man's Land* contract. I asked to see the contract, but he refused. The mood quickly became testy, and Evans announced that Hall would not direct *Amadeus* in America.

Bernie said, "You are going to hold the National Theatre's production of *Amadeus* hostage so you can gain a financial advantage for your client?" Without waiting for a reply, Bernie angrily got up and walked to the office door. But the door was locked, and Bernie had to tug hard at it until someone opened it and let him out. I stayed behind for a few minutes, just long enough to see that the discussion was over.

Bernie was waiting for me on the street with a big smile. "Did you like my act? Why didn't you leave the office with me?"

I said, "It happened so suddenly I didn't have a chance."

Bernie's act must have swayed Evans, because Hall agreed to direct *Amadeus* under the actual terms he had received for *No Man's Land*.

Amadeus, starring Paul Scofield as Salieri and Simon Callow as Mozart, opened in London on November 2, 1979. It was a rousing hit. I immediately started preparations for the Broadway production, with a tryout in Washington, D.C. In it, we would introduce an unknown Ian McKellen to America as Salieri. Also in the cast were Tim Curry, of

Rocky Horror Show fame, who played Mozart; and a relatively unknown Jane Seymour as Mozart's wife, Constanze.

We went to Washington for the first preview on November 4, 1980, at the National Theatre, joined by our partners ABC and Roger Berlind. After seeing the show, Bernie and I discussed changes we thought should be made to the script, especially to its ending. We arranged to meet with the two Peters—Shaffer and Hall—the next morning. It was an amicable meeting, and to our surprise all our suggestions were incorporated in that evening's performance. Obviously, the two Peters had realized the need for the changes and worked them out even before our meeting. Our *Amadeus* then opened on Broadway at the Broadhurst Theatre on December 17, 1980.

In the audience that night was critic Frank Rich of the *New York Times*. Or, at least, he was supposed to be.

Pat and I had known Frank since he was a teenager. I knew his step-father, who was the Washington attorney for the Broadway League, and Pat was close to his mother. When Frank came to New York, he would visit us, and I would arrange for passes so he could see our shows. Frank was a devotee of the theater and extremely bright. His early career at the *Times* was so successful that he rose to become the paper's theater critic.

I also knew Frank's wife, Alex Witchel, before their marriage. As a new graduate from the Yale School of Drama, she came to see me about getting a job. I arranged for her to be employed as an apprentice house manager at the Shubert Theatre in New York, and I supported her application for membership in the Association of Theatrical Press Agents and Managers, whose admission policies were extremely restrictive. A few years later, Alex left Shubert and wound up at the *Times*'s arts and culture section.

One evening, while *Amadeus* was previewing at the Broadhurst, Pat and I were invited to dinner at the home of Edith and Martin Segal. He was then chairman of Lincoln Center for the Performing Arts. A number of other guests were there, including Arthur Gelb, then deputy managing editor of the *Times* and a staunch supporter of Frank Rich.

The custom was that critics could attend one of the last three preview performances or the official opening-night performance. Most chose to attend a preview rather than opening night, which would put them under a tight deadline to get their review into the following morning's paper. But Peter Hall and Peter Shaffer had asked me to see if the critics could come on opening night. So at the Segal dinner party, I asked Arthur Gelb if he could arrange for Frank to attend the opening. Arthur said it would be fine, and I informed the two Peters accordingly. A few days before the opening, I ran into Frank in Shubert Alley and mentioned how pleased I was that he would be at the opening-night performance. Frank reacted angrily and informed me that that was not his understanding. Furthermore, he said, it was not fun to go to an opening and be forced to write a review to deadline. I reminded Frank that it was not about fun, it was about business. The conversation ended on a sour note.

On the Monday after the last preview, our press agent mentioned that Frank and Doug Watt, his colleague at the *Daily News*, had attended that last preview, sitting in the mezzanine—an unusual spot for critics, who usually sat in the orchestra section. I said that that was impossible, as Gelb had promised me that Frank would attend the opening. My belief was confirmed on opening night, when Frank sat directly in front of me. He turned around and saw me, and I noticed a notepad and pen in his hand.

At the opening-night party, I was shocked when Jane Seymour, our costar, arrived to say that Frank had given the show a rave review. I said it was impossible, because he was just at the performance and couldn't have had time to write it. She said, "I just came from Sardi's, and they read the review aloud."

The evening was young, only about ten fifteen p.m., and the *Times* review was not expected for another forty-five minutes. I sought to disabuse Jane and the others about the review they had heard at Sardi's. But I soon found out that she was correct and I was the one who had been misled. Frank had indeed attended the preview and then written his article. He had only pretended to be taking notes during the opening. Feeling betrayed, I phoned Arthur the next morning. I reminded him about his promise that Frank would review the show on opening night. He replied, "Well, he was at the opening night."

"That was a negative pregnant if I ever heard one," I said.

The next day, Pat bumped into Frank on Fifty-Seventh Street. She told him how disappointed I was at his behavior, especially after I had promised the two Peters, based on what Gelb told me, that he would review the opening.

Frank later left his position as theater critic to write articles for the op-ed section and editorial pages and the Sunday arts-and-leisure section of the *Times*. A few years ago, we buried the hatchet. I am sorry the incident ever occurred.

Amadeus took New York by storm. It ran for almost three years and garnered our second Tony Award for Best Play. It was staged around the globe and gained worldwide acclaim. The multi-Oscar-winning motion picture, directed by Milos Forman, was also a huge success. To this day, we still receive our share of royalties from the film. And London's National Theatre earned more in royalties and profits from the American productions of *Amadeus* than it had previously earned from any other show.

The London press jumped on this fact, complaining that Peter Hall and his colleague, Trevor Nunn, then artistic director of the Royal Shakespeare Company, were unduly profiting from plays that originated at their respective not-for-profit London theaters. When a London newspaper reporter called to ask my view, I explained that the theaters were fortunate to have two world-class directors working for minimal compensation and having their not-for-profit theaters share in their financial successes.

Three months into the run, sometime in March 1981, I had dinner with Jane Seymour and a few other people. During the course of the evening, Jane told me that she had been invited to copresent an Oscar with Richard Pryor at the awards show in Hollywood later that month. I gave her a stern look, thinking she would have to miss a performance. But she quickly told me that the show would be telecast on a Monday, a nonperformance day. I couldn't stop her from going, so I let the matter drop. A few days later, Jane's agent at William Morris called me to say he questioned Jane's ability to continue to work with Ian McKellen and Tim Curry, who, she said, were trying to deprive her of the opportunity to present an Oscar on network television.

I promised to look into the matter. I also said I would take a dim view of Jane missing any performances, and furthermore that he should know better than to try to intimidate me. I phoned Robbie Lantz at once, who told me it was a white-hot issue best left up to him. Apparently, Jane had informed Peter Shaffer of her intention to present an Oscar, saying that she would miss a Sunday performance. Peter responded with a letter to Jane detailing an actor's obligations to a show.

That evening, I went to Jane's dressing room and said, "Why didn't you ask me to release you from a performance?" She replied haughtily, "I am an Englishwoman, and when an Englishwoman gives her word, she keeps it."

I reminded her that the Englishwoman had signed a contract to perform *Amadeus* five evenings and three matinees a week, and that I would not want to test her on which promise was more important.

The next day I received a call from Robbie saying that Norman Jewison, the producer of the Oscars, had agreed to allow Jane to arrive on Monday and pre-shoot her presentation. I was happy to return to Jane's dressing room to tell her that all was resolved. But Jane was very unhappy. She complained about having to take the red-eye flight and that as a result she would look terrible on the telecast. There comes a time to end a matter, I told her, and that time had arrived, and I didn't want to hear another word about it. Jane took the red-eye after the Sunday matinee.

On Oscar Monday, I flew to Chicago to meet with Mayor Jane Byrne to protest a proposal to tax theater tickets. Walking into her office at about one p.m., I saw her staff huddled around a television set. The stations were reporting an assassination attempt on President Ronald Reagan. As a result, the Oscars were postponed until the following night. In the end, Jane missed not only the Tuesday evening performance but the Wednesday matinee as well.

Jane looked beautiful on the telecast Tuesday evening, with her long hair curled and draped over one shoulder. On Wednesday, I went to the theater before the matinee and found Ian McKellen with a group of cast members in the area under the stage. Draped over Ian's head was the porter's mop, with its long strands of rope, as he announced in a high-pitched voice, "I'm Jane Seymour and I'm presenting an Oscar."

I don't know whether Jane ever found out about Ian's imitation, but it is one of the memorable performances I associate with *Amadeus*.

Amadeus played at the Broadhurst until October 16, 1983. Ian left the show and was succeeded by the eminent English actor John Wood, who in turn was succeeded by David Dukes and then by Frank Langella. Replacements by top stars like that are extremely rare occurrences on Broadway, and we were fortunate to have actors of their caliber.

Now, there is no doubt that Frank Langella is a wonderful actor. And nobody believes that more than Frank. During his run in *Amadeus*, I enjoyed going to the Broadhurst and chatting with the cast before the curtain rose. One evening, Frank invited me out to dinner. On the appointed day, we went around the block to a local place called Downey's. Frank got right to the point. He said he was as good an actor as any Englishman and was playing Salieri as well as his predecessors Ian, John, and David. What Frank wanted from me was that I get in touch with Elliot Norton, critic for the *Boston Globe* and dean of the American critical fraternity, and ask him to review Frank's performance. Apparently, Frank said, Elliot had great regard for his acting ability.

So the next morning I phoned Elliot and asked if he would come to New York to review the show. Elliot declined at first, saying he had just returned from New York and that he was no longer doing reviews. I explained how important it was to Frank, and based on that, Elliot agreed to do the review. He came to New York, saw the show, and wrote a glowing review of Frank's performance.

Next time I saw Frank, he said, "You see, I knew he would give me a good review."

I was glad that Elliot had come to New York, and I told Frank as much. I thought that was the end of Frank's requests for reviews, but it wasn't. A few days later Frank said, "I want you to ask Frank Rich of the *New York Times* to rereview the show."

Frank Rich had already reviewed the show twice: once with Ian in the lead and again when John Wood had stepped in. Still, I made the appeal. He reported that it was the paper's policy not to do more than two reviews, but that he would nevertheless ask his editor, Sy Peck, about it. To my astonishment, Sy agreed to a third review. A few days later, Frank Rich saw the show, and his review in the *Times* extolled its merits. Langella's performance was wonderful, he wrote, but not as good as McKellen's and Wood's. "While the theatrical technique is first-rate, the underlying passion is elusive," he said.

Clearly, we had gone to the well once too often. Frank Langella was very upset about the incident, so much so that I stopped visiting him, until another incident arose. It was after a Wednesday matinee that I received an irate call from Frank, raging that his photo in the display case outside the theater was no longer there. In its place was a picture of Dennis Boutsikaris, who was playing Mozart. Frank fumed that unless his picture was replaced, he would not perform that evening. I was tempted to say, "Be on stage or I'll bring you up on charges with

Equity." But he was so out of control that I simply said I would look into it.

I phoned Merle Debuskey, our press agent, and told him to replace the Boutsikaris picture. Merle said it was six p.m. and that he didn't think King Displays, the company that arranged the show's artwork, would be open. I warned Merle that he'd better get someone to replace the photo or I would have a raving Frank Langella to deal with. A short while later, Frank's picture was again peering out from the display case; Dennis Boutsikaris's was nowhere in sight.

On October 4, 1984, I went to an opening-night party for Arthur Miller's *After the Fall* at Playhouse 91, an Off-Broadway theater. I was waiting for the elevator, and to my surprise, when the door opened, there stood Frank Langella. A very big man, towering in stature, Frank put his arms out and hugged me. At the same time he whispered in my ear, "Jerry, I was a really bad boy."

I corrected him, "Frank, you were a no-good son of a bitch."

TWENTY-TWO

CAMERON MACKINTOSH AND ANDREW LLOYD WEBBER HIT BROADWAY

B ernie enjoyed the challenge of dealing with difficult personalities. For instance, while I found J. J. Shubert and his personal abuse threatening, Bernie constantly looked for ways to get J. J. on his side. In that respect, J. J. was Bernie's ultimate challenge. Michael Bennett came in a close second. But Bernie didn't stop there. Over the years, Bernie invited all kinds of complicated people into his life. He would bring them home, take them out to dinner, and let them pal around with him.

Back in 1976, Bernie's challenge was a thirty-year-old Brit named Cameron Mackintosh. Little did we know when Cameron first walked into our offices, hoping to sell us some touring shows, that he would become Bernie's newly adopted "son." Nor did we know that, with the arrival of Cameron and Andrew Lloyd Webber, the world of Broadway was about to change forever.

A good-looking man, with a round face, wire-rimmed glasses, and short-cropped dark hair, Cameron was born in 1946 outside London. While still a teenager, he got his first theatrical job as a stagehand at the Theater Royal in Drury Lane. Before long, he was promoted to stage manager for various touring productions. Cameron understood early on that there was a lucrative audience for theater in the boondocks, and he started producing shows to take around the English provinces.

When he first came to see us, Cameron brought with him the poster art for his productions, which made a strong impression on us. In our conversation, Bernie discovered that Cameron could not afford to stay at a decent hotel, and he soon invited Cameron to be his houseguest. A year after that first meeting, he had his first show on Broadway, the Stephen Sondheim compilation *Side By Side by Sondheim*.

Cameron next told us he was producing a new musical by Andrew Lloyd Webber, based on a collection of T. S. Eliot poems titled *Old Possum's Book of Practical Cats*, and that it would be called simply *Cats*. Andrew intended to open it in London, and Cameron said he wanted to bring it to Broadway. Bernie went to London to see an early preview. Pat and I followed a few days later. But Cameron's rights were limited to London, meaning that it was up to Andrew to grant us the American and Canadian rights. At Cameron's urging, he did.

What Bernie and I didn't know was that no other American producers had shown any interest whatsoever in the show. Apparently, they had difficulty imagining a musical whose characters were all cats.

Our plan was to put *Cats* into our Winter Garden Theatre, which seemed a simple enough decision. But in the theater, things are almost never simple. First, we had to cut a hole in the roof and construct separate housing to enable Grizabella, the Glamour Cat, to ride on a suspended tire. Reconfiguring part of the roof was a painful exercise for us. The theater had just undergone a total renovation to repair damages from a nearby restaurant fire.

What followed was even more painful. The theater had been completely repainted in four different colors. The magnificent dome, the frieze, the bas-relief, and the walls were gorgeous. But now Andrew requested that we paint the theater walls black up to the wainscot. We felt this was something we simply had to do, and were thankful at least that it was limited in scope.

Shortly afterward, Andrew requested that we paint all the walls black up to the ceiling. We complied, relieved that we would not have to touch the magnificent dome. The relief was short-lived. The dome joined the walls and ceiling to create a totally black interior. We prayed for a successful show, shuddering to think about the cost of restoring the theater to its original state.

Still, stories about our punching a hole in the roof, together with the show's success in London, generated tremendous publicity for *Cats*. When the show arrived in New York, it had a healthy advance notice. After two weeks of previews, *Cats* opened on October 7, 1982. But reviews ranged from poor to mixed. Frank Rich wrote in the *New York Times*, "While the songs are usually sweet and well sung, 'Cats' as a whole sometimes curls up and takes a catnap. . . . If you blink, you'll miss the plot. . . . But maybe it's asking too much that this ambitious show lift the audience. . . ."

Thankfully, the critics proved to be irrelevant. *Cats* became the longest-running show in Broadway history at that time: 7,485 performances from its first preview on September 23, 1982, to its closing on September 10, 2000. It won seven Tony Awards, including Best Musical.

On the other hand, there were also annoyances. For instance, during the show's run, the *New York Times* weekly theater guide consistently printed a negative comment extracted from Frank's review of the show. I let it pass for quite some time, but after five years or so, I couldn't tolerate reading the comment any longer. I made an appointment to see Abe Rosenthal, who by then was executive editor of the *New York Times*. I met with him and Arthur Gelb, the managing editor.

I asked them, "Why don't you give credence to the half million people who have seen *Cats* in New York, and on the road, and have been delighted by their experience?"

Abe, who would never admit anyone was right, answered, "You've got a point."

Arthur, always extremely defensive about any criticism, made no response. But a week later, the comment was deleted.

Cats was a spectacular achievement in so many ways. We produced four road companies of the show, including bookings at Shubert theaters in Boston, Philadelphia, and Washington, D.C., and an open-ended booking at the Los Angeles Shubert. We also licensed the Canadian rights with great success. Today, no one comes in under budget. Yet, the New York production of *Cats*, originally budgeted at a cost of $3.9 million, actually came in at $5.2 million, showing just how unique this show was. *Cats* spent eighteen years on Broadway and is still touring the country, even making multiple return visits to many places, among them Atlanta, Georgia, where it has toured more than twenty times. The show spawned many road companies that performed protracted, simultaneous, and repeat engagements throughout America and Canada. *Cats*, in fact, was the savior of the road, which by the mid-1980s was in desperate financial shape.

Cats, like *A Chorus Line*, had no stars. The show was the star, meaning that cast members could be replaced without diluting the show's appeal. But, again like *A Chorus Line*, the show gave exposure to unknowns and created stars. *Cats* was also the first Broadway spectacular that appealed to non-English-speaking foreigners. And, just as "Don't Cry for Me, Argentina," the signature song in *Evita*, became a tremendous hit world-wide, "Memory," the signature song from *Cats*, was recorded by great artists throughout the world.

With *Cats* up and running, Cameron prepared to bring to New York his latest London triumph, *Les Misérables*, first coproduced with the Royal Shakespeare Company. Bernie and I flew to London to see it. After we left, as Cameron tells it, he heard that we were not sufficiently impressed to go ahead with a New York booking, so he phoned the Nederlanders. They booked him into the Mark Hellinger Theatre. But that deal fell through when, again according to Cameron, Nederlander changed the booking terms.

So Cameron came back to us, and we put the show into our Broadway Theatre, where it opened on March 12, 1987. After that, it moved to our Imperial Theatre. All told, *Les Miz* ran for 6,680 performances and became the longest-running show in Broadway history, surpassing *Cats*.

At the height of its popularity, there were three concurrent American road companies and at least sixty licensed and unlicensed companies worldwide. *Les Misérables* propelled Cameron into the upper ranks of England's wealthiest citizens. That wealth enabled him to purchase and restore a number of theaters in London's West End and to join Andrew Lloyd Webber as one of London's two most important theater owners.

Not to be outdone, Andrew arrived in New York with *Phantom of the Opera*. It had opened to great acclaim in London on October 9, 1986. But Andrew had struck a deal with Cameron, giving him a 25-percent interest in the show in the United States and Canada, with the stipulation that he manage the show in both countries.

Bernie went to London for the opening and met with Cameron about getting permission to present *Phantom* at our Majestic Theatre. No booking terms were discussed, but based on Bernie's strong relationship with Cameron, everybody shook hands. Cameron said negotiating the booking terms could wait for a meeting in New York.

The streets of the Broadway theater district are fertile grounds for gossip. A rumor soon came to our ears that Cameron intended to book *Phantom* into the Martin Beck. This was confirmed when we learned that Dick Wolf, then president of the theater's owner, Jujamcyn Theaters, had offered it to Cameron for expenses. In other words, no rent. The

Martin Beck—now called the Al Hirschfeld Theatre—at the time had 173 fewer orchestra seats and 136 fewer mezzanine seats but four more box seats than the Majestic, for an overall total of 305 fewer seats.

We needed immediate corroboration and asked Cameron to meet with us. He came alone. We told him about the rumor, adding that we believed we already had a deal. His reply was that he never let friendship interfere with business decisions. He didn't deny that he intended to book *Phantom* into the Martin Beck. Cameron was making a big mistake, but he never gave us the chance to prove it. Bernie and I had already calculated the potential gross weekly box-office receipts at capacity for both the Majestic and Martin Beck. He would make a lot more money with us.

Armed with this information, we met with Hal Prince's attorney, Edward Colton, dean of the theatrical bar. Colton was also our attorney for Shubert theatrical productions. By then Hal Prince, once Andrew Lloyd Webber's director of choice, had had a falling out with Andrew, and the two were not on speaking terms. Colton hoped Bernie would call Andrew and speak to him on Hal's behalf. Bernie did so, and that's how Hal ended up as Andrew's director for *Phantom*.

At the same time, Colton informed us that Hal's contract included a provision granting him the right to approve the choice of theater. In light of our calculations, it was in both Hal's and our best interest to book the show into our theater. Colton was confident that Hal would choose the Majestic.

When Andrew and his business partner, Brian Brolly, arrived, we took them on a tour of the Majestic. Andrew said he was delighted with the theater and that it was perfect for *Phantom*. We were not remiss, of course, in stressing to Andrew the potential financial benefits of presenting the show at the Majestic. Brian pointedly asked if we had discussed booking terms with Cameron, who by this time was behaving in an unusually distant manner. We assured Brian that there had been no such discussions, and Brian said the show would play the Majestic.

At that point Andrew, whose gaze had been fixed on the theater ceiling, excitedly announced that he had just resolved a technical problem in the show: how to get a chandelier to fall from the ceiling. All we had to do, he said, was remove two support columns at the back wall of the Majestic and reinforce and replace them with support beams attached to our adjacent Broadhurst Theatre. In addition, we would have to excavate the under-stage area to install the mechanical equipment needed to operate the show's extraordinary scenic effects.

I said to myself, "Oy!"

But we did it all. *Phantom* opened on January 26, 1988, and was a megahit. Like its predecessors *Cats* and *Les Misérables*, *Phantom* spawned multiple road companies that played throughout America and Canada, and in major cities around the globe.

As for Hal Prince, who up to that point had already won eighteen Tonys for producing and/or directing some of Broadway's greatest hits—*Damn Yankees, A Funny Thing Happened on the Way to the Forum, Fiddler on the Roof, Cabaret, Follies, Sweeney Todd*, and *Evita*, to name a few—he walked away with yet another Tony for directing *Phantom*. Hal also walked away with 4 percent of *Phantom*'s gross, plus the right to direct any company of the show done as a first-class production anywhere in the world.

Hal became a very, very rich man. He expressed his appreciation to Bernie for getting him the job by sending a note that read simply: "Thanks. Hal."

British hits were still playing all over Broadway, but the invasion of new shows from London had definitely slowed down. Cameron followed *Phantom* with *Miss Saigon*. He liked our Broadway Theatre, and wanted us to put in boxes, which had originally been there. We did. But putting *Miss Saigon* in the Broadway meant we had to move *Les Misérables* to the Imperial. Fortunately, that didn't stop its momentum. *Les Miz* ran there for another twelve and a half years.

Miss Saigon, which opened April 11, 1991, ran for nearly ten years and 4,092 performances—more than *Evita*, but not nearly as long as *Cats, Les Miz,* and *Phantom*. One possibility is that it dealt with the Vietnam War at a time when sentiment about the unpopular war was still fairly fresh. Another is that the play cost an astounding $10 million to produce, and it broke the previously taboo ceiling of one hundred dollars a ticket. Still, advance sales topped $35 million, and there's no doubt that the show was a special "East meets West" musical in the great tradition of *South Pacific* and *The King and I*.

We had accommodated Cameron at every turn, so needless to say we were surprised when he took *Phantom of the Opera* to California and put it in the Ahmanson, a competing theater. That was another grievous blow. The show ran there for three and a half years and really helped establish the Ahmanson.

It goes without saying that Cameron is a very good and very canny producer, and he is a demanding negotiator. An entrepreneur, he started his own ticket-brokerage agency and bought an interest in a licensing organization. I believe he also acquired an interest in an advertising agency. If there is a profit center, Cameron will find it.

———•◦•———

A few years later, when Andrew Lloyd Webber showed up with a new musical, *Whistle Down the Wind*, our door was wide open. Set in Louisiana, it's the story of an escaped convict who finds himself in a barn in the presence of a group of children. The children believe the prisoner is Jesus Christ because of wounds on his hands and feet, and they shelter and feed him.

Andrew wanted to book our Shubert Theatre. During our discussion, he asked us to invest $500,000 in the production and advance him $1 million, which he would pay back over the first year of its run. We were okay with those terms and also agreed to book the show for nine weeks at our National Theatre in Washington prior to the New York engagement. None of us had seen the show, but Andrew had presented parts of it at his annual music festival at his estate in Sydmonton, outside of London. We thought it was a hit in the making.

At the time, the musical *Big* was at the Shubert, and, seeing the end of its run in sight, we asked Andrew to give us until November 17. By that time, we figured, *Big* would have closed and the theater would be free. Andrew agreed. With this in mind, we met repeatedly with Jim Freydberg, the play's general manager, anxious to get a closing date. But Jim told us that *Big*'s producer, Irving Feld, owner of the Ringling Bros. and Barnum & Bailey Circus, intended to run the show until the following April, when it would go on tour. We told Jim that after Labor Day, in our opinion, the show would begin losing about $200,000 a week. Irving was a rich man, Jim replied, and the losses wouldn't matter to him.

By mid-August, Andrew's concern about the availability of the Shubert was increasing daily. Edgar Dobie, Andrew's manager, told us that to hedge his bet, Andrew had spoken to Rocco Landesman about booking the show at the Martin Beck. I called Rocco and mentioned our arrangement to hold the Shubert until November 17. If we couldn't deliver by then, we said, we would not try to extend the date. Rocco agreed.

But a few days later, Rocco un-agreed. First he phoned to say he would only hold the Martin Beck until November 8. Since the eighth was in the middle of the week, he was effectively reducing our November 17 date by two weeks. Although we didn't like the change of date, there was nothing we could do about it. Several days after that, Rocco called again, this time to say he had informed Edgar Dobie that he wouldn't hold the Martin Beck and that if Andrew wanted the theater, he would have to sign a booking contract immediately. Rocco, in effect, was stealing the show away from us.

Around the same time, our prediction about the fate of *Big* proved correct. Irving Feld decided that, rich or not, he didn't like losing $200,000 a week, and announced that *Big* would close on October 13. We now started running around to find another show for the Shubert. There were few choices, but I thought the most likely one was *Chicago*.

Although it had originally been booked into Nederlander's Richard Rodgers Theatre, it couldn't stay there because another musical, *Steel Pier*, was signed to start previews on March 27, 1997. *Chicago* would open at the Rodgers but would then have to move. So we approached Barry Weissler, the producer of *Chicago*. He didn't immediately warm to the idea of moving the show into the Shubert, and he also thought our booking terms were too steep. It took some time, but he reluctantly signed.

When *Chicago* opened at the Richard Rodgers Theatre on November 14, 1996, it was a gigantic hit. And I was ecstatic, eagerly looking forward to its opening at the Shubert three months later. But the day after *Chicago* opened at the Richard Rodgers, Nick Scandalios of the Nederlander Organization phoned to see if I would allow *Chicago* to remain there and, instead, take *Steel Pier* at the Shubert.

I told Nick, "I'm sorry, but no."

He replied, "Jimmy said if he was in your place, he wouldn't agree either."

Steel Pier closed within two months. In the meantime, *Whistle Down the Wind* was completely sold out prior to its Washington opening on December 7, 1996. Pat and I went to the opening. But it received devastating notices, and Andrew was deeply hurt.

The question now became, would Andrew close it after Washington, or work on it and bring it to New York? Most concerned of all was Rocco, who called me several times a week to ask if Andrew was going to close the show. I told him it would be uncharacteristic of Andrew to do so. But six weeks into the Washington engagement, Andrew announced the show would not be coming to New York. So Rocco wound up with neither *Chicago* nor an Andrew Lloyd Webber musical.

Ironically, it was not all bad news for him. Andrew had insisted that, as a condition of booking *Whistle* into the Martin Beck, Rocco had to move the front portion of the mezzanine closer to the stage. Doing so added about two hundred seats to its capacity, which made the theater much more suitable and competitive for presenting a big musical.

Still, I think of Rocco every November 8, the anniversary of the date he selected for *Big* to vacate the Shubert.

TWENTY-THREE

TROUBLES WITH PETER HALL
AND TREVOR NUNN

My relationship with Peter Hall, both professional and personal, had been fine, despite the fact that when he was in New York with *Amadeus*, he stayed at Peter Shaffer's house while we were paying him to stay in a hotel. But that petty behavior should have been a sign that he was capable of bigger things.

By the time *Amadeus* closed in New York in October 1983, Peter Shaffer had written a new play, called *Yonadab*. Robbie Lantz sent us Shaffer's script, which told a fascinating biblical story, based on four lines in the Book of Solomon, about a nephew of King David named Yonadab and his relationship with King David's children. The play exemplified Shaffer's great talent for weaving a story together using sensational subject matter, mixing elements of truth and mystery. So we said we wanted to do it with Peter Hall directing.

The right to produce *Yonadab* in America was granted to us by Shaffer. But his loyalty to the National Theatre compelled him to produce the play first in London, where it opened on December 4, 1985. Before bringing the show to Broadway, we had asked for certain rewrites, and they were slow in coming. On top of that, scheduling conflicts were making it difficult to get the cast we wanted.

In the meantime, Peter Shaffer wrote the comedy *Lettice and Lovage*, starring Maggie Smith. We decided to coproduce it with Robert Fox in London and New York. The show opened at the Globe Theatre in London on October 27, 1987, and was a major success. We planned to open it at our Plymouth Theatre on April 2, 1989. Unfortunately, Maggie Smith became ill with a thyroid condition, and then fractured her shoulder, so the opening was put back to March 25, 1990, at our Barrymore Theatre.

By then we had managed to put together a schedule with Peter Hall for *Yonadab*, with an opening date of February 15, 1990. However, in December 1988 we received a letter from solicitors representing London producer Duncan Weldon, stating that his company, Triumph Theatre Productions, was exclusively entitled to Hall's services for three years from the end of his contract with the Royal National Theatre.

I wrote back, hoping to get Triumph to release Peter Hall for our *Yonadab*. Peter then informed me that he might not be able to direct *Yonadab* within our time period, but that he hoped to sort out the problem. The next thing I knew, Hall was directing *The Merchant of Venice* in London, starring Dustin Hoffman. At this point, Hall insisted he needed to read the reviews of *Merchant* before he could finalize the schedule of *Yonadab*. If the reviews were good, he said, Dustin would likely star in a New York production, opening sometime around mid-October.

For us, that timing conflicted with the production schedule and opening date of *Yonadab*, and also pushed *Lettice and Lovage* to the end of April from mid-March. I replied that *Lettice and Lovage* could not be postponed, and told Hall that his work in *The Merchant of Venice* would cause us to forgo *Yonadab* unless we proceeded at the expense of *Lettice and Lovage*. To do otherwise, we would have had to defer *Yonadab* to the fall of 1990. In essence, we were confronted with two equally unacceptable alternatives solely of Peter Hall's making.

When I told the tortuous story to Peter Shaffer, who by nature is a most temperate man, he exploded. He took it as an insult that the whim of an actor—meaning Dustin Hoffman—should determine whether or not *Lettice and Lovage* could go forward. As he reminded me, it had already been delayed a year to accommodate Maggie Smith's health problems. I phoned Hall and told him about Shaffer's reaction. Hall blamed me, saying I was responsible for Shaffer's refusal to postpone the date. Our best-laid plans and preparations for opening *Yonadab* in New York were for naught.

Hall, however, chose to rewrite history. In a letter dated August 30, 1989, to David Aukin, managing director of the National Theatre in London, he insisted that he had kept us informed all along. "I explained this to Shuberts and to Peter, and asked for five weeks' grace. They decided that this did not mean five weeks' grace, and that there would inevitably be much delay while contracts were worked out, negotiations with American Equity, etc., etc. They, therefore, dropped me after they said they could not wait any longer, and were seeking another director. After all the years of work, I am, of course, very bitter about this."

Actually, Peter's problems vis-à-vis *Yonadab* were of his own making.

Yonadab was scrapped, and *Lettice and Lovage* opened in New York on March 25, 1990, at our Barrymore Theatre, to rave reviews. It ran for 286 performances.

But that was not my last encounter with Peter Hall.

In 1997, I read the script of a very interesting play, *The Visitor* by Éric-Emmanuel Schmitt. I met the playwright, with whom I got along very well, and we acquired the rights. Set in Vienna at the time of the Nazi invasion, it's the story of a meeting between Freud and a mysterious stranger who may or may not be God. I engaged Eli Wallach to play Freud but had difficulty casting the role of the Stranger and had not yet lined up a director. That's when agent Robbie Lantz called to say, "Peter Hall is in my office. He has a copy of the script and he wants to do it."

I told Robbie, "I will go ahead with Hall and have already engaged Eli Wallach to play Freud."

Hall was satisfied with this casting as well as with the projected rehearsal date of January 1999. So I now had a director, but no costar. I hoped to enlist the distinguished English actor Derek Jacobi to play the Stranger. Jacobi and I spoke for about an hour in the Shubert offices, when he then confessed that he had also been offered the opportunity to play Uncle Vanya on Broadway. He assured me that he would let me know for certain by the following weekend. He never did.

Casting the part of the Stranger was inordinately difficult, so I told Hall that I needed to postpone the opening by as much as two months to find a costar and to properly promote the play. This did not sit well with Hall, who accused me of trying to get out of doing the show. I insisted, "If we could get a suitable cast, I'd be willing to open first in London. But I can't ask Eli Wallach to appear in London."

Hall asked, "Would you agree to casting Ben Kingsley as Freud and Ian Richardson as the Stranger?"

I didn't think either of them was suitable and told Hall so, at which time he replied, to my astonishment, that he had not submitted the script to them. In other words, he was just coming at me with names anyone could have named, not even knowing if they would be interested. That was the moment I decided it was fruitless to continue.

Shortly thereafter, Hall called to ask for a payment. We had reached an agreement to pay him $60,000 for his services: $20,000 on signing the contract, $20,000 on the first day of rehearsal, and the balance on the opening date. But we had not signed anything. It's not an unusual practice in the business to sign contracts late. Still, I told Hall we would pay him a fee of $20,000.

Hall didn't think this was fair, and I suggested we discuss it on his next trip to New York. I related the conversation to Robbie Lantz, who said he thought I was being eminently fair, since Hall had done no work on the show and no contract had been signed. Robbie generously added that he would waive his 10-percent commission, which meant an additional $2,000 for Hall.

A few weeks later, Hall and I sat down in my office, and he told me about his financial obligations to his children and former wives, and how he had already set aside time to direct a play that was not going to be done. He believed he was entitled to more than $20,000. Against my better judgment, I agreed to pay him $30,000 and told him that Robbie was waiving his fee, which now amounted to $3,000. I added, "You are now $13,000 richer than the first time we discussed this matter."

An ecstatic Hall embraced me and told me, "You're marvelous."

Even though the standard provisions in a director's contract state that the producer is not obligated to produce the play or make additional payments if it does not materialize, I had a check sent to Peter for $30,000.

No sooner had the check gone out when an invoice arrived from him for $30,000, plus £960 for the services of a casting agent—which I'd never authorized—and £41.45 for telephones and faxes. This was the last straw. I wrote Hall that under no circumstances would we pay the casting agent's fee. He had received the equivalent of $33,000, and the matter was closed.

That was still not the end of it. Hall wrote back accusing me of bad faith. As the "emperor of Broadway," he wrote, it was incumbent upon me to show mercy upon my subjects. "Emperors need to be humane and meticulous if they are not to abuse their position."

This evoked my reply: "Your perception of reality is totally at variance with the facts. I am neither an Emperor, exceptionally unprofessional or ungenerous. Nor do I fail to pay my debts. I also don't break my word. I've always respected your work. And, if you choose to end our relationship, it is entirely up to you. Your use of the word 'sincerely' belies the content of your letter."

To my knowledge, *The Visitor* was never produced in the United States.

Bill Kenwright, one of London's most noted producers, had signed on Peter Hall as director of his production company. The financial terms were very generous. And while Hall was under contract to Kenwright, Robbie Lantz called to say that Kim Poster, a London producer, wanted to stage a revival of *Amadeus*, starring David Suchet of Hercule Poirot fame.

I told Robbie that while we would pass on the London revival, we might want to produce it in New York. I requested that he not license the American rights. He asked if Peter Hall could direct. I swallowed my pride and agreed, because Peter had directed the definitive production.

But in light of Kenwright's deal with Hall, it was essential to get his consent to release Hall to direct the revival. I spoke to Kenwright, and he agreed to free Hall, on the condition that Kenwright coproduce the revival in London with Kim Poster. I said that was fine. Kenwright and Poster arranged for the *Amadeus* revival to open at a theater outside London and then proceed to London's Comedy Theatre. Before the opening, Robbie called a meeting with me and Shaffer at his office. There I learned that Kim Poster, who had engaged David Suchet, wanted to be the lead producer in New York.

I said, "We do not want to be anything but the lead producer."

We pulled out, and they were delighted. Bill Kenwright later informed me that Kim Poster had unilaterally changed the agreed-upon tryout theater, and had also changed the London venue from the Comedy to the Old Vic. Kenwright, who had relationships both with the out-of-town venue and the Comedy, then asked Hall to withdraw from the production as a gesture of support. Hall refused, and now Kenwright was furious with him. I was pleased that we no longer had any plans to produce the show in New York.

Not long afterward, Pat and I were in London and attended a rehearsal of the *Amadeus* revival at the Old Vic. Hall greeted me warmly and invited me for coffee. We went to a place next door, where Hall wasted no time in telling me that Kenwright had betrayed him by asking him to withdraw from *Amadeus*. He said the show was in rehearsal and he had an obligation to the actors and everyone involved to continue.

By then the matter had been reported in the London press, and various comments had been attributed to Hall. Kenwright later told me that he had refused to talk to the press, that he and Hall were finished, and that he had been a fool for getting involved with him in the first place.

By then I, too, could not imagine having anything further to do with Peter Hall.

——•••——

Little did I know that with Trevor Nunn, things could get even more problematic.

When Bernie saw *The Life and Adventures of Nicholas Nickleby*, directed by Trevor Nunn, at London's National Theatre in early 1981, he phoned me immediately. Although the show ran for eight hours with a dinner break, he considered it one of the greatest theatrical events he had ever seen. He was determined that we produce it. So we acquired the rights with James M. Nederlander, Elizabeth McCann, and Nelle Nugent. The show had a cast of forty-two, and the engagement was limited to fourteen weeks. Due to its high production and operating costs, we determined that we had to charge a hundred dollars per ticket, an astronomical amount at that time.

Nicholas Nickleby opened on October 4, 1981, at our Plymouth Theatre and ran for more than a year. It was an instantaneous hit. Performances quickly sold out. We garnered our third Tony Award for Best Play and walked away with a Tony for Best Direction. After that, Trevor directed our Broadway productions of *Cats* and *Les Misérables*, and won Tonys for both. With this history, we thought Trevor was a known commodity when *Chess* came along.

Bernie's original idea was to hire Michael Bennett to direct it in London and then bring it to New York. But when Michael pulled out in early 1986 because he was dying of AIDS, Bernie and I decided that the only way to save the show was to get another major director. We asked Trevor.

The request was awkward, because Michael had already cast and designed the show, and it was about to go into rehearsal. However, Trevor agreed, on two conditions. First, he wanted the right to direct *Chess* in New York and not be bound by anything Michael had done in London. Second, he wanted us to produce a U.S. road company of *Nicholas Nickleby*. Having no alternative, we said yes.

Chess opened in London on May 14, 1986. The reviews were only okay, but the score was an instantaneous success. The show ran for about three years and featured Elaine Paige, with whom Tim Rice had been romantically involved for years.

The play was about a world-championship chess match during the Cold War. Glasnost and perestroika had not yet occurred, and the hostility between Russia and America provided the background for the match. While the American character was clearly based on Bobby Fischer, the Russian was probably a combination of two famous players, Viktor Korchnoi and Anatoly Karpov. But it didn't matter who the characters really were; what mattered was the game.

The set was stunning—a black-and-white, under-lit, fluorescent chessboard that revolved and tilted in all directions. It was surrounded by a video wall comprising hundreds of television screens depicting the action taking place during the chess matches. But after seeing the show in London, we decided it needed script revisions before coming to New York. So during the rest of 1986 and early 1987, numerous *Chess* meetings were held and a lot of correspondence was exchanged among Trevor, Tim, Benny, Björn, Robert Fox, Bernie, and me.

In the midst of all this, a controversy erupted between Robert Fox and Trevor. It was precipitated by an ad that Robert had inserted in the brochure of that year's Laurence Olivier Awards. It read, "If you see Trev, please tell him *Chess* is still on." Robert thought he was being funny.

Trevor saw it as "a staggering betrayal both personally and professionally."

Robert apologized to Trevor and the cast, and we hoped that would be the end of that. Not quite. Tim now got furious with Trevor, who had decided not to bring Elaine Page to New York with the show. One of the biggest names in London's musical theater, Elaine was a huge hit in the London show, and Tim was convinced that Broadway would love her.

Trevor didn't care. Nor did he deliver his script revisions on time. We offered to fund another book writer to help make the changes. Trevor asked if we had a writer in mind, but we deferred the choice to him. Sitting in my office, he came up with Richard Nelson. He said he admired his work and would like to call him but that he did not know him.

I suggested he ring the Dramatists Guild to get his number. With the number in hand, Trevor asked to speak to Nelson privately. So we showed Trevor to an office, and after a few minutes he came out, beaming. Nelson would be delighted to work with him, he said. Little did we know that Richard Nelson had previously directed two plays for Trevor when Trevor was artistic director of London's Royal Shakespeare Company. In short, we were the victims of a charade.

Time was becoming a factor. We wanted to try out the show in Washington before its New York engagement. But Trevor announced from London—at least, that's where we were led to believe he was—that he had to leave the show no later than May 10, 1988, to begin directing the forthcoming film version of *Porgy and Bess* in South Carolina. Therefore, he said, he couldn't go to Washington.

Suddenly, he became increasingly difficult to reach. All communications had to be made via his secretary in London. We subsequently learned that Trevor was actually working in Australia on *Les Misérables*.

Our plans for Washington quickly became academic. We couldn't have the set built in time for a tryout and then get it to New York before Trevor's departure on May 10. Thus, Trevor presented us with a fait accompli that required us to open cold in New York.

The set consisted of various geometric structures, vaguely resembling chess pieces, which moved over and across the stage following electroluminescent pathways embedded in the stage. I felt that these moving shapes, each with a stagehand inside, would be disconcerting to viewers, who would sit there waiting for them collide. So now we had a new book writer, a costly major musical that could not try out before coming to New York, a new set that might or might not work, and a deadline which, if not met, would cost us Trevor's services.

In light of all this, we decided to withdraw from *Chess*, and Robert Fox did the same. When we told Trevor, he excoriated us, calling it a cowardly act. He maintained that *Chess* would be an epoch-making musical. He insisted that we wait for his call on New Year's Day. Robert Fox said he wasn't going to sit around waiting for Trevor to phone, so the conference call was postponed until the following day. When it came, Tim, Benny, Björn, Robert, our general manager Tyler Gatchell, and Bernie and I were all on the line. We had no idea where Trevor was calling from.

In a last-minute change of heart, Robert assured us that the show's budget had been cut substantially and that he was now prepared to go forward. Bernie and I said we would think it over and give them our decision the next day. We were faced with the dilemma of abandoning what might be a major hit and letting *Chess* go to another producer and theater owner, or proceeding with what could be a doomed show. In the end, we capitulated and agreed to proceed. In retrospect, that was a mistake.

Chess went into rehearsal in early 1988. We had a wonderful cast but an incomplete book. Richard Nelson and Trevor rewrote nightly after every rehearsal, although none of us were supposed to know this. Tim, Robert, Benny, and Björn were not in New York during rehearsals. By the time the show moved into our Imperial Theatre for technical rehearsals—putting actors on the stage for the first time with all the show's design elements—it appeared to me that Benny and Björn were totally dependent upon Trevor. Robert, Bernie, and I were not, and Tim was disgusted with Trevor. I saw that the set didn't work, and that the stagehands operating within each of their geometric confines could not follow the electroluminescent pathways.

Then Tim noted that some of his lyrics had been changed without his consent. He said he was going to punch Trevor in the jaw. He didn't. But he did announce that he would have nothing more to do with the script. Next, Nelson handed a note to the producers and the creative team reminding everybody that the show's book was not written by Tim, but by him and Trevor. To me, this was a most unprofessional act. Tim's reaction was different. "Fuck him," he said. "I wouldn't want my name on this book under any circumstances."

Word on the street was that *Chess* was in trouble creatively. Plus, it ran a half hour beyond eleven p.m., which required an overtime payment of $25,000 a week. I told Trevor he simply had to cut the running time of the show. He put his arm around my shoulder and benevolently explained, "A show should be just as long as it has to be."

The show opened too long, and the reviews were negative, with the exception of the musical score, which was, and still is, wonderful. The next day, as is the custom, we assembled to talk about the show's future. I insisted again that Trevor cut the show. Trevor said that would be impossible since he was returning to London that night. I warned him, "If that's the case, we will close the show tomorrow."

So Trevor stayed in New York and cut the show. But the boat had sailed. *Chess* closed on June 25, 1988, at a total loss of $6.1 million. Attending the final performance, Trevor found it "breathtaking" and filled with "dazzling dexterity." He said, "I have rarely seen acting as skilled and fresh in a play." He told the cast, "What I saw filled me with pride, with admiration for the writers and the players, and with anger that something so good and so original should have fallen victim to considerations belonging to an agenda which had little to do with the art of the theater."

Tim Rice begged to disagree. He told Trevor the show was far too long; some songs were "clinkers" before they were written; some "noisy rock 'n' roll" was badly staged and performed; and errors of "staggering proportions" were committed. He felt that it was lacking in glamour and choreography, that the costumes were dull and the set too bleak, and that the one big preshow hit, "One Night in Bangkok," was utterly wasted. He said the timing of the show's opening was wrong: it should not have opened just before the Tony nominations were announced but after, thereby giving us the chance to continue the performances without the stigma of no nominations.

Tim went on and on. Some characters were simply not likeable, and the book never merged with the score. "The show would have been a better musical without any book, and indeed a better play without any music."

A month or so later, we received a bill from Trevor for $3,236.72 to cover his transportation to New York and hotel expenses for closing night. He was promptly reminded that he came to the *Chess* closing on his own. He was duly informed that no funds would be made available to pay the bill.

Chess is one of the few shows I have not gotten over. Nor can I forget Trevor's rationale for not being free to go to Washington, especially after his version of events was unexpectedly contradicted one night during dinner with Irwin Winkler, the producer of *Porgy and Bess*.

When I told Irwin about Trevor having to leave *Chess* for *Porgy and Bess*, he said that Trevor's excuse was simply untrue. Irwin explained that when he and Trevor first discussed the film, Trevor gave him specific dates that he would be available to shoot the picture. At that point, Irwin told Trevor, "This is not the way I shoot a movie," and ended Trevor's involvement.

There is a coda to this story. A new version of *Chess*, performed in Swedish, opened in Stockholm in February 2002 and toured Sweden to sold-out houses for nearly two years. Its book was written by a Swedish writer, who also directed the play. Perhaps if we had gone to Washington, and opened in New York after the cut-off date for the Tony Awards, we might have been able to make *Chess* a success. Perhaps.

TWENTY-FOUR

STEPHEN SONDHEIM, THE LEGEND

Dealing with extremely creative and highly motivated people is never easy. This has nothing to do with being British or American; it has to do with temperament. Throw in the "genius" factor, and the process can become exhausting. You learn to develop a high tolerance for ego and capriciousness, in the hope that perhaps a sincere friendship, maybe even a work of sheer genius, will result. With Stephen Sondheim I achieved both—a lovely friendship and the chance to see a genius at work.

Looking back on Stephen Sondheim's youth, it's clear that he was destined for a Broadway career. When he was around ten, just as his parents were divorcing, Stephen befriended James Hammerstein, son of the legendary Oscar Hammerstein II. Noticing Stephen's growing interest in music and the theater, Hammerstein soon became Stephen's surrogate father.

Stephen and James were just fifteen when Hammerstein took them to the tryout opening of *Carousel* in New Haven, Connecticut, before it came to Broadway. Two years later, Hammerstein got Stephen a job as a gofer on his next musical, *Allegro*. Two years after that, Stephen was the Hammersteins' guest at the Broadway opening of *South Pacific*.

Stephen wrote his first complete musical while he was still in high school. Hammerstein went over it with him, critiquing the songs. It was an invaluable lesson that Sondheim clearly took to heart. When he enrolled at Williams College, he declared himself a music major, continued writing and composing—always with Hammerstein in the background—and went on to study with the composer Milton Babbitt, who taught at Princeton and later in New York at Juilliard. After graduation, he spent time trying to sell his songs, went to Hollywood, where he wrote scripts for the television series *Topper*, and tried to win some money as a contestant on the popular quiz show *The $64,000 Question*.

In 1954, Stephen wrote both music and lyrics for a show called *Saturday Night*, which did not get produced. Next, he wrote the title song for the short-run Broadway play *Girls of Summer*. No one took much notice.

By then he had met Hal Prince, who was coproducing a new musical to be directed and choreographed by Jerome Robbins, with a book by Arthur Laurents and music by Leonard Bernstein. Normally, Lenny would also have written his own lyrics, but he wanted to concentrate exclusively on the music, which meant they needed a lyricist. Hal called then-unknown Stephen. The show was *West Side Story*, and Stephen wasn't sure he wanted to do it. He wanted to write music, not lyrics.

But Oscar Hammerstein convinced him that it would be a wonderful opportunity to work with such an illustrious group. He advised Stephen to approach it as a learning experience, which Stephen did. Still, the name Sondheim was such an afterthought that when Brooks Atkinson reviewed the show twice in the *New York Times*, once on opening night and again ten days later, he only mentioned Stephen once. Atkinson praised Leonard Bernstein for his score, Jerry Robbins for his dance, and Arthur Laurents for his story. In the first review, he wrote, "The author, composer and ballet designer are creative artists." No mention of Stephen at all. In the second review, Stephen is listed as the lyricist, but nothing is said about him or his lyrics.

Three years later, when the show was revived on Broadway, Atkinson did note, "It is the impeccable taste of the music, the lyrics and the story that seem so astonishing."

By then, Stephen had written lyrics for the smash Jerome Robbins hit, *Gypsy*. Praising Ethel Merman's triumphant performance and the "genial direction of Jerome Robbins" in his first review of *Gypsy* in May 1959, Atkinson took the time to add, "Jule Styne has supplied a genuine show-business score, and Stephen Sondheim has set amusing lyrics to it."

Nine days later, while still praising Merman and Robbins, Atkinson wrote about Jule Styne, "The music is fresh and lively in the musical-comedy tradition. Taking every situation on its own level, he has written dramatic songs, as well as Tin Pan Alley tunes." He added, "Stephen Sondheim's lyrics are equally hackneyed."

Hardly an enthusiastic rave, but at least by now Broadway knew who Stephen was.

Not that Atkinson's opinions at this point necessarily mattered to Stephen. A few years after *Gypsy*, when he was well on his way as a composer, Stephen told a reporter, "Once the basic idea for a lyric has been set, it's like working out a crossword puzzle. But composing music is genuinely creative. And it's much more fun."

Stephen followed *West Side Story* and *Gypsy* with incidental music for Arthur Laurents's play *Invitation to a March*, then wrote the music and lyrics for *A Funny Thing Happened on the Way to the Forum*. He teamed up again with Arthur Laurents to compose music and lyrics for *Anyone Can Whistle*, which closed after only nine performances, and then again for the play *Do I Hear a Waltz?*, writing lyrics to Richard Rodgers's music.

That play earned him his first solo Tony nomination, along with Rodgers, for Best Composer and Lyricist, as Stephen had previously been nominated as part of musical teams and had won with the team of *A Funny Thing Happened on the Way to the Forum*. In the end, Stephen and Rodgers lost the Tony to Jerry Bock and Sheldon Harnick for *Fiddler on the Roof*.

Then came the 1970s, Stephen's golden decade. He wrote *Company, Follies, A Little Night Music, Pacific Overtures*, and *Sweeney Todd*. He ended the decade with two Tonys and two Drama Desk Awards for each of those five musicals. In other words, he swept the table, winning it all.

In the following years, Stephen won a Drama Desk Award for *Merrily We Roll Along* and one for *Sunday in the Park with George*, and then the Pulitzer Prize for *Sunday* as well. He also won two Tony Awards and a Drama Desk Award for *Into the Woods* and two Tonys and two Drama Desk Awards for *Passion*.

Nearly fifty years after Brooks Atkinson neglected to mention him in what may well be one of Broadway's greatest ever musicals, *West Side Story*, Stephen Sondheim is one of Broadway's greatest-ever composer-lyricists.

Seeing a show in workshop, the way we had seen Michael Bennett's *Dreamgirls*, can save a lot of time and money. If it doesn't work there and you have or are about to make an investment, you now get the chance to cut your losses. But even if the play works in the workshop, that's no guarantee it will be a hit. When Bernie and I saw a workshop performance of Stephen Sondheim and James Lapine's *Sunday in the Park with George*, it was unfinished and only the first act was performed. We were knocked out by it anyway, and agreed to produce it. When the second-act script arrived, however, it did not live up to expectations.

We didn't know James Lapine well, so we relied mainly on Stephen to work with him to rewrite the second act. Meanwhile, we made plans to proceed directly to Broadway and open at our small Booth Theatre, an unlikely destination for an eighteen-member cast starring Bernadette Peters and Mandy Patinkin.

Sunday was Lapine's first Broadway directorial outing, as well as his first Broadway musical as book writer. Although the script still needed further revisions, rehearsals began. Frankly, Bernie and I were holding our breath. Previews started in April 1984, and we soon realized *Sunday* was in trouble. Audiences were walking out in large numbers, and negative comments were appearing in the gossip columns.

Fortunately, Stephen can write new songs to tight deadlines, and he set to work. At the same time, James did numerous rewrites. By the time the show opened, we had one of the greatest first acts of a musical ever written, plus a brand-new second act with beautiful new songs and dialogue.

We expected to win another Tony Award, but the Tony went to *La Cage Aux Folles*, a Jerry Herman musical. In accepting the award, Jerry indulged in self-laudatory remarks to the effect that while his music touched a popular chord, Stephen's was esoteric and less favored by theater audiences. It was the only time I ever heard an acceptance speech that deprecated a colleague's work.

Among the four contenders for Best Musical of the 1987–1988 Tony Award season were Stephen's *Into the Woods* and Andrew Lloyd Webber's *Phantom Of The Opera*. The other two on the list were *Romance, Romance* and *Sarafina!* It seemed to be a horse race between Stephen and Andrew.

The Tony Awards show was held at the Minskoff Theatre, down the street from Shubert Alley. Unlike nearly all Broadway's theaters, The Minskoff had continental seating in the orchestra, which meant no aisles. All the rows of orchestra seats were set in an arc. I was in the center of the arc and from there could see Stephen on my left and Andrew on my right. Of course, since I could see them, they could also see me. *Into the Woods* was not in a Shubert Theatre, and *Phantom of the Opera* was. But lest I be accused of playing favorites, I was determined to demonstrate total neutrality for both shows.

When the Best Book of a Musical award went to *Into the Woods*, I leaned a little forward in my seat so that Stephen and Andrew could see me applauding with enthusiasm for the winner. When the Best Score was awarded to *Into the Woods*, I repeated my performance, and then I repeated it again when the Tony for Best Direction of a Musical was awarded to Hal Prince for *Phantom of the Opera*.

Then, the big moment arrived: the Tony Award for Best Musical. And the award went to *Phantom of the Opera*, a seemingly incongruous result since its book and score hadn't won. When the announcement was made, I responded in exactly the same way as I had on the three previous occasions. I was quite satisfied with myself. I felt I had given equal treatment to both parties. But I was wrong.

After the ceremony, we went to a party given by George Trescher, a noted theater publicist. The place was filled with theater personalities, including Stephen. I went to say hello but received a frosty welcome. At the time, I couldn't understand why.

Two years later, Pat and I were at a party in honor of Jerry Robbins hosted by Mica and Ahmet Ertegün at the Plaza Hotel. We were seated next to Jerry. In front of us were three rows of tables, and I could see Stephen at the furthest table. He couldn't help but see me, so I said to Pat, "Let's go over and say hello."

We gave him a warm reception. He responded by yelling, "You favored *Phantom of the Opera* over *Into the Woods* at the Tony Awards, and I have it on tape!"

I told him he was nuts and that he had no greater admirers of his works than Pat and me. His somewhat mollified response was, "Well, I finally got it off my chest."

After a hiatus of ten years, we reunited with Stephen Sondheim and James Lapine to coproduce their musical *Passion*. It tells the story of an obsessive infatuation between a grotesquely ugly, sick woman and an Italian army officer, who at the same time is having an affair with a married woman. I had difficulty reconciling the basic concept of the play. I didn't understand how such an unappealing woman could be loved by a handsome army officer. I even suggested to James, who wrote the book and directed the play, that he remove the warts on her face and minimize the seizures that left her screaming and writhing on the stage floor. The extent of my success was that one of her warts was removed. It was not until Stephen wrote a magnificent love song for the woman, about how she would die for the army officer, that we saw the meaning of genuine love.

The show was awarded the Tony Award for Best Musical. It ran at our Plymouth Theatre for 280 performances. My opening-night gift from James was a pillbox containing two warts.

Show business is a place where emotions run high, inhabited as it is by creative and emotional personalities. I have enormous respect for their creativity, and without a doubt, working with and getting to know these artists has been the best part of my job. In many cases, they see me as a sort of father figure. I know they want to please me. At the same, they also want to be independent of me.

But some, like Stephen Sondheim whom I respect enormously, have never quite shown their understanding of me and my role. I have always tried to support them completely. Their support of me would have been greatly appreciated.

TWENTY-FIVE

THE BUSINESS OF BROADWAY: UNION HEADACHES

The British and their megahit musicals brought excitement and new audiences to the theater, while American producers sought out new creative talent, especially for musicals. But those of us running the business of Broadway had to find new ways to cope with rapidly increasing costs, royalties, fees, and fringe benefits, as well as demands by unions and guilds for larger salaries. Obviously, money is at the heart of every business. But in this business, with so many people pulling in so many directions, money often becomes the problem rather than the solution.

As inflation weakens the nation's economy, it also changes the financial structure of the theater business, resulting in higher production budgets and operating costs for shows. Those increases partly reflect demands for higher wages, greater pension and healthcare benefits, and longer vacations. But the revenue from a show and a theater is limited to the theater's four walls, so the only recourse to meet higher costs is to raise ticket prices. Raise them high enough, however, and some potential theatergoers are driven out of the market.

A focus on cost-cutting often means confrontations with the unions, whose demands are a huge factor in the theater business. When unions became more militant, collective-bargaining negotiations became more difficult and lengthy. I saw the effects of this firsthand in 1960, when Actors' Equity called a work stoppage that lasted thirteen days. The chief negotiator for the Broadway League in that dispute was Herman Levin, producer of *My Fair Lady*, *Gentlemen Prefer Blondes*, and *Call Me Mister*, among other shows. Herman was a very funny fellow, but the union was hopping mad as usual and didn't like him. They brought in one of their "enforcers" to negotiate. During the heated, all-night negotiations, the enforcer cynically criticized Herman for owning a Rolls-Royce. Herman didn't find the remarks funny. He rose from the table with great indignation and told the Equity members, "I have one. You want one. And you can go fuck yourselves."

This was the first time a theatrical union had tried to establish a pension fund for its members. It was John Shubert who emerged the hero, settling the issue with warmth and compassion by offering to put 1 percent of every actor's wages into a pension fund. After that, Bernie and I attended and later chaired negotiations involving theater owners and producers.

The relationship between theater owners and producers is tricky. At any given time, many producers do not have a running show. Others have running shows, but each may be in a different position financially. Some shows are healthy; some are just getting by. Some are in rehearsals, some are preparing to open, and some are about to close. What it all adds up to is that a union's ability to sustain a strike promotes disunity among the producers. Theater owners, on the other hand, are virtually powerless to control the producers' reactions to a strike threat. Only when union demands are extreme do producers and theater owners present a united front.

One problem complicating negotiations is a basic lack of knowledge about theater economics on the part of many at the bargaining table. Another problem is that both management and union members are constantly changing, so there is little continuity. Despite all this, the surprising fact is that work stoppages seldom occur on Broadway. The potential loss of jobs has a temporizing effect on both sides. The theater business is small and fragile, and the drive to avoid work stoppages generally brings compromise and sanity to the table.

Back in mid-1963, I was asked to chair the Broadway League's negotiating committee to extend the collective bargaining agreement with Local 802 of the American Federation of Musicians. It was the first of hundreds of negotiations with scores of different theatrical unions that I oversaw. The chairman of the musicians' negotiating committee was Al Minuti, a tough and respected union president. This was at a time when rank-and-file union members began asserting their authority in defiance of their leaders.

Day after day, Al and I would find some mutual ground and then agree to meet the next day. The following day, he would start the meeting by saying that no agreement had been reached. We were going nowhere fast. With tensions rising, I pointed to Minuti and said, "There used to be a man who sat at the table where you are sitting who looked like you, spoke like you, and even had the same name as you. But unlike you, he kept his word. Now, will you please leave and ask the real Al Minuti to come to the table?"

Minuti jumped up and demanded that I meet him outside the room.

That was pretty intimidating, and when we got outside, he was apoplectic. "I want you to know that you and I will agree to a deal, but if this contract is turned down by my members, you'll regret the day you met me."

We eventually agreed on a deal, and I fully expected the contract to be ratified. But union members voted it down, and a strike was authorized. With the very real threat of the lights going out on Broadway, Mayor Robert Wagner called the parties down to City Hall, where we stayed for twenty-eight consecutive hours. Toward the end, one rabble-rouser told his caucus colleagues that they did not have to sit there any longer and listen to bullshit. An infuriated Mayor Wagner pointed his finger at the union member and said, "You are in my house, and you'll stay here until I tell you that you can leave."

The mayor then threatened to reimpose a 5-percent admissions tax on theater tickets, which he had been instrumental in repealing. The tax would have a serious impact on union pension and welfare funds. Just like that, the union caved, and the contract was ratified. It taught me a valuable lesson. Politicians will generally support union leaders and their negotiating committees who agree to a contract rather than rank-and-file union members who reject it.

Negotiations with unions are generally contentious. But the most bitterly contentious I ever saw occurred in September 1975, the expiration date for the collective-bargaining agreement between the Broadway League and the American Federation of Musicians, Local 802. Economic times were dire, with the city of New York on the verge of bankruptcy. Times Square and the theater streets were a disaster. Relations with government officials and the media were nonexistent. And the reputation of the Shubert Organization had not yet recovered from the days when J. J. ruled with his irrational iron fist.

At issue was the minimum number of musicians required to be employed in theaters presenting musicals. That number had nothing to do with the demands of the music and everything to do with union demands. During some performances, unneeded musicians sat around the theater playing cards and still drew a paycheck. For the League, the minimums were unsustainable. For Local 802, the minimums guaranteed a livelihood for its members.

Negotiations were especially difficult because I had to deal with three separate union groups. One was the union's incumbent officers and their supporters. Another was a group seeking to oust the incumbent officers. The third was a rump group wanting to take over the union altogether.

Negotiations sometimes took a humorous turn, however. Two amusing exchanges occurred at the outset. The first dealt with a harpist who received special pay for bringing his harp to the theater. One would have thought that you hire a harpist and the harp comes along. Not so. I remarked that such a situation had never arisen before and that the issue was sui generis, meaning unique.

The union president responded, "Just forget the sui and be generous."

At a later meeting, the same union leader told me, "You don't understand the definition of collective bargaining."

I asked, "What is it?"

He said, "You do the bargaining and we do the collecting."

The levity was short-lived. I argued the League's position, which was that the mandatory employment of twenty-five musicians in theaters with 1,100 seats or more was preventing a large number of theaters from presenting musicals. Obviously, if only a dozen were needed but you had to pay twenty-five, the added cost made the show uneconomical. The union negotiator asked what I thought would be a reasonable number instead of twenty-five.

I said, "A theater like the now demolished 1,150-seat Helen Hayes should only be required to employ..."—I picked a number out of thin air—"nine."

One of the Local 802 members shouted at me indignantly, "We're losing sixteen jobs!"

I answered, "I don't follow your logic. If a musical plays at a theater with nine musicians, you're gaining nine jobs."

"No," I was told. "We've got twenty-five, so we're losing sixteen."

I asked, "When was the last time a musical played at the Helen Hayes?"

No one at the table knew. We eventually ascertained that it had been more than twenty-five years, which proved my point that when costs were excessive, musicals were not produced and musicians did not get hired.

The negotiations continued until the contract's expiration date. We failed to reach an agreement, and the union called a strike. Mediators were summoned in by the city. During the strike, when it appeared that we might reach an agreement on a disputed issue, the rump group would show up and union leaders would reject what we were close to agreeing on. The union was determined to close all the musical theaters.

After twenty-five days, and with the mediators threatening to impose a settlement, we struck an agreement. New minimums would be set for each theater, rather than basing them on a theater's specific number of seats. I called a meeting at the Booth Theatre to have the contract ratified by League members. At the meeting, Hal Prince arose, as usual with a sweater tied around his neck and hanging down his back, and glasses tipped up high on his forehead, and announced that it was the worst contract ever negotiated. It would result in the end of musical theater on Broadway, he predicted.

Stuart Ostrow, whose musical credits included Meredith Wilson's *Here's Love* as well as *The Apple Tree* and *Pippin*, seconded Hal. Ostrow even went a step further, saying he didn't need any theater for his musicals, that he could play them on rooftops, in tents, at arenas and other places. I restrained myself from telling them where to get off. The remaining League members, though, appreciated the efforts and felt we got the result we wanted. Needless to say, Hal's gloomy prediction did not cause him to leave the musical theater.

Shortly after the settlement, I felt my position was vindicated. *Rodgers & Hart* opened at the Helen Hayes Theatre with nine musicians. It was the birth of the small musical on Broadway, which flourishes to this day.

———•◦•———

The theater business is tough enough when you have to deal with actors, directors, choreographers, writers, composers, and producers, especially considering that some have egos the size of Times Square, but none are in the same league as unions when the unions are looking for a fight.

In 1993, orchestra minimums were again a major issue in collective-bargaining negotiations with the musicians' Local 802. The minimums had not been changed since the 1975 agreement. We contended that they were outdated and did not reflect changes in the music business, such as new music and sounds, and technological advances making it possible to replicate the sounds of musical instruments.

Historically, Local 802 had adamantly buried its head in the sand when it came to adopting new technologies. I was still chairman of the League's negotiating committee, and at our first committee meeting that January, I told our members that the only way to get cuts in the minimums was to be prepared to perform in the event of a strike. I said I didn't care how they performed—using new technology or recorded music, employing student musicians from conservatories, or finding some other means—as long as the show went on.

At each monthly meeting, I raised the issue, and representatives from every musical show assured me they would be ready to perform. The score of *Cats* especially lent itself to the new technology, so we put it into a computer. The result was so successful that we did a demonstration at the Winter Garden Theatre and invited union members to attend. I reassured the union that we had no desire to eliminate live music. We simply needed to reduce antiquated minimums negotiated for a different musical sound and that we needed to consider modern technology.

Around the same time, during the summer of 1993, relations between the stagehands' union and the musicians' union were severely strained. The New York City stagehands' union Local 1 had arranged to hold its hundredth-anniversary celebration at the Metropolitan Opera House. They hired the Metropolitan Opera's entire union orchestra, and also arranged for the U.S. Air Force Band to perform on the plaza of Lincoln Center.

A few days before the celebration, Local 1 headquarters received a call from the business agent for the musicians' Local 802. He informed them that if they were going to use the Air Force Band—which, of course, was nonunion—they would have to hire an equal number of union musicians. That would mean paying twenty to thirty people to do little more than stand around. The Local 1 representative told the Local 802 man, "You must be kidding."

The Local 802 man assured him, "No kidding is involved."

To which the Local 1 man replied, "Go fuck yourself." And the celebration went on without any union musicians on the plaza.

So, taking a cue from Local 1's stand, at a critical point in the negotiations I announced that if the union struck the musicals, we would perform. But when I later polled committee members from the Broadway musicals, just to be sure, none said they would perform. I was shocked. I had been done in by my own committee. Forced to bluff my way with the union, the best I could accomplish was a reduction of minimums for the smaller Broadway theaters. Minimums in the larger theaters remained the same. At that point, I resolved never again to chair or participate in any labor negotiations on behalf of the League. And I kept my word.

Eventually, after I was no longer directly involved in labor negotiations, it would take a five-day strike and the closure of all Broadway musicals in March 2003 to get a significant reduction in the minimums. Local 802 resisted cuts to the very end, despite the fact that the League abandoned its original position to eliminate all minimums. Finally, the union agreed to smaller minimums in all theaters.

But negotiations were acrimonious from the start. To a great extent, the war was waged in the press. League members claimed they possessed the equivalent of an atomic bomb—a virtual orchestra—and that their goal was to eliminate all minimums. The union responded to this threat by mounting a successful public-relations campaign, claiming that the League was out to kill live music. They urged fellow unions to help save jobs by respecting picket lines in the event of a strike.

Both the League and Local 802 held their breath up to the moment of the strike, waiting to see what the other unions would do. Their decision turned out to be unanimous. They would not cross Local 802's picket lines. Ultimately, the strike was settled when Mayor Michael Bloomberg called the parties to a meeting at Gracie Mansion. Negotiations continued throughout the night, and a settlement was reached. New minimums were agreed on for each Broadway theater.

It was also agreed that minimums would be fixed and nonnegotiable for a period of ten years. The subject of minimums is currently comatose, but it will arise again one day, without a doubt.

TWENTY-SIX

ACTING FOR WOODY

As chairman of the Shubert Organization, I felt that my career prospects were solid enough, but when a second career unexpectedly appeared on the horizon in the early 1980s, I jumped at it. I was going to become a movie star.

Paula Herold, who had once worked for Shubert, called to say she was working for Juliet Taylor, a leading casting agent, and wanted to put me in a movie. I asked whose movie she was referring to.

She answered, "Woody Allen."

I immediately said, "I'm interested." Of course, I also wanted to know what the movie was about.

She said she couldn't say.

I asked, "Who's in it?"

She said she couldn't say.

I asked her, "What's my part?"

She said she couldn't say.

What she could say was that she would send me my "sides"—that is, not the entire script, but pages indicating my part—and that I should be at the Old Homestead Steakhouse in lower Manhattan for my first scene at eight the next morning. She told me what to wear and said to bring a change of clothes to shoot a second scene at the Starlight Roof of the Waldorf-Astoria Hotel.

Since I was in show business, it was only natural that I asked, "What time will the car pick me up?"

"Oh," she said, "We don't have a car for you in the budget."

Having been in the business long enough to understand the meaning of *capricious*, I told her, "Since I'm working for scale and I don't need the job, if there is no car, I'm not going."

She relented and promised me a car. When I got home that night, at about ten o'clock, several pages were waiting for me, with my part indicated on them. But everything was out of context. None of it made sense. I started to read, but since I knew nothing about the movie, I didn't know who I was playing. After trying to memorize my lines, I gave up. I simply could not make heads or tails of my part.

The next morning, a beat-up old car came to pick me up. When I arrived at the restaurant, I was directed first to the makeup truck parked in the street, and I was powdered and brushed. Then I returned to the restaurant, leaving my other clothes in the makeup truck. The restaurant was filled with extras sitting at tables. I sat where I was told to, and Nick Appollo Forte, who was playing the washed-up lounge singer Lou Canova, came over to run through our lines. Only when we started to read the lines did I discover my role. I was a theatrical agent named Sid Bacharach who is trying to steal Canova from a rival talent manager, Danny Rose, played by Woody Allen.

My other scene partner was Mia Farrow, the movie's leading lady and then Woody's girlfriend. So Mia, Nick, and I read our scene together. Mia's line was, "Why are you planning to replace Danny?" And my reply line was, "Business is business."

I decided this movie-star thing was easy.

But Nick yelled at me, "You're not saying it right. You've got to say it with real menace."

A few tries later, I was so menacing that blood was dripping from my teeth.

Places were called. And the camera started to roll. When it came time for me to say my line, I did it the way I thought I was supposed to—menacingly.

"No, no, no," Woody cried out, and ran over to me. "Not like that! You're a nice guy."

I felt like a fool, and we redid the scene several times before I transformed back into my usual gentle sweetheart self.

Later, Nick asked me, "What do you do?"

I told him I worked in the theater. He replied, with pride, that he had never seen a Broadway show. I suddenly realized what a dummy I was for taking his direction.

The next day, we shot the scene at the Starlight Roof of the Waldorf. Howard Cosell, the famous television sportscaster, was in the scene but

With James M. Nederlander, Bernie Jacobs, Nelle Nugent, Liz McCann, and the cast of *Dreamgirls. Photo by C. J. Zumwalt, courtesy of the Shubert Archive*

With (left to right) James M. Nederlander, Bernie Jacobs, Nelle Nugent, and Elizabeth McCann on the set of *The Life and Adventures of Nicholas Nickleby. Photo by Martha Swope © Billy Rose Theatre Division, The New York Library for the Performing Arts*

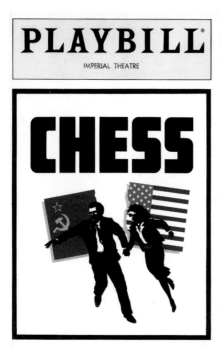

Chess Playbill. *Photofest, used by permission of Playbill®*

Director Trevor Nunn. *Courtesy of the Shubert Archive*

Benny Andersson, Bjorn Ulvaeus, and Tim Rice in London celebrating the decision to do *Chess*. *Photo by Anders Hanser © Premium Rockshot*

With Bernie Jacobs and Jerome Robbins.
Photo by Aubrey Reuben, courtesy of the Shubert Archive

Alec Baldwin and Jessica Lange in
*A Streetcar Named Desire. Photo by
Brigitte Lacombe/Photofest*

Jude Law and Kathleen Turner in *Indiscretions.*
© Joan Marcus

Donna Murphy in *Passion.*
© Joan Marcus

With Stephen Sondheim and Donna Murphy during *Passion*.
Courtesy of James Lapine

With Stephen Sondheim and Scott Rudin.
Photo by Aubrey Reuben, courtesy of the Shubert Archive

With Mia Farrow on the set during filming for *Broadway Danny Rose*, 1984.
Photofest

Some of the fun days with Betty, Bernie, and Pat.
© *Anita & Steve Shevett*

With Hal Prince.

Producer Rocco Landesman.

With Jimmy Nederlander.
© Anita & Steve Shevett, courtesy of the Shubert Archive

showed up late. They said he was delayed in his room on another floor in the hotel. He got a room. I got a rent-a-wreck car to pick me up.

Before we shot the scene, Mia came over to say, "Woody thinks you're very good."

I modestly accepted the compliment. After we shot the scene, Woody came over and asked if I had ever acted before. When I said no, he said, "Well, you're very good." I told him I was pleased for his sake. We then shot two more scenes, one of which was cut from the movie.

Several months later, I heard that a screening of the film was scheduled. I phoned Woody's agent, my old friend Sam Cohn, to get tickets. But Sam told me he couldn't give me any because it was a press preview. I told Sam that if I was asking for too much, especially after I'd done this for scale, to forget about my request. He never came up with the tickets.

The screening was being held at a movie theater in the Plaza Hotel. By coincidence, the cashier there knew Pat and had once told her that if she ever needed anything, just to ask. So Pat asked for two tickets. The cashier got them but warned us that we should be the last ones in, just in case they ran out of seats. We waited outside while everyone filed in. I knew a good number of the people attending, and when they spotted us, they said, "Come on in, sit with us." I had to confess, "We can't because we don't have seats."

When my scene came up, there were loud laughs of recognition. I thought to myself, "A star is born."

The movie was *Broadway Danny Rose*, and praise poured in for my portrayal of Sid Bacharach.

Harriet Slaughter, from the League of New York Theatres and Producers, wrote, "How about letting me be your manager? I'll get you billing above the title next time, and your very own limo."

Sid Garfield in producer Alex Cohen's office decided, "You were never lovelier." Eventually I heard that Alex was getting cast in a movie, and I assured everyone that if he won an Oscar, I would never, ever, speak to them again.

Kathrin Seitz at CBS Theatrical Films told me, "You're very sexy." I agreed, but then wondered, "Only in *Broadway Danny Rose*, or in general?"

Michael Branton, vice president at Lorimar Productions, asked, "After *Broadway Danny Rose*, can *Dallas* be far behind?"

Playwright Jerome Alden informed me, "I have written a new one-character play about Abraham Lincoln, and since you already know the

Gettysburg Address, it wouldn't be too hard for you to learn the rest of the million lines."

Then came an offer from Harry Gould Jr, chairman of the board of Cinema Group. "What is your availability, if and when we do *Flashdance II*?"

I answered, "I am available for *Flashdance II, III, IV, V* or anything else you can think of. I have been maintaining a low profile for some time but have decided it wasn't worth it."

A year or so later, I was at a restaurant, standing at the bar waiting to be seated with my party, when who walked right past me but Woody Allen. I said, "Hello, Woody," but he didn't even look at me. So I walked over to his table. As soon as I got there, he hissed at me, "Never call out my name in public."

His latest picture had just come out. "I just came over to tell you how much I liked *The Purple Rose of Cairo*. He thanked me, peered closely into my face, and asked, "Can you play a doctor?"

I responded, "You know my work."

He asked me if I would be free in September. I said sure, and he told me he would call me. He never did. That movie was *Hannah and Her Sisters*, and my part was stolen from me by Benno Schmidt, then president of Yale University. I have hardly seen Woody since. But that almost wasn't the end of my movie career. Paula Herold called me again, this time to say she had another movie for me, and this time I had a major part. I told her, "I want to read the entire script, because I don't want to be in just any movie."

She couldn't believe I had become so difficult, but said she would send it to me anyway. I read the script and thought it was like a couple of other movies I'd seen, *Greystoke* and *The Gods Must Be Crazy*." I didn't care for it. I gave it to Pat to read.

She read it and said, "If there's going to be a gorgeous leading lady or a great director, do it. But without that, what do you need it for?"

I didn't know how gorgeous the leading lady would be, didn't know how great the director was, and all I knew about the leading man was that he did Qantas commercials. Pat's advice confirmed my opinion, and I said no to my second movie. My part was the newspaper-publisher father of a reporter who goes to Australia to do a story about a guy who lives in the bush.

The film was *Crocodile Dundee*.

TWENTY-SEVEN

A FAMILY GETAWAY AND
SOME SHOW-BIZ FIGHTS

While Pat and I loved living in the city—we had long since moved from Peter Cooper Village to Central Park South—we were fortunate enough to have friends with houses in the Hamptons and Martha's Vineyard. We also traveled to Europe every year. When we wanted to get away for a week or two, there was always someplace we could go. We never wanted a summer house, because Pat was working, and I was working, and Carrie would go away to camp. But Carrie grew up, got married, and had two children. One July Fourth weekend, while Pat and I were in the Vineyard, I phoned Carrie in New York and found her in a playground with her two then-very-young children, alone. I didn't like that. Pat said to me, "It's time we bought a house."

In August 1987, we rented a house in East Hampton. I took a few weeks off and was out there for a while. Whenever I took time off, I found it easy to relax. I have the ability to turn things off inside my head. The office would send faxes every fifteen minutes until I would pick up the phone and say, "Enough already."

We had a good time that month, but we didn't always enjoy seeing the same people we saw in the city. Pat and I decided the Hamptons were not for us. We also visited friends in Connecticut, and Pat thought the area was beautiful. Roger Berlind introduced us to his real-estate agent, and the first day that she took Pat to look at places, Pat found a house she loved. There was only one bedroom, but there were two barns, one of which was used as a three-car garage. Our grandchildren were young, and we wanted something they could enjoy too, so we renovated the house, added four more bedrooms, and put in a pool.

In my typical nervousness, I worried that perhaps we couldn't afford it. I have always been insecure about money. When we were newlyweds, most of our friends had much more money than we did, and were able to hire domestic help. Many moved to the suburbs, out to Long Island or up to Westchester, where their parents bought them $35,000 houses with an acre each of land. We remained in Peter Cooper Village. I always felt like we were the poor ones. I often told Pat, "If only we had enough money to take taxis whenever we wanted."

Since I was head of Shubert, everyone thought I had loads and loads of money. But during my entire career, I was always a hired hand. Because the business was owned by the Shubert Foundation, the New York attorney general in power was constantly looking over my shoulder, checking on salaries and perks, always concerned that the foundation make as much as possible.

What's more, neither Bernie nor I ever invested privately in a show. Acting for Shubert, we were the lead producers on many coproductions, and coproducers of many others. We were solicited almost daily by producers and general managers to invest in upcoming productions. They weren't necessarily looking for our expertise; they were looking for Shubert money, because a Shubert investment was a sort of stamp of approval that would entice others to invest.

Bernie and I were never "angels." We were always salaried employees of the Shubert Organization, and in that capacity we always wore our corporate hats. For us to personally profit from a show, I believed, would have taken profits away from the Shubert Foundation. We were paid to make money for the organization and the foundation. Any personal gain would have been a conflict of interest. I was paid a good salary, yes, but I still worried about money.

We go to our country house for Thanksgiving, and the week between Christmas and New Year's. We also go there for weekends in the summer. Pat drives up on Friday afternoons, but I don't usually get there until late Friday evening. She goes out to dinner and usually returns to find me in the kitchen eating a tuna-fish sandwich. We drive back to the city together early on Sunday evenings. I have come to love the house, and even though our grandchildren have grown up, whenever Pat asks me if I want to sell it, I say no. I like the status quo.

———•·•———

Change is not my mantra, and I think people in the theater world who know me understand that. I also like to think that they see me as even-tempered and relatively easy to get along with. My office door is always open, and people drop by all the time just to say hello or chat. I see them all. Why not? The theater community is a very small world, and bad blood doesn't serve anyone's interest.

Even though I don't go looking for fights, I have never shied away when a fight came looking for me. On rare occasions, arguments became so heated that they stopped just short of turning physical, and that was once the case between Manny Azenberg and me.

A general manager–producer, Manny learned his trade at the office of David Merrick. He left the theater for a spell to work at Madison Square Garden. But he eventually returned to Broadway and became a general manager, as well as Bernie's daily caller. They were friends, although the friendship wouldn't last. Manny comported himself as one of the theater's spokesmen and moralists. He conducted seminars for new producers and was an active member of the Broadway League. He was also, supposedly, devoted to Bernie.

One important principle of Manny's credo was that theater owners did not deserve to be paid rent. They should consider themselves lucky if their theaters are occupied and if the show covers the costs of maintaining and operating the theater. His view had considerable support from others in the business. After all, who would not want to get a theater for nothing?

Manny was also an endless source of fascinating tidbits, which he confided to Bernie. And Bernie loved gossip. As a result of their friendship and Manny's emerging reputation as a Broadway producer, we selected him to be our general manager and a coproducer of many of our later productions including *Children of a Lesser God, Sunday in the Park with George, Jerome Robbins' Broadway*, and *Sarafina!*

In 1978, Manny approached us about a show called *Ain't Misbehavin'*, which was being presented at the Off-Off-Broadway not-for-profit Manhattan Theatre Club. Bernie and I went to the theater, saw the show, and agreed to coproduce it with Manny and three others. It was the first in a series of plays that would involve Manny.

While we were planning that production, I received a surprise call from Leonard Goldenson, chairman of ABC, who said that ABC wanted to get involved with us as a partner. We were delighted to hear this but told Leonard that we would accept on two conditions: that he matched our investment, and that he agreed to invest in all our future productions.

He concurred, and until recently ABC, its immediate successor, Capital Cities/ABC, and its ultimate successor, Disney, were our partners, investing amounts equal to ours, and sharing in profits and losses with us and our other equal partners. This arrangement lasted until 2003, with our production of *Amour*.

Ain't Misbehavin', a small musical, turned out to be a massive hit, running for 1,604 performances, and also had a successful road tour in America and abroad, except in London.

The show was significant for two reasons. It started a new policy whereby not-for-profit theaters were granted royalty and net-profit participation for any production initially presented in their theaters. Also, it was the first in a string of sixteen shows that involved Shubert and Manny.

One of our later coproductions with Manny was the Lincoln Center Theater's South African musical *Sarafina!* The musical, which originated during apartheid at the Market Theatre in Johannesburg, opened at our Cort Theatre in January 1988, where it ran for 597 performances. And after a very successful run, we gave Manny the touring rights for the show.

On top of that, however, he asked if we would guarantee him against any loss if he presented *Sarafina!* at our National Theatre in Washington. I told him I did not think so, and was secretly annoyed that he would even request such a guarantee. Bernie agreed with me. But this became moot when Manny suddenly announced that he would present the show at the National only if we matched the terms he had already negotiated, without our knowledge, with Washington's Kennedy Center.

That was the end of Manny as far as Bernie was concerned, and Bernie never refrained from telling anyone just what he thought. After the *Sarafina!* feud, Manny left Bernie's fold and set up headquarters at the Nederlander offices. Manny was friendly with our competitor Jimmy Nederlander Sr., but certainly not to the extent he had been with Bernie. Things became so bitter among us that, at one Broadway League meeting, when I defended Bernie during an acrimonious discussion, Manny jumped up and screamed that he was going to punch me in the mouth. He even walked around the table and came face-to-face with me, quivering with rage.

I said, "Hit me, go ahead and hit me."

By then people on my side of the table restrained us, but the feud continued. It may have been high-school antics, but I wasn't going to just walk away.

As I've said, I am not one to pick a fight, nor am I one to retreat. My altercation with British actor Patrick Stewart, probably best known for his role as Captain Jean-Luc Picard in the television series *Star Trek: The Next Generation*, is another example.

Patrick Stewart entered my life back in 1988, in connection with Peter Shaffer's *Yonadab*. The play had come to Patrick's attention, and he pursued Peter and me to produce it in New York with him in the title role. This campaign lasted for several years but never came to fruition. Many years later, Patrick came to New York to star in the Shakespeare Festival's Public Theater production of Arthur Miller's *The Ride Down Mt. Morgan*, a play about a man leading a double life. It did not receive outstanding reviews, and no one tried to acquire the rights to produce it on Broadway.

Still, Patrick was determined to see a Broadway production of Miller's play—starring, of course, Patrick Stewart—and mounted a full-court press to convince me to produce it. I was lukewarm about the script, yet gave in, thinking that Patrick would be an instant box-office success and that he and Arthur Miller would carry the day.

We opened on April 9, 2000, at our Ambassador Theatre. Reviews were respectable but not box-office raves. We did very well during the run's first weeks, but the show was rapidly losing advance ticket sales, and empty seats loomed in the near future. I felt obligated to tell Patrick about the bleak prospects, not wanting him to be surprised when he walked on stage and looked out to a sparse audience. He seemed puzzled by the news, but there was no further discussion. Shortly thereafter, I had to go to Los Angeles.

On the Saturday evening, I returned to my hotel room at about five thirty p.m. Los Angeles time. Curtains were up in New York; the shows were underway. Pat and I were going to dinner and the theater that night, so we were in a bit of a hurry when we got a call from the stage manager of *The Ride Down Mt. Morgan*. During the bows at the matinee performance, she said, Patrick had announced from the stage that since his producers were not promoting the play, he was personally asking the audience to spread the word about how marvelous it was and urge others to attend. What's more, she said, Patrick intended to repeat his little speech at the end of that evening's performance, and again after the Sunday performance.

I had never heard of such outrageous behavior, and I told the stage manager to tell Patrick during the intermission, "Under no circumstances are you to repeat this announcement." I said to her, "After you speak to him, call me back." I then asked for his dressing-room phone number so that I could call him myself when the show was over. Pat and I missed our dinner and the play.

An hour or so later, when the manager called back, she said Patrick had screamed at her to leave his dressing room. He said he didn't want to hear anything more from her. Apparently, he repeated his little speech that night. I placed a call to Alan Eisenberg, the executive director of Actors' Equity. It was now close to ten p.m. in New York, and Alan wasn't in. I left a message on his answering machine, asking him to call me regarding an urgent matter.

Meanwhile, our press agent called to say that Patrick's California representative, Kelly Bush, had alerted the New York press to attend the Sunday matinee, after which an important event would take place.

With an eye on the clock, I waited for the curtain to come down in New York, then dialed Patrick's dressing-room phone. When he finally picked up, on the fourth ring, I told him, "You have committed one of the most unprofessional acts I have ever experienced."

He screamed at me that I was calling him unprofessional and hung up the phone.

At around twelve fifteen that Saturday night, Alan Eisenberg phoned back. I explained what had happened and asked him to call Patrick. I said, "You must warn him not repeat his curtain speech at Sunday's performance."

Apparently Patrick got the message and refrained from making any further announcements. But on Monday, the New York papers were filled with news about the occurrences at the Ambassador Theatre. The news even spread throughout the country and abroad.

Not only were Patrick's comments totally unwarranted, but so were those of Arthur Miller, who announced his complete support of Patrick's position.

I asked for an accounting of the total amount we had spent to promote the show, broken down into print media, radio, and television
expenditures. It came to a significant sum. I also ascertained that it was
the only dramatic show airing a television commercial. So, that Monday
morning, I filed a charge with Actors' Equity demanding an apology
from Patrick. Later that day, I received a telephone call from Sam Cohn,
Patrick's agent, asking if I would meet with him and Patrick on Tuesday
morning.

I asked Sam, "Do you have a written apology to present to me?" He
said he didn't. "Then I'm not interested in seeing either you or Patrick."

Sam called back a few hours later, asking me to meet with him,
Patrick, and Arthur Miller. I again asked, "Do you have a written apology
for me?"

"No," he answered. "But . . . you won't meet with Arthur Miller?"

I said, "Not until I receive a written apology."

No meeting took place. I then decided to have the cast assemble in a
semicircle on the stage at the conclusion of the Tuesday evening performance. Patrick was in the middle. I was on the fringe, facing the cast. I
said that while I had never divulged financial data to a cast, under the
circumstances I felt it necessary to do so. I spelled out the exact amount
we had spent, which happened to be more than for most plays, and
reminded them that we were the only dramatic play to have a television
commercial. Without once looking at Patrick—as I far as I was concerned,
he was a nonperson at the gathering—I said, "We support the play
completely, and I know you will do so as well."

Their response was warm and encouraging.

An Equity hearing on the charge was scheduled for the following
Thursday. In the meantime, Sam phoned to read me a statement purport-
ing to be an apology from Patrick. To use a legal phrase, it amounted to
a plea in confession and avoidance. Patrick admitted to having said
what he had, but then proceeded to try to justify his actions. A copy of
the purported apology was also sent to Equity, along with a note from
me saying that this did not constitute an apology. They readily agreed.
So we had a hearing, and I stated our case.

Patrick sat there with a legal pad on which he had written about
seven pages of comment. He spoke and again made a plea in confession
and avoidance. Except, this time he buttressed the avoidance portion by

stating that what he did was common practice in the English theater. Later, I phoned Robert Fox and Bill Kenwright and told them what Patrick had said. They both maintained they'd never heard anything like that in their careers. They agreed that "Patrick has some fucking nerve to do what he did."

Equity rendered a decision and instructed Patrick to furnish me with a written apology. Shortly thereafter, Patrick began telling people how upset he was and that he hoped he and I could be friends.

That will never happen, I assured those same people. "I will not have anything to do with him, either professionally or otherwise."

So it is to this day. As far as the play's fate, it did not sell out during the rest of its run, nor did it recoup the investment. It did, however, sell a large number of tickets at the discount ticket booth in Duffy Square. We all know the aphorism "No good deed goes unpunished." My reward for producing the play, losing a large amount of money, affording it a theater and an outstanding physical production, cast, and staff, at least to me confirms the veracity of that saying.

One of our partners in the production was noted film and Broadway producer Scott Rudin. Several months after the Equity decision, Scott was in the middle of preparing a movie and called to say that Patrick's California agent, Kelly Bush, had contacted him. Apparently, she wanted to tell Scott how pleased she was that one of her clients would be working in his new movie. But Scott said he never wanted to lay eyes on her again and that if she came within a thousand feet of where he was shooting, he would have her arrested for trespassing.

It's unfortunate that, in the theater, business relationships become strained for any number of reasons. A producer refuses to book a show with us because we don't have a theater they find desirable. Or the booking terms are not to the producer's liking. Or we have disappointed the producer. Or the producer has disappointed us on some prior occasion. But the business has relatively few players, and slights are often overlooked simply because of the need to get work done. Certain actions, however, go beyond the pale, and such was the Patrick Stewart episode.

TWENTY-EIGHT

THE WORST OF TIMES

In late April 1986, at six thirty a.m., I received a phone call from Betty Jacobs. She said, "I think something is wrong with Bernie."

I asked right away, "What happened?"

She said Bernie was acting very strangely. I rushed over to their place as soon as I could. Bernie was sitting on the edge of his bed in his pajamas. He was disoriented and kept asking me what time it was. Each time I gave him an answer, he repeated the question. By this time, Betty had called Bernie's regular doctor, who made arrangements to have him examined by a neurologist.

At New York Hospital, a doctor took me aside to speak privately about Bernie, who was then around seventy. I told him about Bernie's family, his behavior patterns, his pride in his memory, his skills as a lawyer and businessman, our relationship, and his hypochondria. The doctor then asked Bernie to come into his office and posed some simple questions, such as who's the president of the United States. Bernie couldn't accurately answer any of the questions.

Later that afternoon, the doctor phoned to say that Bernie was suffering from transient global amnesia, a rather common occurrence, and assured me it would improve within twenty-four to forty-eight hours.

Bernie started to recover. I could discuss matters with him, and he was able to resume labor negotiations. His reasoning was intact but his memory was not the same. He became withdrawn, and in no way like the old Bernie, my partner, my friend and fellow sufferer. I urged him to see a psychiatrist to no avail. Bernie carried some sort of pills with him, but they were ineffective. Nevertheless, during these years I never hesitated to discuss problems with Bernie and listen to his opinions. We made decisions together as we always had done.

Bernie was a statesman of the theater, and his contributions to Shubert and the industry are well known and respected. He was an active Broadway League participant and a major voice in the business of the theater. He was generous in his dealings with producers and supportive of their shows. He was a unique talent. Even after his "episode," Bernie continued to chair League meetings, but as the years went on, some colleagues became increasingly aware of Bernie's memory problems.

Alan Eisenberg, who chaired a particularly long and protracted negotiation on behalf of Equity, was a great admirer of Bernie's. He never made an issue of Bernie's memory lapses, and indeed he and other Equity members supported Bernie. However, I too was growing increasingly concerned.

I knew I could still rely on Bernie, and I believed he was capable of chairing union meetings, but I felt he didn't need the strain or the responsibility. I reminded him that I had resolved not to conduct any union negotiations and suggested that he do the same. I honestly believed I had convinced him. Unfortunately, I had not. He suddenly announced that he would chair a round of negotiations.

Things only got worse from there. A group of League members consisting of Michael David, Edgar Dobie, Alan Wasser, Herschel Waxman, and Manny Azenberg met with Bernie. Bernie, Phil, and I called them "the Gang of Five." Couching the terms as best they could, they told Bernie that they did not want him to conduct negotiations.

Bernie was crushed. It would have been one thing if I had been able to talk him out of it. But to be done in by his own group, and embarrassed in front of the union that loved and respected him, was the ultimate insult. As far as I was concerned, the Gang of Five's action was intolerable, so much so that it drove me to change my position and tell Bernie he should conduct the negotiations. Which he did.

When they were finished, Bernie announced that he would no longer chair any negotiations, leaving the League to conduct them without him or me for the first time since we started in the business.

———•◦•———

But that was not the final chapter concerning League union matters. This time there would be serious effects on my health. In late spring 1996, three years after I stopped conducting union negotiations, I received a call from a *New York Times* reporter asking about the role

Bernie and I had played as advisors to various unions' pension and welfare funds. Apparently, an unnamed "disgruntled associate" had gone to the *Times* with public tax records listing fees we had been paid. I was asked: "How much money are you and Bernie paid as counsel? How long have you represented the employer trustees? Who appointed you? Do League members know about your roles?"

I told the reporter that the payments were proper and well known by both League and union officials. I said, in no uncertain terms, "Our work for the union funds was no secret." I then added, "I see no impropriety in receiving a fee. If it was not a proper activity, I wouldn't do it."

Irving Cheskin, who was the League's director for pension and welfare matters, was quoted in the article as saying, "It's been going on a long, long time because we asked them to."

In fact, we'd been advising the funds since the 1960s. When the foundation took over the business and I became chairman, the League and the unions asked us to continue because, as Irving was quoted saying in the article, "We all felt there should be no change."

But the article's general tone was accusatory and took the position that our dual roles were in violation of the 1974 Employee Retirement Income Security Act.

While no one involved with the League or the union funds seemed to object to our role, the article explained that "many other producers, theater owners and stage executives voiced surprise, calling it unusual and saying that it posed questions of conflict of interest."

Those producers, theater owners, and stage executives were unnamed and otherwise unidentified. I was astounded by the nastiness of the article. We immediately consulted our attorneys and received confirmation that, since our services had been requested, our fees were reasonable, and all parties involved knew what we were doing, there was no conflict of interest and no violation of the statute.

After getting that clean bill of health from our own attorneys, and somewhat encouraged by the fact that the *Times* article also reported that, according to federal officials, "Mr. Schoenfeld and Mr. Jacobs were not the subjects of any pending case," I told Bernie we should resign as counsel to all the funds. Bernie agreed. And we did.

A Labor Department inquiry was in fact opened, but was not pursued. The reason it wasn't pursued was because we clearly had done nothing wrong. The matter ended, but not without lasting ill feelings on Bernie's and my part. But especially on my part. It affected me so badly that I had a breakdown.

Too much was happening at the same time. Pat's sister, who had been briefly ill with cancer, died that spring of 1996. Pat and Cynthia had always been very close. It was a difficult time for Pat and piled even more pressure on us both. We were also in the middle of a stressful move. After thirty-three years on Central Park South, we had decided to buy an apartment uptown. Never one to wear out a pair of shoes looking for a pair of shoes, Pat found an apartment she loved on a Monday, I saw it on Wednesday, and we bought it on Friday. Paying for it, in addition to the upkeep on the Connecticut house, only added to my anxieties.

I simply could not cope. I tried to be supportive to Pat, but I quickly went down the tubes. At one point, we were planning to fly to San Diego to see a show. But I was incapable of making a decision. I told Pat, "I can't go." She said, "Yes, you can." I agreed to go, then changed my mind and said, "I can't." She promised to come along. I said that would be fine, and then promptly talked myself out of it. I was seeing a psychiatrist, but he wasn't helping much. The best he could do was to tell Pat, "You've got to take over because Jerry is in very bad shape."

We both knew that. The accusations in the *Times* and the possibility of a full-blown Labor Department investigation, Pat's sister's death, Bernie's health problems, plus the stress of moving...I just couldn't handle it all.

I did go to San Diego, and Pat came along, but it was hell for us both. Carrie at least saw what Pat and I could not. She told her mother, "Dad's been here before. He'll go to the brink, but something will stop him; it always does. He will always perform."

Carrie's insight made Pat a little less frightened. But I didn't know which way to turn, what was right, what was wrong. I couldn't eat, sleep, or think. Everything frightened me. I was panicky. I wasn't sure I could make any decision or take any action. And I didn't know if either of us would ever come out of this dark tunnel.

A friend who had been through depression recognized how serious mine was and suggested I see a noted psychiatrist he knew, who happened to be on vacation in Westport, Connecticut. He phoned the doctor, who said, "Tell him to come up immediately."

I was in Westport the next day. We talked for a long time, and he promised he could straighten me out in eight to ten weeks. He also said that if I had come earlier, it would only have taken four to six weeks. Interestingly, he said my psychological condition had been determined by the time I was seven. I couldn't wait to fill the prescriptions he gave me.

Unlike prescriptions from previous doctors, these were not narcotics. He gave me a cocktail of vitamins and antidepressants, some sleeping pills, and some thyroid medication. It wasn't long before I was sleeping again.

The full effect of the medication hadn't yet kicked in when we received devastating news. Betty Jacobs called to say that Bernie had been rushed to the hospital and needed to undergo two heart bypass surgeries. Bernie survived the first, but the second surgery, on August 26, 1996, led to a fatal stroke. Bernie died the next morning.

————•◦•————

Deep down, we all knew the high risk involved in the two operations. Still, Bernie's death was totally unexpected. I was not at all prepared for it, nor were others in the Shubert Organization, or his friends and colleagues in the theater. My depression only deepened.

The void created by Bernie's death had to be filled, and I had to do so immediately. No one could really take on Bernie's unique role and discharge his duties. I couldn't add all his responsibilities to my own. I would have to restructure the work functions of some of the company's executives. I notified the board members and gave them my recommendations regarding the delegation of Bernie's responsibilities.

I nominated Phil Smith, our executive vice president, to become president and a member of the board of directors. I knew Phil was anxious to move into Bernie's office across the hall from mine, but it took months before I was emotionally ready to allow him to do so. Phil's duties would include negotiating booking contracts with various general managers and producers, selecting heads of various departments and their subordinates in our theaters, participating with League members in collective-bargaining negotiations in New York—and with Peter Entin, our head of theater operations, in cities where we operate theaters—and booking our road theaters.

I assumed sole responsibility for booking shows and selecting theaters, for embarking on new productions and investing in the productions of others. I created a new department, which I named Creative

Development, and initially staffed it with Dessie Moynihan and an assistant. Dessie proved to be an excellent choice. With a PhD in theater and experience teaching at Sarah Lawrence College, she was a valuable assistant to me, and was well liked and respected by the creative people in the theater.

Robert Wankel, who was already CFO, took over Phil's job as executive vice president. Phil's expertise in box-office management and the sale and distribution of tickets enabled him to work closely with Bob in managing Telecharge, our computerized ticketing system, and, subsequently in expanding the Telecharge operations to new venues, restaurants, hotels, and service organizations. I delegated additional responsibilities to Bob, including managing our nontheatrical real estate, our financial portfolios, and our extensive insurance coverage.

The roles and duties of the company's executives in charge of our various departments expanded and became more complex. A number of senior executives were elevated to vice president in view of their added responsibilities. I also made a point of repairing my relationship with our competitor Jimmy Nederlander. And I reestablished a cordial association with my old antagonist Manny Azenberg.

True to the new psychiatrist's word, relief came in about ten weeks. For the first time in a very long time, when I walked down the street I began to feel free: free from tension, from anxieties, from the failures that I saw as my own.

I stopped personalizing failures and accepted that when I made a decision and it didn't work out, it was not my personal failure. Maybe it was the failure of a show, or of a division, or of a hundred different causes. But it wasn't personally Jerry Schoenfeld's failure. Plus, all I had to do was make another decision. I was a new person. I didn't recognize that new person, but I sure loved him. I have been completely satisfied with my happy ending. But I still wonder why I was afflicted with this condition and what I might have been able to accomplish if anxiety had not plagued me for most of my life.

Of course, I will never know. On one hand, it's unfortunate that I suffered from the depression that drove me to the psychiatrist's office. On the other hand, if I had not experienced it, I might never have appreciated what it really means to enjoy the pleasures of life.

———•◦•———

I still miss Bernie. In his obituary, the *New York Times* described him as a man with sad, dark-rimmed eyes and the look of a basset hound, "a basset hound who could tell any potential master to take a walk."

They wrote: "A somber man, sparing and blunt with his words, Mr. Jacobs very much coveted his privacy. He rarely granted interviews, and his name seldom appears in books about the theater. But behind the scenes, he exercised untold influence."

Although Bernie often kept his emotions buttoned up, the *Times* said, he could be full of enthusiasm. "But he did not let that enthusiasm carry him away into a financial mistake. He was most persuasive in business dealings, a demon in contract negotiations. Sam Cohn, the theatrical agent, said that negotiating with Mr. Jacobs was like 'the worst migraine you've ever had in your life.' Mr. Jacobs never hesitated to speak what was on his mind. His reply to Mr. Cohn's comment was, 'I don't like Sam.'"

My lifelong friend and lifelong partner, Bernie Jacobs, was eighty years old.

TWENTY-NINE

CLEANING UP TIMES SQUARE: PART I

Long before I became chairman of the Shubert Organization in 1972, it was blatantly obvious to me that the health and welfare of the business depended on the health and welfare of Broadway, and that the squalid state of the theater district—especially Times Square—was a cancer that could, one day, destroy us. Times Square had been in decline for years. Pornography, prostitutes, pimps, and drug dealers, unsafe streets littered with trash, and all kinds of hustlers and criminals infested midtown Manhattan.

One problem was that the Broadway community had no collective voice. We were neither appreciated nor rewarded by our home city and state nor by the federal government for our economic, educational, entertainment, and cultural contributions. We had been left to our own resources for survival. And we were totally unprepared for the urban decay that was engulfing us. The very people who should have supported us were either apathetic or actively attacking us. Not just local politicians and City Hall, but, inadvertently, the U.S. Supreme Court.

Many small theaters, especially Off-Broadway for-profit houses, were in desperate financial straits. So when the U.S. Supreme Court began handing down decisions permitting nudity and dancing as a form of free expression, developers took notice. One real-estate developer, Irving Maidman, who owned several small theaters on West Forty-Second Street, quickly converted them and other available spaces into strip joints and burlesque houses. Nudity was in vogue. No more pasties, no more G-strings—total nudity was in. Eventually Maidman lost his properties, and I have every reason to believe that many of them fell into the hands of the Mob. But the trend he had begun seemed irreversible.

Around the same time, a spate of judicial decisions made the definition of obscenity so obscure that law enforcers and judges simply threw their hands up in despair. In turn, the city enacted an ordinance downgrading street prostitution to an offense punishable by a mere fifteen-dollar fine. As a result, New York became a magnet for hookers, and Times Square turned into New York's red-light district. Movie theaters became X-rated theaters. Old hotels became whorehouses. Dilapidated buildings became massage parlors. Vacant stores became pornographic book stores, peep-show joints, and screening houses for pornographic films.

Conditions steadily deteriorated. At its peak in the early 1970s, about 430 sex-related businesses existed in midtown Manhattan, from Thirtieth to Sixtieth Streets, from the Hudson to the East River. Going to the theater meant putting your life at risk. Things were so desperate that we moved the start of evening performances from eight thirty p.m. to seven thirty p.m. so that theatergoers could leave the neighborhood an hour earlier. When shows ended, patrons fled, and the district became a wasteland, except for people looking for sex, paying for sex, or exhibiting sex. Where in the 1920s there had been about eighty theaters in the area, by 1970 there were thirty-three.

Public reaction to the sex business in Times Square was generally that as long as it didn't affect their neighborhoods or the city's overall well-being, it wasn't their problem. But that was not our perception. I could see the cancer spreading rapidly, driving out non-sex-related businesses and driving up felony crimes.

Pat, Carrie, and I often walked through Times Square in the evenings and on weekends, and I constantly criticized everything we saw. I complained so much that I was driving Pat out of her mind. Finally, she told me, "You have three choices: shut up, move out, or do something about it."

Faced with three equally disagreeable options, I chose the latter. In the beginning, I was the lone ranger of the Times Square reclamation effort. My theater colleagues were indifferent. The media wrote that I was wasting my time, convinced that cleanup efforts would fail. I was a one-man band with no supporting players, and I knew I needed to enlist the support of local residents west of Times Square. They were the voters who elected our legislative representatives in the city and in Albany. I, like most of my colleagues, merely worked in the area and lived elsewhere.

I arranged meetings with community leaders and explained what I was hoping to do. I gave talks at the Broadway League and everywhere else I could to enlist support. I tried to allay people's general mistrust of the business community. We were perceived as not caring about residents of the area where we worked. I needed to show local residents that our interests and theirs were intertwined. I enlisted the support of the Police Department and met with our local precinct commanders. I drove around in police cars after the shows let out to get a better picture of what was going on where. I took government officials into porno establishments so they could see the conditions firsthand. I established a relationship with the priests at Holy Cross Church on Forty-Second Street and at St. Malachy's the Actors' Chapel on Forty-Ninth. Wherever I went and whenever I spoke to anyone, I made a point of never asking for anything, for myself or for the Shubert business.

When I started my campaign, I didn't know anyone in city government, and no one in city government knew me. I thought my best plan of action was to discuss the problem face-to-face with then mayor John Lindsay. But he wasn't an easy man to get to. The only person I knew who knew him was Hal Prince, so I asked Hal if he could arrange an appointment. Hal came through, and when I got to City Hall, I was greeted by the mayor and the commissioners of several city agencies.

This was a unique opportunity, and I took full advantage of it. I did not hold back. To me, this was an "apple pie, motherhood, American flag" issue. I told them that the theater district was sinking into an abyss of pornography, crime, and filth. I said people shunned the area, that tourists from all over the world were warned to avoid Times Square at all costs.

I mentioned Marriott's plans to build a hotel in the heart of the theater district and that I was in favor of the idea. I explained how this Marriott Marquis hotel project would help transform an area that had become New York's black hole. What had been the site of the Astor Theatre had turned into that strange attraction called Ripley's Believe It Or Not! and then had become a junk store. It was located on a key block, leading directly into the theater district. But the area was so dreadful that decent people stayed away. Those who did venture to the theater fled once the curtain came down.

I explained how we had had to advance curtain time to seven thirty p.m. so theatergoers could get home earlier and more safely. I told the

Mayor that Forty-Second Street was a plague infecting the entire Midtown West area. That the district was polluted by hundreds of massage parlors, peep shows, burlesques, X-rated movie houses, and pornographic book and video stores. Crime was up. Tourism was down. And the theater was endangered. I ended by saying, "It's about time the city did something."

Once that was off my chest, I thanked Mayor Lindsay for the meeting and left. I later learned that Lindsay turned to the people in the room and asked, "Who was that son of a bitch?" And in the silence that followed, he added, "You know, he's right."

Lindsay established the Times Square Task Force, made up of the commissioners of some twenty city agencies, including the police, fire, sanitation, health, buildings, and transportation departments. I got to know the commissioners and other high officials who could make the turnaround a reality.

As a corollary to these efforts, we decided to stop talking about Broadway as "the fabulous invalid" and started taking a more positive approach. We began to change how we did business with the public, making it easier for theatergoers to buy tickets. We started accepting credit cards. Up to this point, the idea of paying credit-card fees was unheard of to theater owners. Even something as obvious as reserving tickets by phone was only introduced in 1973–1974.

Once the curtain rises, an empty seat in a Broadway theater is like an empty seat in an airborne plane. It's a missed opportunity. That's why, when Mayor Lindsay called me early in 1973 to discuss a way to sell discounted tickets, I was all for it. He asked for my support to put a discount ticket booth in Times Square, proposing that the traffic island in the middle of Forty-Third Street on Broadway would be the ideal location. He also said the city had a trailer that could be used as a box office. I differed with him on the ideal location. I said the booth should be placed in Duffy Square, on Forty-Seventh Street in the center of Times Square. I picked this site because I believed it would transform Duffy Square. At the time, the square was like an outdoor flophouse. The public benches and the warm air wafting from the subway gratings attracted vagrants and prostitutes. By putting the trailer there, I believed, we could turn the area around and create a safe haven for theater patrons to purchase tickets for a variety of shows.

The deal was that the public could buy tickets at half off the box-office price, but only on the performance day. In other words, they could buy discounted tickets for seats that would otherwise go empty. The mayor agreed, and I presented the idea at a Broadway League meeting. I proposed that the booth be operated by the not-for-profit Theater Development Fund, and I volunteered Shubert's Phil Smith to provide logistical support for its operation. The booth idea was supported by most of the League's membership, and the trailer was placed in Duffy Square. The few theater owners and producers who were not on board stubbornly held out for a few years but eventually capitulated.

Shubert contributed an initial $10,000 to the Theater Development Fund, and the now-famous TKTS booth opened on June 25, 1973. It was such a success that an offshoot later opened downtown at the World Trade Center, and another at South Street Seaport. The TKTS concept has since been replicated in other cities here, as well as in London. It became the template for discount ticket-sales booths everywhere.

Mayor Lindsay's efforts didn't stop there. He also made it possible to build new theaters by amending New York City's zoning laws. New laws allowed real-estate developers who incorporated a new legitimate theater into a theater-district building project to receive a bonus allowing them to construct larger buildings than would have been possible before. The mayor cleared the way for the construction of several theaters, including the Circle in the Square, the Gershwin Theatre on Fifty-Second Street between Broadway and Eighth Avenue, and the Minskoff Theatre on Broadway between Forty-Fourth and Forty-Fifth Streets. He rejigged the zoning lines and increased the so-called "floor area ratio," which meant we could build bigger stages and larger auditoriums in the new theaters. That didn't necessarily make them better theaters, but it certainly improved the stage portions.

Sadly for Shubert, the provisions of the consent decree from all those years ago still loomed large. It prevented us from acquiring an interest in any additional theaters without court permission, and enabled our competitors, the Nederlanders, to lease the Gershwin and Minskoff theaters. It never seemed fair.

Lindsay left City Hall in 1973 and was replaced by the former city comptroller, Abe Beame, the man who had originally lost to Lindsay two terms before. Standing just five feet two inches tall, Beame was born in Great Britain and raised on New York's Lower East Side. He was an old-style "Democrat machine" politician. We got along well, and in January 1976, he formed the Mayor's Midtown Citizens Committee to deal with Times Square's problems and to propose solutions. He named me its chairman.

On paper, the committee sounded like a great idea. But there was also real support for it. Media editorials cynically dismissed it as another fruitless step in a long trail of failed attempts to save Times Square. Mayor Beame's appointments to the committee consisted of a disparate group, ranging from priests, newspaper reporters, and political activists to architects, real-estate developers, theater people, and restaurateurs. All of us were deeply concerned about breathing new life into Times Square, and it wasn't long before we produced a list of problems and our recommended solutions. Unfortunately, we were soon mired in controversy.

One of the men Beame appointed to the committee was Seymour Durst, a well-known real-estate developer and chairman of the Broadway Association, a group of developers and business owners in the Times Square area. Durst also owned a building on West Forty-Sixth Street, between Sixth and Seventh Avenues, containing the Luxor Baths. If you wanted a Turkish bath, the Luxor was the place to go.

Early on, Durst complained to me that he was not getting adequate police and fire-department protection to deal with problems created by a whorehouse operating on the fifth and sixth floors of his building. His only alternative, he said, was to sell the building. I advised him to choose a buyer carefully or it might fall into the wrong hands and thwart the committee's efforts. He promised to tell me who the buyer was before he actually sold the building. But he didn't. Shortly afterward, Mayor Beame called to say that Durst had sold the building to the operator of the whorehouse. I said I couldn't believe it, since he'd given me his word that he wouldn't sell without letting me know. The mayor now asked, "What should we do about it?"

I said, "Not we, you, since you appointed him."

A couple of months into our work, Durst resigned from the committee.

The committee soldiered on, and with high hopes we sent our report to the mayor in July. In our opinion, at the heart of Times Square's problems were "quality of life" crimes, including prostitution, vagrancy, drunkenness, peddling, drug pushing, drug taking, panhandling, and graffiti. We thought this was groundbreaking stuff. Sorry to say, our report sat around for eighteen years before anyone took notice of it.

It was the early 1970s, and Father Bruce Ritter was a man with his own agenda. A former Franciscan friar, Bruce had taken over a building on Forty-Fourth Street, next to the St. James Theatre. There he ran Covenant House, a charity that provided shelter for runaway teenagers. In those days, Eighth Avenue was known as the "Minnesota Strip" because so many young girls from around the country, many from the Midwest, ended up there plying their trade as prostitutes.

Covenant House had sixteen beds, and Bruce was looking for money to expand. He told me that, at that time, he could only provide an overnight stay for his homeless flock and that he wanted to do more. He asked me to come up with financial support for his project. I raised the matter with our board, and we gave him some modest start-up funds. Bruce was a zealot and eventually expanded Covenant House to sixty-four beds, enough to provide more extensive stays for the runaways. That was fine, of course. But when he converted a building on Eighth Avenue between Forty-Third and Forty-Fourth Streets into a sanctuary and held church services there, neighbors began complaining. Some of Bruce's residents were hustling passersby, including theater patrons on Forty-Fourth and Forty-Fifth Streets. Hoping to mediate the situation, I arranged a meeting, which went nowhere. Bruce kept repeating that if he could save the life of just one teen, that was far more important than all the legitimate theaters on Broadway. There was no reasoning with him, so I took the matter to City Hall.

By this time Abe Beame was gone, and the inimitable Ed Koch was mayor. A lawyer and former congressman, Koch served three terms as one of the city's most popular figures. When he arrived at City Hall, he appointed a lawyer named Herbert Sturz as his deputy for criminal justice. Herb soon moved from there to chairman of the City Planning Commission, making him an important man to know. Herb agreed to meet with us. Bruce came with his lawyer and a few Covenant House officials. I showed up with two priests, Father Robert Rappleyea from Holy Cross Church on Forty-Second Street, and Father George Moore of St Malachy's the Actors Chapel on Forty-Ninth Street.

Quickly grasping the gravity of the situation, Herb asked for a little time to find a solution. Father Rappleyea was no friend of Bruce's. He deeply resented the fact that Bruce had set up a sanctuary right in his parish without the cardinal's consent. Meanwhile, Fathers Rappleyea and Moore arranged for me to meet with the bishop. I described the street conditions and Father Bruce's obstinacy. The meeting was unproductive and I concluded that the archdiocese was not interested in getting involved in an internecine battle among its priests.

True to his word, Herb Sturz arranged with Governor Hugh Carey to turn a large facility on Dyer Avenue and Forty-First Street, near the Lincoln Tunnel, into the new home for Covenant House. All parties were satisfied with the new arrangement.

Robert Rappleyea, one of the most inspiring men I have ever met, invited me one evening to the rectory, where he called a meeting of fifty civic associations, representing midtown businesses and 165,000 locals. Everyone was complaining about the conditions in Times Square and the theater district. I got up and I asked, "Have you complained to Fred Ohrenstein and Richard Gottfried?" They were the politicians who represented the theater district in Albany. Some people responded that they couldn't reach them by phone.

I asked, "Are we a united community?"

The room answered in unison, "Absolutely."

"Fine," I said, "then keep calling Ohrenstein and Gottfried and tell them that if they don't support the bill prohibiting loitering, they won't be reelected."

Despite his well-known First Amendment reservations, Ohrenstein introduced a bill in the New York State Senate to outlaw loitering, and Gottfried took it into the assembly. The bill passed. It was the first important piece of legislation that we were able to get on the books.

With a vocal group of voters behind us, politicians began to pay more attention to our mission. The day after the Thanksgiving parade, for example, I walked through Times Square, which looked like a garbage dump. Normally, the city wouldn't pick up trash from the parade until after the weekend, but I wasn't going to put up with the wait. I phoned City Hall and got someone on the phone. "Clean up the goddamn streets," I said. We've got millions of people coming here this weekend, and it looks like a dump."

The civil servant said to me, "Do you know it costs $80,000 to do that over the weekend?"

I answered, "Do you know that if these streets didn't have these theaters, you wouldn't have enough money to pay sanitation workers? We generate a lot more than $80,000 over that weekend. Clean the goddamn streets."

A few hours later, that person called back to say, "You won."

I said, "What did I win?"

He said, "They're picking up the garbage. But now you have to write a letter to the sanitation commissioner to thank him."

Like a dummy, I wrote a letter thanking a man for simply doing his job.

Around the same time, the New York State Department of Commerce released a survey, published in the *New York Times*, revealing a fascinating fact: the number-one draw for tourists to New York City was a Broadway show.

A poll of New York State residents showed that some 37 percent believed Broadway was the most appealing thing about the city. That was echoed by some 33 percent of those surveyed in other areas. The next favorite attractions were museums, cited by 17 percent of the respondents. As a result of that survey, the state produced a $1 million publicity campaign for Broadway. Brochures were produced, commercials appeared on television, and ads were placed in newspapers and magazines.

Officially called the Broadway Show Tours Campaign, it gave the world the famous tagline "I love New York." It was a monumental success. Visitors spent $181 million more in the first nine months of the campaign than during the previous nine months. It brought much-needed taxes into city and state coffers, and helped create six hundred new full-time travel-related jobs.

We had never seen anything like it. Inexplicably, however, it was not repeated. The campaigns that followed Broadway Show Tours focused instead on New York State's mountains and lakes. Despite our repeated efforts to mount a new Broadway campaign, it never materialized.

———•·•———

When Ed Koch became mayor, I asked him if he wanted to continue the work of the Mayor's Committee. I explained that, in this context, the word *mayor* meant each successive mayor, not just Mayor Beame. In his typical straightforward fashion, he said, "Why not, you're doing a good job."

Shortly after that, I received a visit from Richard Ravitch and Irving Fisher, the developers of Manhattan Plaza, a middle-income housing project located on Forty-Second and Forty-Third Streets between Ninth and Tenth Avenues. The huge project would include hundreds of apartments, a restaurant, a health club, tennis courts, a swimming pool, and other amenities. But Ravitch and Fisher told me that because they could not service the city's $95 million mortgage, the project would have to be converted into an unrestricted, subsidized Section 8 housing development.

Until then, the only Section Eight I'd ever heard of was an army discharge for a disability. I retained a lawyer named Al Walsh, a former commissioner of the city's Department of Housing Preservation and Development. Walsh explained that if this plan went forward, the middle-income housing amenities in Manhattan Plaza would not exist. There would be no tennis courts, no swimming pool, no other amenities. In effect, Manhattan Plaza would become another tenement building.

Here I was fighting an uphill battle to clean up the area, and Manhattan Plaza was now going to become just another eyesore. It was a downturn I could not accept. Among other things, it posed a threat to the west side of the theater district, so I paid a visit to Roger Starr, who had taken over as housing and development administrator.

I told him, "You have no right to change the project from what was already approved by the Board of Estimate, and I will not support your plan."

The Board of Estimate was the city agency responsible for budget and land-use decisions. He shot back, "I have written off midtown."

"But I haven't," I said, and then threatened, "If this does not go back to the Board of Estimate, we'll bring a lawsuit."

Furious, I went to see Seymour Durst, in his capacity as president of the Broadway Association, and invited him to join the League in my contemplated lawsuit against the city of New York.

That's when Roger Starr phoned to say, "We have a $95 million mortgage on that property, the city is in terrible financial shape, and we could lose it. You're doing a great disservice to the city of New York."

I reminded him, "This is the last pot of gold this city has, the development of this area and the waterfront, and you're going to throw it away."

Several weeks later, Pat and I were having dinner with producer Alex Cohen and his wife, Hildy Parks Cohen. A former actress in the original cast of the long-running soap opera *Love of Life*, Hildy now produced television shows. Alex was an important-enough producer to be nearly on par with David Merrick. But unlike David, who was very debonair, Alex had a potbelly—his stomach came into the room first—and he walked with his feet turned out. He had thick lips and a snorty way of talking that gave him a tough demeanor. Hildy was very pretty, although she could be as tough as he looked.

That night, when talk turned to Manhattan Plaza, Alex said to me, "You know what we should do with this project? If it's going to be for the poor, let's make it for our poor. Turn it into the theater's bedroom."

I said right away, "That's the answer. You're right." But I also knew that Alex's approach would be more emotional than practical, and I said, "Alex, leave it to me. You stay out of this."

I broached the subject with Actors' Equity and they immediately wanted the entire project for their members. That would never be accepted, I explained, but we all agreed that theater-industry employees were ideal as Manhattan Plaza's core population. Although Durst was willing to join us in the lawsuit, we decided not to proceed with it. Instead, we came up with a 70-15-15 compromise. Seventy percent of the housing would go to actors, ushers, porters, doormen, cleaners, matrons, porters, stagehands—the whole performing-arts gamut. Fifteen percent would be reserved for the elderly and handicapped, and 15 percent would go to local residents. The plan went through.

But then we had trouble getting people to move in. Potential residents were not willing to walk across Forty-Second Street to get to the building. That's how bad Forty-Second Street was. Alex convinced his driver to move in, and we also got some stagehands to rent, and from there it snowballed. Within a year we had more than three thousand people on a waiting list. Manhattan Plaza became the anchor for the development of Forty-Second Street. Together with the newly formed 42nd Street Development Corporation, we helped create Theater Row. Massage parlors, porn houses, and sex shops that had littered Forty-Second Street west of Ninth Avenue, across from Manhattan Plaza, were shut down and turned into a string of functioning Off-Broadway theaters.

A few years later, a plan emerged to redevelop Forty-Second Street between Seventh and Eighth Avenues. This time developer Seymour Durst became an obstructionist. He initiated several lawsuits to prevent the redevelopment, believing that the plan's subsidies would compete with his ability to develop his own properties. His lawsuits delayed the redevelopment of Forty-Second Street until 1993, when the Disney Company leased and restored the historic New Amsterdam Theatre on Forty-Second Street near Seventh Avenue.

It's doubtful that Disney would have moved in had it not been for the nearly twenty-five years we spent laying the groundwork. Along with Disney came redevelopment of Forty-Second Street, the last remaining blight on the new Times Square. But as we will see, it would take many more battles with politicians and others before today's vibrant Times Square would become a reality.

THIRTY

OUT OF LOVE,
AND STUBBORNNESS

Taking on many of Bernie's duties after his death in 1996 made my days considerably longer. For years, I'd taught a theater course at Yale. I had schlepped up to New Haven every Friday, and especially enjoyed my time there while Lloyd Richards was dean of the drama school. He was one of the founders of the Eugene O'Neill Theater Center in Waterford, Connecticut, where he nurtured young playwrights, put on their plays all summer, and was responsible for helping launch the careers of Wendy Wasserstein, Lee Blessing, David Henry Hwang, and Christopher Durang, among others.

My contribution to my students at Yale Drama, all those aspiring young actors, directors, craftspeople, and playwrights, was to impress upon them that theater is a business. I firmly believe that to be successful in theater you need a fundamental knowledge of how the business works. But I didn't just lecture; I also imposed on people I knew—producers, actors, writers, directors, stage people—to join me in the classroom and talk about all aspects of the theater business.

Then, back in the early eighties, I got it into my head that the Shubert Organization could help students experience the business first-hand by setting up an intern program. Yale was too far away, so I approached my own alma mater, NYU. But NYU wasn't interested and turned me down. By then Schuyler Chapin was dean of the Columbia University School of the Arts. When I pitched my idea to him, he understood right away and started a graduate course called "The Business of the Theater." He named me an adjunct professor, and I gave up Yale for Columbia. I taught the course in both fall and spring semesters for years, invited theater people as guest speakers, and even brought my students to Shubert to hang around and see the business on a daily basis. When we were producing a play, I had my students read scripts, or sit through all-night negotiations with producers, playwrights, and other theater owners. It was a thrill to me that my classes were always full.

Eventually, I found that teaching both semesters was a bit much, so I cut back to a spring session only. It may be half as many classes, but it is still a year-round thrill. And I am constantly amazed that wherever Pat and I go—I mean anywhere in the world—we bump into my students. They're out there. They're everywhere. I'm Mr. Chips. And I love it.

With Bernie as my sounding board, it felt comfortable when we decided to take a chance on a new show, as long as we both agreed. We were willing to take risks when they seemed worth it to both of us. But now, alone, I had to think twice as hard before making a decision. That said, a new Edward Albee play wouldn't normally seem like a risk that Bernie would have objected to. After all, Albee, author of *Who's Afraid of Virginia Woolf?* among many other extraordinary plays, is one of America's most distinguished playwrights. But this play was different, and this play I produced for the sheer love of it.

The play had the strange title *The Goat, or Who Is Sylvia?* It was about a man who has a love affair with a goat, to the disbelief and consternation of his family. After the opening at our Golden Theatre on March 10, 2002, the *New York Times* review wrongly described *The Goat* as a play about bestiality. I was so annoyed by the critic's trivializing misinterpretation that I phoned Albee to tell him the *Times* didn't get it. He wasn't in, so I left a message. The review hurt the play somewhat, and a few weeks after opening, its producer Liz McCann called asking if I could help continue the play's run by reducing the booking terms. I said yes. A few days later, Albee called to say, "I can't thank you enough for helping my play."

It was a memorable phone call—the first time any playwright whose work we had helped in similar circumstances had ever shown any appreciation.

I told Albee that the *Times* critic had completely misunderstood his play. "It's about the boundaries of love."

"No," he said. "The play is about love having no boundaries."

"I can see that," I said, adding, "I'm grateful for your call."

Again he repeated, "I'm grateful for what you did for my play." And closed by saying, "We better hang up now, before we both start crying."

My appreciation of *The Goat, or Who Is Sylvia?* was confirmed when it received the 2002 Drama Desk and Tony Awards for Best Play, as well as the 2003 Pulitzer Prize.

Unfortunately, my decision to bring *Le Passe-Muraille* to Broadway did not fare as well, even though my love of the play still endures. Again, I think Bernie would have agreed to produce the show. Robbie Lantz had recommended that I see it, so Pat and I flew to Paris. It was a small musical composed by the famous Michel Legrand. We attended an evening performance and afterward dined with Michel.

Based on a short story by Marcel Aymé, a popular French writer who is memorialized with a statue in Montmartre, the musical is a fantasy about a man who can walk through walls. I found it charming and thought James Lapine would be the ideal director. We acquired the rights to adapt and produce it in the United States and other countries, then retained Jeremy Sams to adapt the book, which was written by Didier van Cauwelaert. We changed the play's name to *Amour*.

At first, James was reluctant to direct the show. Then he said he would only do it Off-Broadway. I worked out the play's budget and decided it could not survive financially in an Off-Broadway theater. I pressed James to change his mind, and he finally relented.

Work began before contracts were signed, which sometimes happens in the theater. To create the magic needed to simulate the leading man's passing through walls, closed doors and other obstacles, we hired an illusionist. The set was beautiful. It simulated a Paris street with an angular perspective converging upstage, where there was a replica of the Sacré-Coeur. Unfortunately, it did not work. Some of the set's sections didn't meet, allowing the audience to see through the apertures and into the wings. We sent the set back to the shop for modifications. When we put up the new set, two large portions toppled over—one onto the stage and the other into the orchestra pit. Fortunately no one was injured, but this required more work, forcing us to cancel two preview performances.

I met with James's agent, George Lane, and offered very generous financial terms for James's work as the play's director. But Lane would first agree to a financial arrangement and then change his mind or bring up new terms. The process was becoming exasperating, and I finally told James that his agent was not doing him any good. To my surprise James replied, "That's what he gets paid for."

This went on for weeks, until we were less than a month away from rehearsal. In order to resolve the dispute, I offered another beneficial option. The next day, Lane phoned to say that James had become livid at my new offer. This was the last straw. I warned Lane, "Don't ever call me or any one else at Shubert again, because you are persona non grata here." I never spoke to him again.

The morning of the first rehearsal, James arrived at my office at exactly eleven ten, or fifty minutes before the rehearsal call. I reminded him, "You haven't signed your contract yet, and if you don't or won't, I will terminate the show."

James replied, "I know." He signed the contract there and then.

I loved the show, but most of the critics did not, and it closed on November 3, 2002, after forty-eight performances. About four years later, *Amour*, directed by Darko Tresnjak, was presented at the Norma Terris Theatre of the Goodspeed Opera House in Connecticut. This modest production did not involve any illusions; all the passages were simulated, and it had a new scenic design. It was still a revelation. To this day, Michael Price, artistic director of the Goodspeed Opera House, says *Amour* remains one of Goodspeed's most successful productions. I loved it in Paris, when it was called *Le Passe-Muraille*, and loved it even more when I saw it in Connecticut as *Amour*.

----•◦•----

When I love a show, I am willing to do whatever it takes to make it work, as I did with *The Goat, or Who is Sylvia?* and with *Amour*. But just mention *Zerline* to Pat and watch her raise her eyebrows and mumble, "Jerry can be very stubborn."

Somewhere in heaven Bernie is nodding. "Yes, he can."

Pat is right about me being stubborn. If I don't want to pursue something, no one can make me do it. But when I do want to do something, no one can stop me.

And that was the case with *Zerline*. I loved that play, and I was also pretty hooked on Jeanne Moreau.

Back at the end of the 1980s, Pat and I were in Paris and went to see Jeanne Moreau in this little play, in a tiny theater in Montmartre. We both thought it was absolutely wonderful, and that night I told Pat, "I am going to bring *Zerline* to New York."

The French title was *Le Récit de la Servante Zerline*. Based on a short story by Austrian writer Hermann Broch, it was only sixty-five minutes long, about a German maid who had spent her life working for a fading wealthy family. It took place in the 1920s. She talked about what she saw and did in the house, especially about getting into and out of the wrong beds. In London, acquiring the rights would have taken no time at all. But France operates differently, and at a glacial pace. It took a very long time to find out who owned the rights—it turned out to be someone in Germany—and then to acquire them. I'm talking years.

While all this was simmering, Jeanne Moreau won the 1988 Molière Award, the French equivalent of a Tony, for Best Actress in *Zerline*.

While I was trying to get the rights, I was also trying to meet with Jeanne. That took years too, but on one trip to Paris, five or six years after we had seen the show, we managed to make a dinner date with her. We were to meet at a famous Left Bank steakhouse, but when we got there, we were told that Madame Moreau was on a major diet and would not be joining us for a meal. However, she would be there in time for dessert. By the time she arrived, Pat and I were absolutely full.

Jeanne, whose mother was British and who therefore speaks perfect English, sat down and promptly abandoned her major diet. She ordered five dishes of ice cream. I kept repeating that I wanted her to come to Broadway to do *Zerline*. In between scoops of ice creams, she said she would love to, and promised to come to New York to look at some possible theaters. Nothing happened for another four or five years. By now, Pat was saying, "Forget it."

We managed to acquire the rights to the play, after nearly a decade, and I commissioned a translation. We then went back and forth with Jeanne. First she was coming to New York, then she wasn't, then she was. And all the time Pat was saying, "Forget it."

Eventually, Jeanne did come to New York. We showed her some theaters, and when she left, I assured Pat this was going to happen. That is, until we discovered there wasn't room in Jeanne's schedule, and we'd have to wait another two or three years. Everyone tried to talk me out of it. Pat didn't even have to say, "Forget it"; it was written all over her face. Still, I refused to give up. I kept pressing Jeanne for a date, until finally from Paris she sent word that she didn't want to do it.

Even then I wouldn't give up. If I couldn't have Jeanne Moreau, which I was now reluctantly willing to concede that I couldn't, I would find someone else. I was still determined to stage *Zerline*.

I convinced Elizabeth Ashley to do it—I loved her and she was the perfect choice. We helped produce it with the Hartford Stage, in Connecticut. Elizabeth was very good, but the play didn't work as well as I hoped.

But I did it. With no regrets. I never second-guessed myself. I wanted to do it, and I made it happen, even though it took nearly twenty-five years.

In the theater business, as in life, when it comes to some relationships, unfortunately, neither affection nor persistence is enough to sustain them. Sometimes they simply arrive at a dead end. That was the case between producers Alex Cohen and David Merrick, and between Alex and me.

Alex was often quoted as saying, "Any moron can make money, and in show business any cretin can make money. My considerations have never been financial. A flop in my head is a show or an experience I didn't care for. And a hit in my head is something I enjoyed doing very much. You'd be surprised how many of my flops have been hits and hits flops."

And Alex had experienced enough of both to know.

The most prolific producers of plays imported from London, and occasionally from Paris, during the twentieth century were Alex Cohen and David Merrick. And considering the profusion of successful plays and musicals that had originated in London, that's saying something.

Alex actually spent so much time in London that he bought an apartment in Knightsbridge overlooking Hyde Park. He became as much a fixture in the London theater community as he was in New York. At one time I suggested that he produce classical plays with internationally recognized English stars and create an all-star classical theater company. As with other ideas I presented to Alex, he responded enthusiastically, but then I never heard anything further.

David and Alex were fierce competitors, and there was no love lost between them. Although Alex was a master publicist and promoter, he never had Merrick's deep financial resources or David's instinct to go for the jugular. Over breakfast one morning at the Savoy Hotel, David told Alex that he was going to see John Osborne's great play *Look Back in Anger*, and mentioned that he had a spare ticket. Alex accepted the ticket and went along.

David said, "The deal is if we like it, we'll do it together." Alex agreed. They both loved the play. And the next thing Alex knew, David was producing it in New York alone. They never did another deal together.

Alex got his revenge a few years later, however. It was the late 1960s, and he was trying out *Hellzapoppin'*, starring Soupy Sales. He had booked it into our Broadway Theatre. But the show was dying out of town, and he was on his way to tell us that he wouldn't be bringing it to New York after all. Along the way, as Alex told the story, he bumped into someone who told him that David was having a problem. He was producing a play called *The Happy Time*, and the director, Gower Champion, was insisting that Merrick book the show into our Broadway Theatre. Armed with this knowledge, Alex came to see Lawrence Shubert Lawrence Jr. and told him *Hellzapoppin'* was ready for the Broadway, and that he wanted to keep his booking. When Merrick heard this, he became furious. He then insisted on buying Alex out of his Broadway Theatre booking, to the tune of $50,000. Alex got the last laugh.

Alex Cohen later produced a number of network television specials. They were celebrations of corporate events, like CBS's fiftieth-anniversary special, *CBS: On the Air*, and the *Night of 100 Stars*. He also had a ten-year contract to produce the Tony Awards. Before the contract's 1986 expiration date, feelings in the Broadway League toward Alex were outright hostile. League members thought they were not getting a proper accounting for the Tony Awards receipts, for sponsors' benefits, for air travel, hotel reservations, limousine services, the Tony Ball, the special *Playbill*, guest tickets, and so on.

Alex's response was, "Fuck 'em. They get 11 percent of the contract price for the Tonys and that's it."

I told Alex he was part of a tripartite arrangement comprised of the League and the American Theatre Wing, which owned the trade name Tony, and him and CBS, which broadcast the Tonys. I reminded him that he was not a Lone Ranger, and that if he insisted on maintaining his current terms, the League and the Wing would not renew his contract. Bernie, Alex, Alan Morris—a good friend who represented Alex—and I met for lunch at the Plaza Hotel. After telling Alex the old terms wouldn't fly, we agreed to a modification that was considerably more beneficial to the League and the Wing, and told Alex that we were going to recommend it to the League.

At the next League meeting, the matter came up when the League and the Wing were casting for a new producer. I brought up Alex's proposal. The League members not only rejected it out of hand, they refused to allow Alex to bid on a new contract. As far as the League was concerned, Alex was finished. When Bernie and I gave Alex the news, he said, "All you had to do was to tell them to agree and you didn't do it."

I tried to make Alex understand that he had created an impossible situation and had been wrong to assume that his proposal was a fait accompli. I also reminded him that he had once told me that he lost money on the Tony Awards and didn't care whether his contract was renewed. He said I should have understood he didn't mean it.

Nevertheless, our relationship finally ended. To the very end of Alex's life, we only spoke once more, when Pat and I were visiting Lester and Sue Wunderman in Mougins, France. Lester was a marketing genius who, rightly, has a place in both the Direct Marketing Association Hall of Fame and the Advertising Hall of Fame. Sue was for many years director of editorials at WCBS-TV. Her first husband had been Ted Cott, the former NBC radio man.

The Wundermans' house was on the same street as Alex's. One afternoon, Lester brought me a copy of *Variety* that he said Alex wanted to give me. I wondered, "Is it a peace offering?" Lester said he didn't know.

The next day, Lester announced that Alex and Hildy were inviting Pat and me to their home for a drink. But Hildy, who wrote scripts for the Tony Awards show, had cautioned Lester that I shouldn't regard the invitation as "a Thanksgiving gift." I declined the invitation. Lester asked me to reconsider, saying that my not going would make things difficult for him and Sue since they were friendly with the Cohens. So off the four of us went to Alex and Hildy's.

On our arrival, Alex escorted me on a personal tour of his home. When we went upstairs, he told me that life is short and we should let bygones be bygones. I agreed, but it was for naught. After that, whenever I saw Alex at a party or an opening, he acted as if he didn't see me.

Alex passed away on April 22, 2000.

His old nemesis, David Merrick, passed away three days later.

THIRTY-ONE

DANCING WITH DIVAS:
MAE, MARIA, AND JOAN

In the theater business, a hit is defined as a show that recoups its investment. A hit show is not defined by the profits it brings in or the duration of its run. Many shows have relatively long runs but do not recoup their investment. Shows that run for short periods, when properly budgeted, and with star casts, can generate large profits. But stars also generate their own kind of energy.

You hire them to bring in an audience. And they want to be well compensated for that. *A Chorus Line* and *Cats* were exceptions. They proved that megahits can make money without stars. But most shows can't. And stars know that. They want big money, which means everyone else gets less. Stars also don't want to get locked into long runs. So we needed to work out a new formula whereby everyone involved would benefit from their appearance. That usually means having them participate in the production's profits. But no matter the arrangement, it also means having to cater to their whims and fancies—and I spent nearly a lifetime perfecting that art.

The first star I ever had any contact with was back in the very early days, when J. J. sent me to settle a problem with Mae West. She was in a revival of her hit show *Diamond Lil* at the Broadway, and was upset because someone was impersonating her in a show way downtown. So Pat and I first went to see the Mae West impersonator. She was working at a tiny, dreary club somewhere on Second Avenue and Twelfth Street, which in the 1950s was a very shady area. The impersonator's act was dreadful, and I would be surprised if she was making fourteen dollars a week. No one could ever seriously have considered her anything but a bad impersonator.

Then we made our way back uptown to meet the real Mae West in her dressing room. Pat and I set out to assure her that she was inimitable. But what we saw when we arrived was a sad disappointment. There was no doubt that she had huge star quality, but Mae West was a little old lady at this point. She was really the one impersonating Mae West.

Handling her was easy. But then she was "old school," a grand lady who was happy for the attention paid to her.

———•◦•———

Then there was our friend Maria Schell, Austria's greatest and most beautiful actress, famously called "the blond angel." Maria was one of the two women with whom I'd fallen in love from the screen. For the record, the other was Hope Lange.

Maria was in a slew of classic films, including *The Last Bridge* and *The Brothers Karamazov*, and had worked with many of Hollywood's greatest leading men, including Gary Cooper and Marlon Brando. She was now starring in *Poor Murderer* at our Barrymore Theatre. Unfortunately, the play received poor notices and closed after a run of only eighty-seven performances.

Maria was devastated that the show was closing, and urged me to try to diminish the power of the critics to close a show before it had had a chance to prove itself. There was little I could do. But I had an idea for an all-star theater featuring American and English box-office stars in revivals of great plays. I asked Maria if she would join me in inviting noted theatrical personalities to participate. She was enthusiastic about the idea, and we wrote to many stars. Our plan was still being formed, and we knew it would take at least two years to implement, but we believed we could line up some of these actors. Realistically, of course, they could pull out if they received more enticing offers. Surprisingly, we received a very large number of acceptances.

Maria and I needed an artistic director for the project, and she suggested her younger brother Maximilian Schell. An excellent actor and dramatic-play director, Max was in New York, and Maria arranged an appointment.

I told him our idea and asked if he would be the artistic director. Max agreed. I offered to pay him an initial $10,000. We decided to prepare a list of possible plays, and I explained that each play should have an "A player" or two. In other words, we needed stars to draw in an audience. But Max was not familiar with the term, and asked what I meant by an A player.

I explained, "An A player is someone who would sell tickets regardless of critics' reviews. Now, there are many B players who might be better actors than A players, but they wouldn't sell enough tickets to overcome negative reviews."

Max immediately wanted to know, "What kind of a player am I?"

I found myself in a sticky situation. I didn't want to insult Max by telling him he was a B player and risk losing him as artistic director. In fact, I didn't want to be drawn into giving an answer at all. So I said, "Your question is irrelevant, since you are not being engaged as an actor."

Not satisfied, Max kept pressing me. "But am I an A player or a B player?"

Again, I ducked the answer. Unfortunately, Max wouldn't let the matter drop. So I told him the truth. "You're a B player."

He was shocked, but fortunately still agreed to prepare his list of plays. Maria later told me that Max was very sensitive and that I had hurt his feelings.

When Max's list arrived, his first choice was *Tales from the Vienna Woods*, which he had directed at London's National Theatre. It was a play noted for its length and large cast. His second choice was *Hamlet*, starring Maximilian Schell. I wrote back that during the first season, classical plays should not be on his list, and added that *Vienna Woods* would be too large and costly a production. After that, neither of us bothered to pursue the plan. What I had thought would be a wonderful project fizzled out. The following summer Max appeared in *Everyman* at the Salzburg Festival in Austria. I received a postcard from him that read, "Seventy-three thousand people were turned away because there were no tickets available. Not bad for a 'B' player."

Some time after that, Max came to New York with his wife, famous Russian actress Natalya Andrejchenko, and invited Pat and me to dinner. As we were walking out of the restaurant, Max asked, "Do you still think I'm a B player?"

I put my arm around him, looked into his eyes, and said, "Yes, Max, but you keep working at it and one day you'll become an A player."

In 2001, he gave a stunning performance on Broadway in *Judgment at Nuremberg*. Pat and I went to the opening night, and then visited him in his dressing room. I congratulated him on his performance.

"Max," I said, "you are an A player."

That finally put this long-simmering matter to rest.

Maria, meanwhile, clearly had passion in mind when she invited Pat and me to her wonderful summer home in the Bavarian Alps on one of our European trips. It was a kitschy place, in true Bavarian style, complete with a barn that had been converted into a guesthouse. She wanted Pat and me to feel comfortable—romantic, even—so she fixed up the place as if two young lovers were visiting. There was a loft bed that we climbed up into, and to set the mood every night, a fire roared in the fireplace. The beds were covered with eiderdowns—those heavy duvets that always slip off the bed and are designed for cold winter nights in Bavaria. It was a very warm and cozy love nest. Except that this was the middle of August. Between the warm weather outside and the fireplace and eiderdowns inside, it was as hot as hell. But Maria was a wonderful hostess and a dear friend.

Many years later, Max sent me a copy of a loving film he had made about her called *My Sister Maria*. In it, he recounted her beautiful life story. He also explained how she was fading away, completely disoriented, and institutionalized. It brought Pat and me to tears. I asked Max for Maria's phone number, and when he sent it, I called her. We spoke for a long time. But I have no idea if she knew who I was. Maria died in 2005 at age seventy-nine.

<hr />

Joan Fontaine was so different from Maria. Joan acted like the huge movie star she was, and movie stars are just not the same as the rest of us.

For years, every Christmas Eve, Pat and I went to a party hosted by John and Isabel Stevenson. Everybody who was anybody showed up at their apartment on Park Avenue. The Stevensons were wonderful people, although Isabel had an odd habit of pinching pennies when it came to feeding guests. John always bought the best wines, but Isabel would invite eighty people for Christmas Eve, buy food for twenty, and then divide everything into four. They had carolers, and guests brought their children. We took Carrie and our grandchildren with us, but we always went out to dinner first.

On December 24, 1979, their apartment was so thick with people that there was barely room to stand. I was wedged in between several people in the large living room, when a theatrical agent I knew threaded his way through the crowd towards me with gorgeous woman at his elbow. My heart skipped a beat. It was Rebecca. It was Jane Eyre. It was Joan Fontaine.

He introduced us, then drifted into the crowd, leaving Joan and me standing face-to-face, practically touching. After a few words, exchanged in each other's ears, Joan whispered, "You're one of the most exciting men I've ever met in my life."

I quickly looked over my shoulder to see if she was referring to someone else. There being no one recognizable behind me, I said, "Are you referring to me?"

She answered, "Yes."

Not knowing how to reply, I leaned over and whispered, "Better than Larry Olivier?"

She said, "Much better."

I was surprised, but my surprise did not end there, because now she said, "I would love to have lunch with you."

I said, "And I would love to have lunch with you. Call me and we'll make a date."

She sternly replied, "I don't call men."

I said, "I can't possibly write down your telephone number in this crowd, and since you are not in the telephone book and I am, I would love to hear from you and take you to lunch."

And call she did. I took her to lunch at Sardi's, and for over two hours she told me that despite my thinking she was a happy woman, she wasn't. She had married four times, two of her husbands had walked out on her, and her daughter did not speak to her. When I asked about her sister, Olivia de Havilland, she told me the subject of siblings was reserved for our next luncheon and that I should read her book.

About three months later, I was standing in the driveway of the Beverly Hills Hotel in Los Angeles, waiting for a car, when suddenly I heard a voice cry out, "Jerry!"

I looked around, and it was Joan. She ran toward me and I swept her up in my arms, spun her around, and whispered in her ear, "Better than Orson Welles?"

She said, "Much better!"

A few months after that, I was walking into Inigo Jones, a London restaurant, and as my guests and I were being escorted to our table, I noticed three people sitting on a banquette in front of a window. They were in silhouette, and I couldn't make out who they were until a familiar voice cried out, "Jerry!"

When she jumped up, I said, "Joan!" She covered the distance between us, bent me over backward on the banquette, and kissed me. I whispered in her ear, "Better than Cary Grant?"

She said, "Of course. He was nothing!"

When the musical hit *42nd Street* was set to open at our Winter Garden Theatre on August 25, 1980, I invited Joan to the opening with Pat and our guests. She insisted all of us first come to her house for cocktails. Her apartment on East Seventy-Second Street was beautiful and befitting a star of her magnitude.

A few years later, Pat and I went to John Gardiner's Tennis Ranch in Phoenix, Arizona. As I checked in, I noticed a magazine on the desk, *What's Doing in Phoenix*. Since I couldn't possibly have known what was doing in Phoenix, I opened the magazine and found that Joan was appearing in *Dial M for Murder* at the Windmill Dinner Theatre.

I asked the receptionist to call Joan. She wasn't in, so I left a message asking her to call me. At around six thirty that evening, while I was dressing to go out for dinner, the phone rang, and her first question was, "Jerry, where are you?"

I said, "In Phoenix."

She said, "Are you alone?"

I said "No, I am with my wife."

"Oh," she said, "I'll try to be brave."

I invited her to lunch the next day, and she created a stir of recognition among the hotel's guests in the restaurant. After lunch, I escorted her to her car, and she said, "Just my luck, I like your wife."

After that, I continued running into Joan from time to time. Whenever I did, she'd put her hand inside her blouse over her breast and move it up and down, saying, "I love this man."

I wasn't vain enough to believe that I was the only object of this affection, but I was delighted by it. A few years later, we met at the airport in Rome on our way to Nice. Joan was traveling with a male companion, and when we boarded, she gave her friend instructions to sit with Pat so she could sit with me. During the flight, I told Joan about *Love Letters*, a show being produced in Los Angeles, and asked if she would like to costar in it. She said she would love to. I then spoke to the producer, who was delighted with the prospect of having Joan in the play, and promised to let me know when she could fit Joan into the schedule. When she finally got back to me, I called Joan, who was then living in Carmel, California.

But now she replied with great indignation and reprimanded me, saying, "Don't you know I don't do those things anymore?"

Her tone was so unfriendly and abrupt that I had nothing more to say than good-bye. I thought this was the end of a long unrequited love affair. But many months later I received a call from Joan, saying she was upset about an untrue magazine article stating that she was missing performances in a play. She wanted legal advice as to how she should proceed. Adopting the same tone she had used when I'd spoken to her about *Love Letters*, I said, "I recommend you get a good libel lawyer," and closed with "Good-bye."

I never heard from Joan again.

THIRTY-TWO

DEALING WITH LIZA AND AL

My experience with Liza Minnelli was exhilarating at times, exasperating at others. She came to us through the famous Broadway producing team of Cy Feuer and Ernest Martin, who were in charge of the Ahmanson and Mark Taper Forum theaters at the Los Angeles Music Center. They approached us in the mid-1970s to coproduce a new play, *The Act*, to be directed by Martin Scorsese, with a score by John Kander and Fred Ebb of *Cabaret* and *Chicago* fame.

The Act centered on a fading movie star trying to make a comeback in Las Vegas. With Liza as the star, the play had all the earmarks of a hit in the making. So much so that we acquiesced to an arrangement whereby the Music Center would recoup its half of the $800,000 capitalization from the profits of the Los Angeles engagement. That would not pose a problem since the number of season subscribers virtually assured a return of the Music Center's investment. We would recoup our investment from our New York–engagement profits. Beyond that, we would split profits equally.

But shortly after rehearsals started in L.A., we realized that *The Act* was in trouble. Marty Scorsese, who wasn't a stage director, was directing the show as if it were a movie. He framed the stage between his index fingers and thumbs, and when the cast was ready, he would call out, "Action!" It wasn't working, and the show was rapidly going nowhere.

Cy Feuer decided we had to replace Scorsese and volunteered to take over on an interim basis. We agreed, knowing that he had previous directing experience. The show opened to poor notices and Sam Cohn, this time representing Kander and Ebb, urged us to close the show in Los Angeles. "It's doomed to failure," he warned.

I told Sam, "We're not about to lose our $400,000 investment. We won't close it under any circumstances."

We were, however, willing to hedge our bet. So, before the end of the run, we engaged one of the theater's star musical directors, Gower Champion, to redirect the show with New York in mind. Gower did a good job with the material he had. The show opened on Broadway at our Majestic Theatre on October 29, 1977, to a large advance, thanks entirely to Liza's box-office appeal.

We thought we were on our way to recouping our investment and turning a profit. Unfortunately, shortly after we opened, Liza became ill and missed a Saturday matinee performance early in the run. That caused a real problem for us. The audience wanted to see Liza and tried to exchange their tickets for the following Saturday matinee. But that wasn't easily done, since ticket holders for that matinee also wanted to see Liza, and there were few available tickets. Then Liza missed further Saturday matinee performances and soon began to miss others as well.

As the missed performances piled up and tickets backed up, I got a call from Cy Feuer announcing, "Liza only wants to play seven performances."

I asked, "Did you hear this from Liza?"

He said, "No."

I told him, "Leave it alone."

He did, but the request didn't die. A couple of weeks later, Cy called again and said that Liza's lawyer and agent, Mickey Rudin, wanted to meet with Bernie, Cy, and me the following afternoon at the Algonquin Hotel. Mickey was a powerful guy in the business and not someone to fool around with. He represented Frank Sinatra, Lucille Ball, and many top celebrities both in Los Angeles and Las Vegas. So Bernie and I met Cy and Mickey in the lobby of the legendary Algonquin, which resembled Grand Central Station at rush hour. It was filled with smoke and conversation. Every table was full.

Bald, fat, and looking like he'd come straight out of central casting, Mickey was sitting in an armchair, puffing on a big cigar. His large stomach protruded in front of him, preventing him from leaning forward when he spoke. That, combined with the noise in the room, made it impossible for me to hear anything he was saying except "seven performances."

I shouted back, "Eight performances." He shook his head. I tried again, "We need the eighth performance to recoup our investment. Come to our office tomorrow and we'll show you the books."

Rudin showed up the next day, alone, and began the conversation by saying to me, "I like you, kid, but I'm just a hired gun. Now, Liza will get

With Mayor Michael Bloomberg:
"We've had our ups and downs, but he's still been a great mayor."
Courtesy of the Shubert Archive

With Wendy Wasserstein.

With Jackie O.

Carrie, Fiore, Sam, and Julia.

With Sam.

With Julia.

Pat and I, married fifty years.

In Paris: "And I still don't
know how I got here."

With my great friend Hugh Jackman.

The Hirschfeld drawing of Bernie and me.
© *Al Hirschfeld, reproduced by arrangement with Hirschfeld's exclusive representative, the Margo Feiden Galleries Ltd., New York, www.alhirschfeld.com*

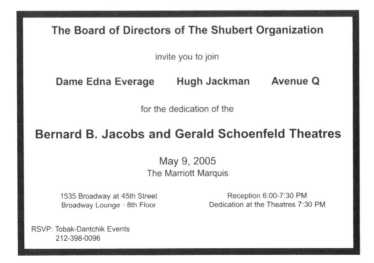

The Board of Directors of The Shubert Organization

invite you to join

Dame Edna Everage   Hugh Jackman   Avenue Q

for the dedication of the

Bernard B. Jacobs and Gerald Schoenfeld Theatres

May 9, 2005
The Marriott Marquis

1535 Broadway at 45th Street   Reception 6:00-7:30 PM
Broadway Lounge · 8th Floor   Dedication at the Theatres 7:30 PM

RSVP: Tobak-Dantchik Events
212-398-0096

The invitation to the big event.

The big night: the naming of the theaters.
With (*left to right*) Pat, Mike Sovern from the Shubert Board,
Betty Jacobs, Dame Edna, and Hugh Jackman.
© *Joan Marcus*

The *Avenue Q* puppets of Bernie and me.
© *Joan Marcus*

"How did I get here?"
The marquee of the newly renamed theater.

sick again; she'll have her period, a migraine; she'll have relapses. I'm just telling you this as a friend."

I warned him, "I don't know why you are talking to us like this. We are not without friends in this business. If she doesn't perform eight times a week, we're going to close the show and sue her for $400,000."

He just stared at me. When I repeated the story to various people over the next few days, I was told I should have my head examined for talking tough to Mickey Rudin. He wasn't somebody you threatened.

A few days later, Bernie and I went to Philadelphia for the opening of our musical *The Prince of Grand Street*, which we were coproducing. During dinner at Rose's Restaurant across the alleyway from our Forrest Theatre, our theater manager came in saying that Bob Corpora, the stage manager of *The Act*, was on the phone. I left the restaurant to take the call. Bob said Mickey Rudin had just left Liza's dressing room and was going onstage to announce that Liza would only perform seven times a week. After that, he was going to instruct the box office to stop selling tickets for the eighth performance.

I ordered Bob, "Tell Mickey Rudin that if he takes one step toward the stage or the box office, he is going to be thrown out on his ass."

Thankfully, Rudin backed down, and it never came to that. From that instant I did my best to avoid any contact with Liza Minnelli. That is, until one day when I was walking off the stage at the Majestic as she was walking onto the stage, and we met in the entranceway. One of us had to let the other pass. Suddenly Liza threw her arms around my neck, kissed me, and gave me a tender greeting. "Hello, boss."

A couple of weeks later, Bernie and I were in Los Angeles when Cy Feuer told us Mickey Rudin wanted us to meet in his office. As soon as we entered Mickey's office, Bernie eyed what was called a Quotron, a machine that gave up-to-the-minute prices of stock-market shares. Bernie hadn't seen one before and was immediately convinced that Mickey was on the cutting edge of technology.

But the real point of the meeting was Mickey's announcement that Liza had been offered a late-July engagement in Sun City, South Africa. The weekend engagement would pay her a quarter of a million dollars. He said, "If you let her out of her contract on July 1, Liza will reimburse you for the gross receipts of each cancelled Monday night performance until the end of the *The Act*'s run."

Since July was then one of the year's least profitable months, we accepted. In effect, Liza was foregoing $25,000 for each week between February and July. She would leave the show about two months early, and we would recoup our investment. In total, Liza missed twenty-seven performances. We put in a claim with our insurance carrier under our "star nonappearance" policy, which provided for a three-performance deductible. At first, the insurance carrier rejected our claim, saying that Liza was seldom out for more than three consecutive performances. That was not the case, I argued, because Liza suffered from one illness and many relapses. At that point, the insurance carrier accepted our claim, applied the three-performance deductible, and paid us for twenty-four missed performances.

All concerned seemed happy with the outcome, especially Mickey Rudin, who for many years sent me complimentary tickets whenever Frank Sinatra played Carnegie Hall. *The Act* received six Tony nominations and won Liza the award for Best Actress in a Musical.

Al Pacino, who came to us the year after Liza, was no easier to deal with, and, for a time I thought he was a little strange. Al has wowed Broadway several times, winning his first Tony Award in 1969 in *Does a Tiger Wear a Necktie?* He followed that with *Camino Real* and then *The Basic Training of Pavlo Hummel,* for which he won his second Tony.

In 1979, at the urging of Moe Septee, a Philadelphia theater operator who had produced *Pavlo Hummel,* Al agreed to return to the stage in David Wheeler's Boston production of *Richard III.* Moe then asked us if we would be interested in coproducing the show on Broadway. The prospect of Al Pacino doing Shakespeare delighted us, and we arranged to meet Al and Moe to discuss it. Sitting in my office, Al kept shrugging his shoulder as if it was stiff and painful. I wondered if something was wrong with him, but I didn't ask. We told Al that we would produce the same show that played in Boston.

The next day, I was walking down Forty-Fourth Street, and ran into Anna Strasberg, wife of Lee Strasberg, the founder of the Actors Studio. She said she was pleased that Al had come to see us. I said I was concerned about Al's health and described the way he kept shrugging his shoulder.

Anna explained, "Don't you understand? He is Richard III."

So Al was in character, even off the stage. I began to wonder if I had a nutcase on my hands.

The show went into rehearsal, and I greeted the cast. I saw no point in attending the rehearsals, since the show was no different from the Boston production. On the Sunday that the cast was going to travel to Philadelphia, I happened to be playing tennis with Sam Cohn, and we decided to stop by the Cort Theatre, where they had assembled, to wish them good luck. Al shook my hand and said, "Promise me you won't come to Philadelphia to see the fucking show."

That was music to my ears, since I had no desire to go.

By this time, the lure of a star of Al's magnitude had brought in large advance ticket sales in New York, and we seemed assured of a financial success. Unfortunately, the show received negative critical reviews in Philadelphia. Previews were scheduled to begin on Thursday, May 10, 1979, and continue until the play's opening on the Thursday of the sixth week. Al liked lots of previews.

On Monday morning of the first preview week, Samuel "Biff" Liff, Al's agent, phoned to say, "Al's not ready."

I asked, "What do you mean?"

He replied in a louder voice, "Al's not ready."

I told Biff, "Please speak English and tell me what you mean."

Biff answered, "He's not ready. He's not going to perform on Thursday."

Before becoming an agent, Biff had been David Merrick's production stage manager, one of the theater's most important jobs. Biff knew everything there was to know about producing a show, having learned it from the toughest producer in the business. David's motto was, "It is not enough that I succeed; others must fail."

I told Biff that Al had better be ready on Thursday or we would close the show and sue Al for $450,000, the cost of the production.

Biff replied, "Jerry, you've got trouble."

I said, "Biff don't tell me I've got trouble, you've got trouble."

Biff once again said, "Jerry, you've got trouble."

I said, "Biff, if you say that to me once more, I'm going to hang up."

That did not stop Biff, who repeated, "You've got trouble."

So I made good on my promise, said, "Good-bye, Biff," and hung up.

When I returned from lunch, I found Biff, Moe Septee, and Porter Van Zandt, our production stage manager, waiting for me. I ushered them into my office, and Biff started the conversation right where he'd left off. "Jerry, you've got trouble."

I said, "Biff, if you say that to me once more, I'm going to ask you to leave."

At that point, Moe said, "Can't we resolve this?"

I replied, "If you write a check for $75,000 payable to the production company for the sold-out first four previews, we can settle the matter."

Moe said, "I don't have that kind of money."

I ended the meeting by telling the group, "Al better be on stage, or we're going to close the show and sue him."

All was quiet on Tuesday. On Wednesday, I went to Yale University to teach my course. Afterward, I called my office and was told that Sy Peck, the cultural editor of the *New York Times*, had phoned. This was disturbing news, and I wondered whether or not to call him back. I weighed the pros and cons and decided I had to. When I got him on the phone, he already had the whole story of Al not opening the previews. I told Sy that if the story ran, it would severely hurt the show, since the public wouldn't know when Al would be ready and therefore wouldn't buy tickets. I begged him not to print the story. After a long hesitation, he said he wouldn't.

Late that afternoon, Moe Septee was on the phone. He said he couldn't thank me enough for what I had done and that Al would go on.

A few minutes later, Biff called me to say, "Jerry, you were magnificent."

I didn't know what either of them was talking about or why Al had changed his mind.

The next day, I received a call from Al's lawyer, Arthur Klein, on another matter, and I asked, "How come Al agreed to go on?"

Arthur said he had simply told Al to get his ass up onstage on Thursday night or "Jerry will sue the shit out of you."

That evening, I went to the Cort Theatre and waited to see if the curtain was going up. It did. The following Monday, I got a call from Biff saying that he and Al wanted to see me. As they walked down the corridor to my office, Al snarled at me, "You didn't come to Philadelphia to see the fucking show."

"Fuck you," I said. "You told me not to come."

When we sat down, Biff said, "Al would prefer not to perform before critics on opening night."

I said, "Fine with me. We will invite the critics on the Tuesday, Wednesday, and Thursday of the last preview week so that their reviews will appear on the following Friday."

Al asked, "Would you do this for me?"

I said, "I'd be glad to."

Truth be told, I would have done it for anyone.

After this was resolved, Al and I had our first decent conversation. As he was leaving, I said I would attend the Saturday evening show. Pat and I were there, as promised, along with some guests. At the curtain call, Al was dripping with perspiration and panting heavily. I told Pat and my guests I had to go backstage to see Al, and that I'd meet them later. When I knocked on Al's dressing-room door, he yelled, "Come in!"

I found him lying on a chaise, still drenched and still out of breath. Thinking that I had to do something drastic, I ran across the distance between the door and the chaise and threw myself on top of Al and hugged him. I whispered in his ear, "Now do you believe I really love you?"

We both burst out laughing.

The opening-night party was held in the Belasco Room on the third floor of Sardi's. Al arrived about forty-five minutes late. The crowd was packed in like sardines, but he spotted me as if I were the only person in the room. He jumped into my arms, proclaiming, "Jerry, I owe you one."

I told him, "That's the nicest thing anybody ever said to me."

A year or so after that party, I had an appointment with a friend of Al's. The meeting had nothing to do with Al, but on the way out he said he'd just seen Al, who asked him to remind me that he owed me one.

I said, "I know."

He said, "Al wants to play Hamlet."

I answered, "Tell Al that's not the one."

Years passed, and Al was again on Broadway starring in *Salome*. I went to see him backstage, and we fell into each other's arms and reminisced about the one he owes me.

THIRTY-THREE

THE ANTICS OF MAGGIE, KATHLEEN, AND ALEC

Whenever a show is in previews, it's always been my habit to visit the cast, make sure they're happy, encourage them, pat them on the back. So, as usual, when *Lettice and Lovage*, a play written specifically for Maggie Smith, was in previews in 1990, I went to our Barrymore Theatre to visit her. But she seemed less interested in seeing me than I was in seeing her.

She politely told me, "I'm happy. You don't have to come and baby me or mother me. If I find there's something wrong, I'll be perfectly at ease to get in touch with you. I hope you don't mind me saying this."

I answered, "I'm delighted you're here and glad that you've been so frank with me."

Needless to say, I didn't go back to see her until opening night. Then, sometime after the show was running, Maggie gave an interview to the *New York Times*, during which she commented that the producers had never bothered to come by to say hello. I was shocked and wrote to Maggie, reminding her that I had stopped by and that she'd basically told me not to come back again. I said I was very upset that she felt we were neglecting her.

Maggie phoned immediately. "You are 100 percent right. I certainly did say you needn't pay any attention to me. I will write a letter to the *Times* and tell them so."

I said she didn't have to. But, lady that she is, she did.

—•—

I tried to be equally gracious when Kathleen Turner overstepped the boundaries.

In London in 1994, Pat and I had attended a performance of Jean Cocteau's *Les Parents Terribles*, directed by Sean Mathias. I thought the play was outstanding and arranged to see it again on a later trip. In the interim, I learned that Sean was actor Ian McKellen's partner, so when the curtain went down, I was not surprised that Ian greeted me and escorted me to the greenroom to meet Sean. I told Sean I would like to do the play, and arrangements were made with the National Theatre to bring it to New York. When I returned to New York, Kathleen Turner contacted me and made a strong pitch to play the part of the mother. She was so passionate in her plea that we cast her. The rest of the cast consisted of Roger Rees of *Nicholas Nickleby* fame, Eileen Atkins, Cynthia Nixon, and Jude Law. It was Jude's Broadway debut.

After the play opened at our Barrymore Theatre on April 27, 1995, there was constant discord among cast members. After all, this was a show with more than one big-name star. I visited them at least once a week before curtain time to quiet them down.

The dissension reached its peak during the run on the July Fourth weekend. I received a call from the stage manager, who told me Kathleen had announced that she was not coming in on July Fourth, a performance day. She said she would be spending the holiday at her home in Amagansett, Long Island. I told the stage manager to tell Kathleen she would be well advised to fulfill her obligation and perform that day, holiday or not.

At five thirty p.m. on Tuesday, July 4, the stage manager called to say Kathleen was grilling chicken on the beach and wouldn't be in. I couldn't wait until the next business day to file charges with Actors' Equity against Kathleen. Even before the filing got cold, Kathleen's agent—who else but Sam Cohn—called to see if he and John Breglio, Kathleen's attorney, could meet with me.

I said, "Yes, provided Kathleen also attends the meeting."

When they arrived, I met them in our reception area. Kathleen was in a highly agitated state. I escorted them into our conference room and told Kathleen, who kept folding and unfolding her hands, that nobody had given her permission to miss a performance. The only one who could have given her permission was me, and I had not. She was trembling, and a wave of compassion came over me. So I told the three of them, to their great relief, "I will withdraw the charge."

The other cast members were not as tolerant, especially Eileen Atkins and Roger Rees. Kathleen is a very likeable woman, but to the English cast members, in particular, her conduct was inexcusable.

Two days later, Kathleen's doctor called to say he had found nodules on her vocal cords and that she could not speak for a week. Since we were sold out for the weekend performances, I asked her doctor if she could commence her silence on the following Monday without any detriment to her health. He replied that he'd given Kathleen a cortisone injection and that yes, the following Monday would be all right.

Before the evening performance, I went to the theater to give Eileen Atkins the news that Kathleen would miss more performances. She was sitting in her dressing-room chair facing the makeup mirror. I put my hands over her eyes and whispered in her ear, "I have something to tell you, but promise you won't get upset and jump all over me."

She agreed, and I related my conversation with Kathleen's doctor. But instead of being upset that Kathleen would be out again, Eileen reacted quite differently. She was now outraged, and castigated me for suggesting that an actor with vocal problems should risk her health to perform. I explained about the cortisone shot, but she was still enraged.

That said, Kathleen did perform over the weekend, was silent the following week, and thereafter resumed performances. It took a long time to stabilize the cast before things finally quieted down.

To this day, I am very fond of Kathleen, and I think the experience helped reinforce to her the importance of fulfilling contractual obligations. She is a wonderful actress who simply made a mistake. It happens.

———◆•◆———

A few years later, when Alec Baldwin made a mistake, it was a wall that suffered.

There was a certain poetry in the fact that when Alec and Jessica Lange opened in their 1992 revival of *A Streetcar Named Desire*, it was at our Barrymore Theatre, the same house where this famous Tennessee Williams play had debuted forty-five years earlier with Marlon Brando and Jessica Tandy. This time Alec played Stanley and Lange played Blanche, and it was a great production. Unfortunately, it was not the happiest of companies.

Jessica's blond hair came down in front of her eyes, and she had a habit of flipping her head back to toss her hair out of her face. It was very distracting. On top of that, her voice was faint, and she couldn't be heard past the second row. She was doing a very nice acting job, but she wasn't projecting, and that tossing her hair incessantly was driving me crazy. I sent word to the director, Gregory Mosher, "You must tell Jessica that she has to project and also stop flipping her hair."

Gregory agreed with me, as did the preview audiences, who after the show told us that they could not hear Jessica well. Alec, on the other hand, had received a rave review from Frank Rich at the *New York Times*, who said Alec's Stanley was "the first I've seen that doesn't leave one longing for Mr. Brando."

I knew that Alec and Jessica were not getting along. But I was floored when Alec walked into my office and, without even a hello, said cryptically, "I will pay for the renovation of the wall in my dressing room."

I asked, "What are you talking about?"

He said, "I am so frustrated. I can't work with her."

I was worried because I knew about Alec's temper. "What happened?"

"Instead of hitting her," he confessed, "I put my arm through the dressing-room wall."

A few years later Alec and Jessica reunited to make a television version of the play. The film earned each of them a Hollywood Foreign Press Award for Best Performance in a made-for-television movie.

THIRTY-FOUR

BACK TO TIMES SQUARE,
AND BEYOND

It was the early 1990s and Times Square still suffered from what I regard as "quality of life" crimes. They include illegal vending, begging, prostitution, and all the sex-related businesses that plagued Times Square for decades. They occur in many major American cities but were especially prevalent throughout midtown New York and, frankly, still have not been satisfactorily resolved. I presented an idea to the Mayor's Midtown Citizens Committee that involved creating a court to deal solely with quality-of-life crimes. The committee embraced the idea enthusiastically, and I started working to implement it.

The mayor's guy, Herb Sturz, and I met for breakfast in late 1992 to discuss the idea. I confessed that "quality of life" seemed too tame a name for the court. Herb suggested calling it the Midtown Community Court and locating it in the theater district, where most of these crimes occurred. I said I'd recommend to Shubert's board that we offer the Longacre Theatre on West Forty-Eighth Street between Broadway and Eighth Avenue for the court. The board agreed, but then the owners of two new buildings across from the Longacre opposed the idea. It was a typical NIMBY—"not in my backyard"—situation. So we had to find another location.

Next, I lobbied Judge Robert Keating, chief administrative judge of the criminal court, who lent his strong support for the court. After him, I went to David Dinkins, who had just succeeded Ed Koch as mayor. We found an old, unused courthouse on West Fifty-Fourth Street between Eighth and Ninth Avenues. The location was ideal, as it was next door to the Midtown North Police Precinct, whose jurisdiction included a large portion of the theater district and Times Square. I then set out to raise the necessary $2.4 million to convert the building into a new modern courthouse. But since I was accustomed to being asked for money and not to requesting money, I had no idea how to proceed. I asked Pat, who always had her hand out for her charities, "How do I find funders who are willing to give to this project?"

Pat advised me, "One way is to ask somebody to go through the book at the library that lists foundations and their interests."

Pat left on a trip to California, and called me a few nights later in the office, forgetting the three-hour time difference. It was ten p.m. in New York, and I answered just as she realized what time it was. She asked, "What are you doing in the office so late?"

I told her, "I'm reading this foundation directory you told me about, but I'm only up to the letter *G*. What now?"

Pat said, "Close the book and think of five CEOs you can call. Tell them you want some money."

That's exactly what I did, starting with me. The Shubert board unanimously voted to grant $300,000. Within three weeks I'd procured the remaining funds from the *New York Times* ($300,000); Morgan Guaranty Trust Company and Booth Ferris Foundation ($300,000); New York Telephone Company, now Verizon ($300,000); the Rockefeller Foundation ($200,000, solicited by Herbert Sturz); and American Broadcasting Company ($75,000). The balance was contributed by smaller donors. Lewis Davis acted as pro bono architect to design the new criminal court with his firm, Davis Brody Associates.

Despite doubters—like Paul Schecter, former counsel to the New York County district attorney, who made the unforgettable comment "It's a bad idea whose time has come"—the plan came to fruition. The Midtown Community Court opened in October 1993 and quickly demonstrated how wrong Schecter had been. The court was embraced by the area's residents, as well as by the not-for-profit theater organizations that occupied the building's upper floors.

The idea was a success from the very beginning, and has been replicated in thirty-eight cities across the country, as well as abroad.

The court represents a major innovation in the criminal justice system. It also stands as a testimonial to the efforts of the Mayor's Midtown Citizens Committee and the many people responsible for its success, particularly Mayor Dinkins, Herbert Sturz, Judge Robert Keating, Chief Judge Judith Kaye of New York's Court of Appeals, the court administrators John Feinblatt, Amanda Burden, and Julius Lang, and the

Community Court's first judge, Judith Kluger. Later Rudolph Giuliani, Mayor Dinkins's successor, made quality-of-life crimes a major component of his administration.

The Mayor's Midtown Citizens Committee is still at the heart of a highly successful partnership between the public and private sectors, the business and residential communities, and the city and its agencies. Its success is reflected in the amazing conversion of Times Square from a cesspool to a figurative Garden of Eden filled with beautiful new buildings, clean and safe streets, a vibrant theater district, a new Forty-Second Street, and bright neon signs reflecting the history and character of old Times Square.

I am proud to say that the committee has been one of my life's most significant experiences. Its original members were relative strangers who bonded in a common cause. We sublimated our individual interests for the benefit of the whole. We are an action-oriented group, and with the help of successive mayoral administrations we changed the landscape of Times Square. It wasn't easy, and it didn't come quickly. But our accomplishments are many: a new residential development called Manhattan Plaza; construction of the Marriott Marquis hotel, currently the most successful hotel in the Marriott chain; the substantial eradication of concentrated pornography; creation of the Midtown Community Court; a sensitive and effective interaction among city agencies, particularly the police and fire departments and the buildings, sanitation, and health departments; plus a host of significant new office and residential developments.

The tawdry, unsafe, dirty sex businesses in Times Square, on Forty-Second Street and the surrounding streets, are substantially gone. Once again, Times Square, with its glamorous signs and thriving theater district, is a magnet attracting local residents and tourists in record numbers.

——•◦•——

I promised myself that establishing the Midtown Community Court would be my last crusade. But sometimes new windmills come along that must be fought.

In September 2000, the press reported that New York City was bidding to become the site of the 2012 Olympics. The plan, called NYC 2012, was created and initially funded by the deputy mayor for economic development, Daniel L. Doctoroff. He was a big investment banker who had joined Mayor Bloomberg's team at one dollar a year, on the condition that Bloomberg allow and actively support his efforts to bring the Olympics to New York. Their plan envisaged developing an Olympic stadium on the west side of Manhattan near the Jacob K. Javits Convention Center and over the west-side railroad yards between Thirtieth and Thirty-Fourth Streets, and Eleventh Avenue and the West Side Highway.

The plan called for major transportation improvements and the use of existing and new venues for various Olympic events in the city's boroughs and the nearby New Jersey Meadowlands. Bloomberg and Doctoroff argued that it would be a great economic boon to the city of New York, and they were right about that. But their suggested location for the stadium was another matter entirely. Furthermore, no third-party negotiations about the stadium had taken place. It was like a return to the days of the master builder Robert Moses.

Questions arose as to who would pay for the stadium and what financial benefits would accrue to the city. There were also the transportation consequences of putting it in already congested midtown streets, near the Lincoln Tunnel, the Hudson River, and of course the theater district. When it soon became apparent that the stadium would not be economically feasible, the plan morphed into a stadium for the New York Jets football team. But the team only played eleven home games, and seating for football was different from seating for the Olympics, again raising questions of economic feasibility.

My years of experience with Midtown West and its waterfront had long ago convinced me that the area was a gold mine. In my view, it was without a doubt the city's most valuable remaining undeveloped waterfront property. But I was also convinced that a stadium near the already congested streets near the theater district and the Lincoln Tunnel, and within the Clinton historic-preservation district, would only result in further traffic jams, noise, and air pollution.

I brought the stadium plan to the Shubert Organization's board of directors. They unanimously opposed it, but didn't want to be the first to say so publicly. So I began meeting with representatives from local community boards and neighborhood groups, and with our local New York State senator and assemblyman, our U.S. senator, our member of the New York City Council, and our U.S. congressman, as well as representatives of Madison Square Garden.

Some voiced quiet support, but only the management of Madison Square Garden was willing to support us publicly. They agreed that the mayor's plan was folly. Their location between Thirty-First and Thirty-Third Streets and Seventh and Eighth Avenues was a stone's throw from the proposed stadium site, making them particularly vulnerable. The Garden management saw the plan for what it was: self-serving and detrimental to the city's interests. In the end, they were the first to publicly oppose the mayor and Doctoroff's plan. Bizarrely, after their opposition, rumors circulated that the mayor might not be renewing the Garden's lease. Clearly, things could get nasty.

Doctoroff continued to lobby intensively for the plan and announced that regardless of any opposition, including litigation, a shovel would be in the ground in February 2005. Accordingly, the city mounted a major campaign to enlist real-estate developers, construction unions, the hotel association, New York civic associations, community boards, the Regional Plan Association of New York, New Jersey, and Connecticut, and the financial community. The city was looking for vocal support and financial backing, while also seeking to diffuse Madison Square Garden's opposition.

In the midst of this frenetic activity, an article appeared in the *Wall Street Journal* quoting Professor Andrew Zimbalist of Smith College, a recognized expert on stadiums. Zimbalist argued, in effect, that there was no history to show that a stadium has any positive economic impact on an urban center. At the same time, I learned that a professor at the Wharton School of the University of Pennsylvania, Lynne Sagalyn, was an expert on the subject of stadium financing and infrastructure.

I met with both professors and reported their views back to the Shubert board. Based on the experts' opinions, and without my advice or vote, the board decided it could no longer wait to voice its opposition. We did so with the simultaneous support of our competitor Rocco Landesman at Jujamcyn, and Tom Short, president of the International Alliance of Theatrical Stage Employees, among the most important theatrical unions in North America.

When yet another presentation was scheduled by the deputy mayor and the New York City Partnership, a civic association made up of leading New York businesses, labor unions, and others, I decided to attend. After all, we were a member of the Partnership and fully entitled to express our views. The meeting was held in the twenty-third-floor headquarters of Martha Stewart Living, a perfect backdrop overlooking the site of the proposed stadium. I had prepared a simple three-line statement that I intended to read at the meeting. I believed it was incumbent on the city to hear the views of all concerned people so that the public could make an informed judgment about the stadium's merits.

Doctoroff and Jerry Speir, chairman of the Partnership, had told me they were not opposed to my reading the statement. But then the Partnership's director unilaterally ruled that I could not. I suggested that she read it, but she replied that no one could read any statements. With that I told her that she obviously did not respect due process, and I left the meeting. When I returned to my office, I phoned Jerry Speir and explained what had happened.

I decided to have Shubert host a breakfast at the University Club on Fifty-Fourth Street, and I invited fellow members of the Partnership and representatives of other interested groups, excluding the press. My guest speakers were Professors Zimbalist and Sagalyn.

The night before the breakfast, a blizzard blanketed the city in snow. I assumed that only a few people would show up. Yet more than a hundred people came. Even Donald Trump was there. He came because a few years earlier, when he was holding a press conference and a blizzard struck, I was the only person who attended. He was now returning the favor.

Shockingly, my guest speakers were not given sufficient time to complete their remarks because the director of the Partnership, who was partly orchestrating the event, took it upon herself to limit them.

The stadium issue progressively intensified. Former mayor Ed Koch, the *New York Times* and other newspapers, and public citizens all urged opening up the development to public bidding to see if any party was willing to pay more than the city, the state, and the Jets had offered. Shortly thereafter, Madison Square Garden made a surprise preemptive bid to buy the development rights. Their plan was to build a platform over the railroad yards and develop apartment houses, office buildings, a park, and other amenities. But no stadium. That turned the debate scorching hot.

The Bloomberg administration and the Jets blasted the Madison Square Garden bid as "a desperate last-minute attempt to derail a project that would create thousands of jobs, more than $1 billion in tax revenue and allow New York to realize its Olympic dreams by building a world-class sports and convention center."

Since the project involved state funding and transfer of the land by the Metropolitan Transit Authority, attention now focused on gaining the necessary approval by the three-member Public Authorities Control Board. At this point, the Jets on one side and Madison Square Garden on the other undertook furious lobbying campaigns in the form of television and print ads.

In the end, two of the three Control Board members abstained from voting. A stadium on the West Side became a dead issue. Despite a belated attempt to relocate the stadium to Queens, New York City lost the 2012 Olympics bid to London. I still believe the best interests of the city were served, although Mayor Bloomberg angrily told me that my opposition was detrimental to Broadway theater. Obviously, I disagreed.

In my opinion, Bloomberg has been a great mayor, just not a great judge on the financial benefits of a stadium in the city. We never opposed the Olympics. We just didn't want them on the west side of Manhattan.

THIRTY-FIVE

"PASSING STRANGE": MAYBE NEXT YEAR

On May 30, 2007, Pat and I went to see a performance of *Passing Strange* at the Public Theater. As I watched the show, I observed the audience reaction. It was extremely positive, as was the reaction of our guests. I enjoyed the show very much, and looking around me, any doubt I had that the musical was skewed to a younger audience was dispelled: the audience was made up of people of all ages. It was not a "house crowd," but rather a joyous, enthusiastic, diverse group of theatergoers— men and women, young and old, black and white.

The title *Passing Strange*, despite a program note of explanation, in no way describes the show. The star, Stew, is the coauthor, lyricist, and composer. I'd never heard of him or his band from the West Coast called the Negro Problem, and it seemed nobody else had, either.

It's a difficult show to describe, and I did not want to put any label on it that might discourage any segment of the theatergoing audience from attending. But then, I really didn't have to label it. The critics did that, calling it a rock 'n' roll musical, a biographical story of a young middle-income black youth from Los Angeles striving to find his way in life. It was funny, exciting, tender, joyous, and uplifting.

The next morning, after discussing the show with Pat, I phoned Oskar Eustis, the artistic director of the Public Theater. I said, "I saw *Passing Strange* last night and want to produce it on Broadway."

He seemed surprised and said, "Yesterday I got a call from Liz McCann, who also wanted to acquire the production rights.

We knew Liz very well. She was a successful producer. So I said, "Why don't I call her and see if we can coproduce it."

Liz was very pleased when I called, and we embarked on a journey to raise $5 million for the show. Since Shubert had not previously sought outside investors for our shows and Liz McCann had, I decided each of us would try to raise half the money from nontraditional investors. I didn't enjoy the process, but we raised more than our half. As I recall, we produced the show with Liz for slightly over $3.1 million, leaving us a reserve of about $1.9 million, which was great. But when we announced the show, there was no response from ticket buyers. The public knew practically nothing about the show, we discovered. So we spent the reserve to cover operating losses and to pay for print, television, outdoor, radio, and Internet advertising.

Passing Strange opened at our Belasco Theatre on February 28, 2008, to the season's most ecstatic reviews—in fact, the most ecstatic reviews for a new musical in many seasons. But instead of a deluge of ticket buyers, there was only a trickle. The show was in deep financial trouble, and in order to continue, we had to raise additional funds. We needed to be in a position to contend for the Tony Award for Best Musical. After factoring in weekly losses to the day of the Tony Awards, we calculated that we needed $1 million. The only alternative was to close the show.

In the past, I had advised others in a similar dilemma to "never chase a show with additional funds; just close it." But I presented the matter to our board of directors and told them we stood a good chance of winning the Tony Award for Best Musical. They agreed that we should join the chase. However, we failed to raise the full $1 million and had to top up the investors' portion with an additional $325,000.

We were nominated for seven Tony Awards, including Best Musical, Best Book of a Musical, Best Original Score (Music and/or Lyrics) Written for the Theater, Best Orchestrations, Best Performance by a Leading Actor in a Musical (Stew), Best Performance by a Featured Actor in a Musical (Daniel Breaker) and Best Performance by a Featured Actress in a Musical (de'Adre Aziza).

We continued our advertising campaign with print ads in the *New York Times*. The ads were still unproductive. Our losses continued to deplete the additional financing, and the Shubert Organization became the funder of last resort. The show's cast was remarkable, making themselves readily available for interviews and brief performances to promote the show. As a group they were the most willing, pleasant, and supportive people I have ever worked with.

For some inexplicable reason, the week before the Tony Awards, which were held on Sunday, June 15, 2008, we saw a spike in our daily ticket sales and weekly gross receipts. So much so that we experienced our first profitable week in a long while. Our confidence rose, and all of us in the Shubert and McCann offices became optimistic about our chances to win the Tony for Best Musical. Our optimism was fueled by several newspaper articles predicting that *Passing Strange* would win the Tony.

Not surprisingly, a number of people told me that they would vote for *Passing Strange*. Of course, since the ballots are secret, I would never know if they kept their word. During the ten days before the Tony cutoff date, our office and the Liz McCann office checked the list of Tony voters who had not yet seen *Passing Strange*. I personally called a number of them to say I noted that they hadn't seen *Passing Strange* and hoped they would. By the time I arrived at Radio City Music Hall, where the Tony Awards were held, my confidence level was high. But our cash reserves were not, and I knew that if we didn't win, we would probably not have the financial means to keep the show running.

The final award of the Tony broadcast is the award for Best Musical, so I didn't learn our fate until a few minutes after elevn p.m.—four hours after the first award's announcement. Then it happened very quickly. We lost.

I still wonder why *Passing Strange*, which received the most glowing reviews for a musical show of the past several seasons, did not attract an audience, no matter what marketing efforts we used. We were in the press, on the radio, on television, in the subways; we did "wild posting" advertising outdoors; we had an exciting website; our cast was featured in leading magazines and trade papers, too numerous to count; we were on ABC's *The View*. Our cast responded willingly to all our publicity efforts, all to no avail.

Perhaps it was because the show was not properly described in the media. Looking back, I think that the February 29, 2008, *New York Times* review by Charles Isherwood stated it best: "Call it a rock concert with a story to tell, trimmed with a lot of great jokes. Or call it a sprawling work of performance art, complete with angry rants and scary drag queens. Call it whatever you want, really. I'll just call it wonderful and a welcome anomaly on Broadway, which can use all the vigorous new artistic blood it can get."

Perhaps no one had heard of Stew or our cast members. Perhaps the show fell victim to the generation gap, and our older audience stayed away believing it was a rock 'n' roll show. Perhaps we discounted too many tickets to make a profit. Perhaps it was "too new" a musical. Perhaps the hundreds of Tony voters who said *Passing Strange* was a shoo-in did not vote for it. Perhaps the road venue operators and League members outside of New York voted for *In the Heights*, which won the award that year, because they thought it was likely to tour, possibly in their own cities across America.

Maybe we lost for some or all these reasons, and maybe for reasons I haven't thought about. I'll never know how close the vote was, or wasn't. But it will take me a long time to get over the loss. My one consolation is remembering the fact that *Dreamgirls* lost to *Nine*, and *Sunday in the Park with George* lost to *La Cage Aux Folles*.

Just before *Passing Strange* was due to close, Spike Lee asked me if he could film a performance. I thought that was a great idea, not just because I loved the show, but also because the film would document a work that I believed was important and needed to be seen. Spike wanted the cameras on stage. I said fine. It was announced that the show would be filmed during the last three performances. They were all sellouts.

The curtain came down for the last time on July 20, 2008, after a run of twenty previews and 165 performances. Maybe next year will be our turn.

THIRTY-SIX

TOMORROW'S BROADWAY

Today's Broadway audience consists of the under-forty patrons and the over-forty patrons. The education of the former, in my opinion, has generally been lacking in art and culture, while the latter has enjoyed a far richer arts and cultural education. As the years go by, the under-forty segment will, of course, completely eclipse the over-forty segment. Future audiences may well be comprised of people with little formation in arts and culture. That is an ominous portent for the future of the theater.

At the same time, I fear that Americans are overly engrossed in sports. The print and electronic media are preoccupied with sports; the public seems drugged on sports. Governments can't resist spending valuable tax dollars on sports and stadiums. Colleges and universities are tripping over each other as they compete for lucrative television coverage and for students whom they reward for athletic prowess rather than academic qualifications.

It is a bleak picture, in my view. Especially in New York City, the home of Broadway, where politicians are falling over themselves to give away billions of taxpayer dollars to build new baseball stadiums and other sports facilities.

The logical question is: What is the future of the Broadway theater? I could say great, but I don't believe it. We need to create a new audience, we need to get children interested in the theater, and that means we need to expand the teaching of all arts in our public schools.

Many years ago, we created a program with the Board of Education called the Drama Enrichment Curriculum, which at its peak had 110 participating high schools, each with one senior class for students interested in the theater. The Broadway League provided those students with free tickets to four shows each semester, and the chance to attend monthly lectures at the Shubert Theatre. Guest speakers featured fabulous talent, such as Tennessee Williams, Lena Horne, Michael Bennett, and other top professionals of the day.

I vividly remember the day Tennessee Williams was the lecturer. Producer Morton Gottlieb introduced him as someone whose plays are presented every day in some corner of the world. When Morton mentioned the name Tennessee Williams, the entire audience of inner-city children rose en masse, cheering and screaming. Tennessee did not know how to respond. Shivers of elation came over me. We need a lot more of that kind of experience. It is essential, not just for Broadway's health but for the country's cultural health, that we give our children this gift.

On October 17, 2001, Pat and I attended a dinner party at the home of Mort Zuckerman, publisher of the New York *Daily News* and other magazines and periodicals. The occasion was to celebrate the screening of a new movie, *Life as a House*, produced and directed by our mutual friend Irwin Winkler. Another guest at the party was Joel Klein, the former assistant attorney general in charge of the Antitrust Division of the United States Department of Justice. By then Joel had left the Justice Department to work for Thomas Middlehoff, chairman and chief executive officer of Bertelsmann, one of the world's largest music, TV, radio, and book publishers.

Three months later, I was invited to lunch with Middlehoff, to discuss an option that Bertelsmann held to purchase the Lyceum Theatre. Joel joined us, as his position at the time covered real estate, financing, and other services for the company's North American divisions. So Joel was no stranger to me when, on July 30, 2002, he was sworn in by Mayor Bloomberg as schools chancellor. And as soon as I heard about his appointment, I arranged to meet with him. I wanted to pique his interest in introducing art and culture into the curriculum of New York City's public schools.

Our first meeting led to others, and little by little our Blueprints for the Arts was developed, thanks to a strongly motivated chancellor and his staff, particularly the New York City Department of Education's Dr. Sharon Dunn, who was special instructional manager for arts education, and Paul L. King, director of theater programs, plus the support of Mayor Bloomberg. Our plan sought to create comprehensive programs for theater, dance, music, and visual arts.

To implement the Blueprints program required recruiting teachers and providing instruction in those disciplines. Teachers qualified in these areas simply did not exist, as a result of many decades during which the arts were eliminated from the curriculum. The teachers then had to be certified by the Board of Education, a long and arduous process.

But some success is visible. The Theater Blueprint is now part of the curriculum in more than 350 participating schools, out of the more than 1,400 schools in the public-school system.

The Shubert Foundation has shown its support for the program by contributing more than $880,000 to date, accompanied by a commitment to donate more as needed. Invaluable assistance for the program has also been given by Fred Gershon of Music Theater International, a leading licensee of musical theater texts, scores, and teaching aids for schools throughout the country. More substantial support is still needed, and I hope that others will support the cause.

Despite all its shortcomings, the theater continues to lure writers, directors, designers, actors, producers, and theater owners, who make it their life's work.

Why? I could be cynical and say money. But I don't think anyone in the business would give that as a reason. I could say it's about the people you meet. But I don't know of many enduring relationships, unfortunately. I could say it's about the excitement of being on a Broadway stage, and in a very real sense that's true, but very few people actually get there, and those who do don't necessarily linger.

So, what is the theater's mysterious attraction, which despite the hardships, odds, and frustrations draws you to it? You do it because you love the theater.

Still, for someone who plans on spending a lifetime in the business, love alone is not enough. To make a successful living at it, you have to understand the business of the theater. You have to understand our product and how illusive it can be. We have to satisfy the audience, which can be fickle. We have to satisfy the critics, who can make or break a play. We raise millions of dollars to bring our product to market with the full understanding that it can become worthless overnight. It's a harsh, relentless business.

Unfortunately, too many people working in Broadway theater today are not knowledgeable about its history, and some show little or no interest in learning about it. Some people have a mercenary view of the business, and some take an insular view on how and to what extent, if any, theater relates to the outside world. The same can be said about too many who write about Broadway: they don't know how the business works, nor do they seem interested in learning. For example, when evaluating a Broadway theater season, their barometer is attendance and gross weekly box-office receipts. While those numbers may sometimes be impressive, they fail to take into account the number of theatergoers who purchase discount tickets and the amount of gross receipts attributable to those.

In addition, the success or failure of each show depends on attendance and gross weekly box-office receipts for each individual theater. If a season's total attendance and gross receipts were equally divided among all Broadway theaters, the overall financial results would be disastrous. A show and a theater can be considered a success only when there is a large attendance at full-ticket prices. When reporting fails to include such important data, it distorts the picture of Broadway's financial health, which in turn creates problems with unions and guilds, and with government relations. Only when reporting is complete and presented in a way that's understandable can the results of a show and a theater during a particular season be accurately measured.

Unlike other forms of live entertainment, whether on a stage, on a playing field, or in any other venue where admission is charged, Broadway receives almost no ancillary revenue from television. There are a few exceptions, but the three-dimensional stage does not necessarily lend itself to two-dimensional television. In addition, Broadway does not receive low-interest government loans, subsidies, or tax-exempt bond financing, which already-wealthy sports-venue operators receive so that they can build new stadiums. There are no government enticement subsidies for theater to come to New York City or to do business in the city. Nor does Broadway receive any sort of corporate retention deals not to leave the city.

Ironically, movie and television productions that originate in New York City continue to get substantial support in the form of lower state and local taxes. I don't begrudge them these incentives, which help support the creative arts, but it is frustrating that no similar consideration is given to Broadway and its long-term survivability.

Perhaps it's too much to expect city and state lawmakers to devote some time and attention to the question of how Broadway will cope with its future. So far, they haven't recognized the urgency of addressing Broadway's plight and of helping to provide substantive solutions.

The Broadway theater and its many components—producing, creating, acting, the technical side, the economics of the business, the environs of the theater district, plus the plays and musicals themselves—have all undergone fundamental changes. All are vastly different today from what they were during the mid-twentieth century.

The Broadway community and I, representing the Shubert Organization, have attempted at every turn to deal with this ever-changing landscape and, especially, with the neglect that has imperiled Broadway. We were the leading protagonists in the revitalization of Times Square. We spent a fortune restoring our antiquated theaters. And we did it alone, with little or no concern or support from New York City, New York State, the federal government, the print and electronic media, or our educational system.

And Broadway continues to go it alone. Unfortunately, though our efforts to date are significant, they are not sufficient to have a meaningful effect on Broadway's long-term prospects. I'm afraid that the status quo will continue until the day a theater owner is forced to demolish a theater or to file for bankruptcy. Perhaps then the government will step in with some form of support. By then it may be too late.

I have never forgotten what Ed Koch told me when I asked him why the city didn't do more to help us. He shrugged, "Why should I help you, Jerry? You can't move."

———•◦•———

Until 1958, the names of most Broadway theaters remained constant. But after that year, a new trend began, and as of 2005 approximately one-quarter of all Broadway theaters had changed names. The National, for example, was renamed the Billy Rose, then the Trafalgar, and then the David T. Nederlander Theatre. The ANTA became the Virginia and subsequently the August Wilson. The Alvin was renamed the Neil Simon, the 46th Street Theater became the Richard Rodgers, and the Coronet became the Eugene O'Neill.

On June 15, 2004, at the meeting of the board of directors of the Shubert Organization, board member Stuart Subotnick announced, "I have had extended discussions with the other members of the Board, except for Mr. Schoenfeld, concerning the renaming of the Plymouth Theatre and the Royale Theatre as the Gerald Schoenfeld Theatre and the Bernard B. Jacobs Theatre respectively, and based on those discussions, I would propose they be renamed accordingly."

Three other theaters had been renamed in recent memory: the Mansfield had become the Brooks Atkinson, the Ritz had became the Walter Kerr, and the Martin Beck had become the Al Hirschfeld. Atkinson and Kerr were *New York Times* theater critics, and Hirschfield was the noted *New York Times* cartoonist. Odd, then, that after the Shubert board announced it was renaming two theaters for Bernie and me, the *Times* would lead the charge against the move.

Charles Isherwood, writing in the paper, decided, "The lexicon of Broadway, including the names of specific playhouses, conjures not just a street or a business but also a history, a cultural tradition and even an ideal.... An organization that should be at pains to combat the notion that Broadway has become a minor byway of American culture is taking advantage of it for the aggrandizement of current and former executives."

I would argue that Bernie and I were not just "current or former executives"—that we had played an integral part for more than forty years in maintaining and improving American theater in general, and Broadway theater in particular. We more than paid our dues by changing Broadway for the better. I hope this memoir sets out our case.

The Plymouth, which now bears my name, was built by the Shubert brothers in 1917. It was one of the first theaters designed by the famous theatrical architect Herbert Krapp and it backs onto its Krapp-designed twin, the Broadhurst. The Plymouth features lavish eighteenth-century interiors and a pair of handsome balconies overlooking the street. A 1,079-seat house with a single balcony, it housed Shakespeare and Ibsen right from the beginning, and saw great names in early twentieth-century Broadway playing there, legends such as John and Lionel Barrymore, and Edward G. Robinson, who acted in several shows there in the 1920s.

Spencer Tracy played at the Plymouth, as did Barbara Stanwyck, Clark Gable, and Raymond Massey, who starred in Robert Sherwood's Pulitzer Prize–winning *Abe Lincoln in Illinois*. Frederick March, Tallulah Bankhead, Montgomery Clift, and E. G. Marshall played there in Thornton Wilder's *The Skin of Our Teeth*. Gypsy Rose Lee also played there, as did Yul Brynner, Richard Burton, Henry Fonda, Harry Belafonte,

Peter Ustinov, Charles Boyer, Claudette Colbert, Ruth Gordon, Anthony Quinn, Alec Guinness, Jeremy Irons, and John Cleese.

It was at the Plymouth where they staged *Irma La Douce*, *The Caine Mutiny Court-Martial*, *Equus* starring Anthony Hopkins, and *Ain't Misbehavin'*. It was where Neil Simon triumphed with *The Odd Couple*, starring Walter Matthau and Art Carney. And where George C. Scott followed a few years later with Simon's *Plaza Suite*. More recently, Eugene O'Neill's *Long Day's Journey Into Night* with Vanessa Redgrave, Brian Dennehy, Philip Seymour Hoffman, and Robert Sean Leonard was there. As was Chita Rivera's *The Dancer's Life* and the Tony Award–winning, *Heidi Chronicles*.

The Royale, now bearing Bernie's name, opened ten years after the Plymouth. It was taken over by the Shuberts two years later and at one time was leased to CBS, where they produced radio dramas. Designed by Krapp in the modern Spanish style, with a vaulted ceiling and wonderful murals, it has two balconies and 1,078 seats, just one seat fewer than the Plymouth.

Mae West played there in *Diamond Lil*, and Julie Andrews debuted there in *The Boy Friend*. Laurence Olivier and Joan Plowright starred there in John Osborne's *The Entertainer*; Martin Sheen was there with *The Subject Was Roses*; Bette Davis played there in Tennessee Williams's *Night of the Iguana*; and Lauren Bacall, Barry Nelson, and Brenda Vaccaro performed there in Abe Burrows's *Cactus Flower*. Then came Andrew Lloyd Webber and Tim Rice with *Joseph and the Amazing Technicolor Dreamcoat*, followed by Bernadette Peters, who won a Tony there in Andrew Lloyd Webber's *Song and Dance*. *Art* was at the Royale, as was the hugely successful *Grease*.

Among the stars who worked the Royale stage were Bert Lahr, Betty Grable, John Gielgud, Margaret Rutherford, Bob Fosse, Richard Burton, Laurence Olivier, David Niven, Gloria Swanson, Phil Silvers, Eartha Kitt, Anne Bancroft, Max von Sydow, Martin Shaw, Frank Langella, Alan Alda, and James Gandolfini.

Now, four years after seeing that marquee light up with my name, as I preside over the Shubert Organization and attempt to cope with its problems, I remain steadfastly optimistic and devoted to its continuance in the twenty-first century. If one hundred years of existence have not overwhelmed the Shubert Organization and Broadway, then this significant part of American culture, one hopes, will endure.

The Shubert Organization and The Shubert Foundation are both still here, stronger, more respected, more secure, and just as determined as in 1972, when Bernie and I took over the reins, to perpetuate the American theater.

EPILOGUE

Jerry never talked about retirement or dying. He always told anyone who asked, "They will drag me feetfirst out of Shubert Alley."

And that's pretty much what happened. He was never ill. He never suffered. He was never diminished.

Ironically, for a man who spent so much time in the theater, on the night Jerry died he'd gone to the movies. But it wasn't just any movie; it was the premiere of Hugh Jackman's *Australia*.

Jerry and Hugh had formed a warm friendship when Hugh was in New York in *The Boy from Oz*. Jerry was always going backstage to tease Hugh and have some laughs with him. After that, they would get together whenever Hugh was in New York. Jerry was constantly urging him, "Come back to Broadway." Hugh always promised Jerry that he would.

Australia premiered at the Ziegfeld Theatre on November 24, 2008. We sat just behind Hugh, his beautiful Australian movie-star wife, Deborra-Lee Furness, and various members of their family.

When the film ended, Jerry jumped up and hugged Hugh. "The film is good," he said. "Now cut this out and come back to Broadway."

Jerry died of a heart attack that night.

Two and a half months later, a celebration of Jerry's life was held at the Majestic Theatre. We planned it purposely to fit into Hugh's schedule. He'd been the master of ceremonies for the dedication of Jerry's theater. We wanted him to be the master of ceremonies for the celebration of Jerry's life. It was February 9, 2009. More than two thousand people stood on line, waiting to get in. The Majestic only holds 1,700. So three hundred people had to stand at the back. That's how much Jerry meant to them.

Bill Haber produced the show, and later told me that he doesn't want to be on Broadway anymore "because it's no fun to be there without Jerry."

But on that wintry Monday afternoon, it was fun.

Everyone came with a smile. So many of the people who knew and loved Jerry were there—Helen Mirren, Angela Lansbury, Whoopi Goldberg, Robert Fox, Andrew Lloyd Webber, Tim Rice, Jeremy Irons— all sharing their love of him. There were songs and speeches and tears.

It was pure Jerry Schoenfeld.

At the end, Mayor Bloomberg summed up Jerry, as he had when he celebrated with us the opening of the Schoenfeld Theatre, telling the audience, "Right now, Jerry is busy creating new shows with Bob Fosse and Michael Bennett. And he's arguing with God about air rights. And God knows he won't hear the end of it."

The year before Jerry passed away, his friend Robbie Lantz died. Six months after Jerry, his friend Sam Cohn died. Now I'd like to think that when Jerry's finished arguing with God, the three of them are somewhere having lunch, trying to do a deal.

Seven and a half months after hosting the celebration at the Majestic, Hugh Jackman made good on his promise to Jerry. He returned to Broadway with Daniel Craig in *A Steady Rain*.

And it was at the Gerald Schoenfeld Theatre.

I went backstage after opening night to see Hugh, and the first thing he said to me was, "Pat, he's here. He hasn't gone away. He's here in the wings. I can feel him here."

How did he get there?

That's how.

— Pat Schoenfeld, New York City, 2011

INDEX